BUSINESS/SCIENCE/TECHNOLOGY DIVISION
CHICAGO PUBLIC LIBRARY
400 SOUTH STATE STREET
CHICAGO, IL 60605

Chicago Public Library

REFERENCE

Form 178 rev. 11-00

Romantics at War

Education at War

GEORGE P. FLETCHER

Romantics at War

Glory and Guilt
in the Age of Terrorism

PRINCETON UNIVERSITY PRESS

PRINCETON AND OXFORD

Copyright © 2002 by Princeton University Press
Published by Princeton University Press, 41 William Street, Princeton, New Jersey 08540
In the United Kingdom: Princeton University Press, 3 Market Place,
Woodstock, Oxfordshire OX20 1SY

All Rights Reserved

ISBN: 0-691-00651-2 (cloth : alk. paper)

British Library Cataloging-in-Publication Data is available

This book has been composed in Sabon

Printed on acid-free paper. ∞

www.pupress.princeton.edu

Printed in the United States of America

10 9 8 7 6 5 4 3 2 1

BUSINESS/SCIENCE/TECHNOLOGY DIVISION
CHICAGO PUBLIC LIBRARY
400 SOUTH STATE STREET
CHICAGO, IL 60605

RO2OO3 44480

For my three children who express
their Romantic urges in different ways,

DEBORAH, who searches for meaning
in far-off lands.

REBECCA, who writes and sings of
yearning for home.

GABRIEL, who at an early age plays
Beethoven as his favorite.

May none know the horrors of war.

U 22 .F588 2002
Fletcher, George P.
Romantics at war

CONTENTS

Coming to grips with the issues in this book has brought me to an understanding of where I stand in the cross-currents of intellectual history. Just imagine having to take a stand on all the following issues: Must legal thinking always be rational, or is there room for nonrational thought within the system? Do Romantics have any place in the law, and if so, what should their distinctive contribution be? How do we resolve the classic dispute about the units of agency — do only individuals act or is it possible to take group action seriously as a basis for attributing collective guilt? And what about the basic word that runs throughout this discussion of crime and punishment — *guilt*? What does this word mean, and does it lend itself to attributing blame to nations who commit aggressive war as well as to individuals who commit crimes?

Searching for my position on these spectra of opposites has engaged me for many years. In my early professional work, circa 1970, I would have been loathe to describe myself as sympathetic to nonrational "right-brain" thinking or to describe myself as a Romantic. I was too closely identified with the analytic philosophical tradition. The intellectual heroes of my youth were Herbert Morris, H.L.A. Hart, and Ronald Dworkin. These were scholars who brought analytic rigor to legal studies and I am grateful that I spent many years in their tutelage.

It is obvious, however, that I showed an early and seemingly eccentric appreciation for methods of legal thought that were clearly at odds with the analytic tradition. Two articles in the *Harvard Law Review* provide a window on a mind-set that from my current perspective I can see as the beginnings of the arguments in this book. In 1972 I was engaged in searching for a new way of thinking about the foundations of tort law — an alternative to the arguments of efficiency then in ascendancy. The conventional view about the leading *Palsgraf* case, which arose from a notoriously complicated accident with multiple causes, was that the majority opinion by Judge Cardozo was analytically more rigorous than the dissenting opinion by Judge Andrews. The latter was supposedly muddle-headed because it reasons that the question of proximate cause in accident cases resembles a "spring, starting on its journey . . . joined by tributary after tributary . . . reaching the ocean, com[ing] from a hundred sources." My own take on this debate was that Cardozo's definitions of the "risk reasonable to be perceived" as equivalent to "the duty to be obeyed" placed too much faith in definitions and the seductiveness of particular words. The nonrational invocation of an image of a stream appealed to me as a human way of judging — the best method under the circumstances.

Four years later I pursued this theme in developing a contrarian conception of the history of larceny. My thesis — probably better documented than anything I have written since — stressed the image of the thief coming stealthily at night as the historical foundation for defining the boundaries of larceny. The word-oriented, "left-brain" profession of law professors had great trouble with this argument. The standard way lawyers think about the contours of crimes is to pretend that our words carry the power to stake out boundaries between the lawful and the unlawful.

I see now that skepticism about verbal definition in legal thinking connects strongly to the study of comparative law, particularly the analysis of legal systems across diverse linguistic families. Monolingual American lawyers take their pet phrases like "reasonableness," "fairness," and "due process" very seriously. In the post-legal-realist age they know that "general propositions do not decide concrete cases." Yet they invest the central words of the common law tradition with a liturgical function. Merely reciting the right words supposedly signals a sound approach to the problem. It never seems to occur to English-speaking scholars and judges that lawyers in other traditions have no comparable words in their vocabularies. If our idiom of legal analysis is local and contingent, we should have greater humility about the ability of our parochial language to capture deep truths about the law.

Bruce Ackerman was probably the first to join forces with me when in 1977 he developed his own distinction between two ways of thinking about legal problems. He saw in my emphasis on right-brain responses to images a pattern of unreflective thought that he dubbed "ordinary observing." He regarded it as an advance in the legal thinking to move from this kind of thinking to "scientific policy-making," a method that at the time signaled the application primarily of economic analysis. Neither Ackerman nor I realized at the time that we had both distanced ourselves from the conventional faith in verbal definitions held by the mass of lawyers and judges. My method favored the human response to images — below, as it were, the level of verbal distortion; his, the invocation of a universal mathematical and economic system — above and beyond the distortions of language.

At stake in my 1970s articles was another attitude toward law that I have come only in the fullness of time to understand. When I did research in particular problems I found a recurrent pattern of contradictions in the sources of law. Most people assume the law is a consistent set of propositions — something like a rule book for solving cases. Both of these 1970s articles emphasized the dramatic conflict of ideas that surged beneath the surface of the law. In the 1972 article on tort theory I stressed the conflict between the deontological principle of reciprocity and the utilitarian standard of reasonableness. In the 1976 work on the history of larceny the critical question was whether we should recognize the imperfect and incomplete nature of a law of theft based on a shared image of thieving.

In these conflicts between legal ideas, there was always a thesis and an antithesis. In the Hegelian style of thinking, where opposition generates new combinations of ideas, one should expect a synthesis to emerge from the historic tensions in the law. But in fact the dramatic confrontations of legal ideas do not resolve themselves in a stable equilibrium. The constant juxtaposition of opposites is characteristic of all living dynamic political cultures.

The recognition of inescapable contradictions could have led me to a Marxist theory of law — if I had believed in the possibility of *Aufhebung* or "transcendence" in a revolution or an equivalent historical transformation. Lack of faith in stable resolution eventually led me to think of my approach to law as a Romantic theory of irreconcilable conflict.

It was not until I read Isaiah Berlin's *Roots of Romanticism* a few years ago, however, that I understood that the word "Romantic" was the right label to attach to this phenomenon that had long intrigued me. His erudition and eloquence have me in their spell. I feel about Berlin as I have about few other scholars that if he and I have both read the same text — particularly one in the Romantic movement — his understanding is likely to be more accurate than my own.

The Romantics were interested, to be sure, in glory and in war, but they were not particularly engaged by the law and by the subject of guilt. These subjects represent, as it were, an open square in the periodic table of ideas, and I seek to fill it with the arguments of this book. I try to reason from various sources toward a position on nationhood and guilt that would seem most suitable to a Romantic sensibility.

In my many travels and many years of studying comparative

law, however, I have never encountered anyone intrigued by the same questions of Romanticism in law. In October 2000, however, at a conference sponsored by the Humboldt Foundation in Bamberg, Germany, I had a remarkable meeting with a German-speaking Chinese scholar of criminal law from Taiwan, Ms. Yu-Hsiu Hsu. We happened on the subject of Romanticism in law and she offered me several original ideas about the way German Romantics would think about legal problems. This conversation was a turning point in the process that Judge Andrews might have described as a "spring, starting on its journey . . . joined by tributary after tributary . . . reaching the ocean, com[ing] from a hundred sources." Yu-Hsiu was an essential tributary because she gave me the confidence to believe that the turn toward Romanticism had sources other than my own eccentric stream of thought.

But there was yet another tributary to join the accumulating flow of ideas. In the early 1990s, I—as well as many other people interested in political theory—found an enormous attraction to the problem of communal loyalties. I began to take values like group loyalty and national patriotism seriously in a way that was novel for me. The "communitarians" writing at the time were interested primarily in the problem of identity and, as Charles Taylor put it, in the "sources of the self." I was concerned about the moral issues raised by having a personal stake in a particular narrative of family and nationhood. Placing these loyalties at the center of my moral thinking put me at odds with the Enlightenment tradition and its emphasis on the equal treatment of all.

In this period I found myself drawn more and more to the subject of national identity. I was willing to argue that the sense of nationhood had played a greater part in American history than most historians were willing to admit. These thoughts led to a full-scale theory of constitutional history, which appeared in book form in April 2001.

The last of the influences that shaped this book comes from my long-standing commitment to the problems of crime and punishment. I have written more about those topics than about anything else, and therefore the issues of criminal responsibility invariably enter into my perception of the world. The central mysteries of the criminal law dwell, I believe, in two questions: first, what is the meaning of "guilt" — the word we use all the time to describe responsibility for criminal behavior. And second, what is the meaning of "punishment" — the practice of making people suffer for their guilty violations of the law? However obvious these concepts of guilt and punishment may be to some, I am constantly mystified by the depth of these problems.

My thinking about these diverse themes took on an additional impetus in April 2000 when the Yale Law School invited me to give the Storrs lectures in 2001. I committed myself to three lectures in November 2001, and by the late spring of 2001 I had picked the title for the series: *Liberals and Romantics at War: The Problem of Collective Guilt*. The controversial problem of collective guilt — the negative side of national pride — lies at the intersection of all the themes that have occupied me for years: Romanticism, collectivity, nationalism, and guilt all entered into the scope of the lectures I had in mind.

The lectures were drafted and ready to be delivered when September 11 took us by storm. In November, when I spent a week at the Yale Law School to give the lectures, the subject of war, crime, and guilt had a salience that I had not expected.

I am very much indebted to the Yale community of scholars and students for attending the lectures and challenging me in question-and-answer periods after each session. Worthy of special mention in this regard are Anthony Kronman, Bruce Ackerman, and Paul Kahn, who respectively introduced the three lectures with words of support and sympathy for the project that still resonate in my mind. I was particularly impressed by Dean Kronman's remarks both at the first lecture and the dinner afterward. It was a great pleasure to hear the thoughts of someone who seemed to understand aspects of my work better than I did myself. I want also to thank Elizabeth Stauderman who, without prior consultation with me, decided to use Blake's painting *Jerusalem* — presented in the design of the dust jacket — to capture my attachment to the Romantics.

Among the many faculty and friends who graced the lectures not only with their presence but with critical comments, I would like to express my appreciation to Jack Balkin, Dany Celemejer, Russell Christopher, Jules Coleman, Mirjan Damaska, Eve Epstein, Owen Fiss, Rebecca Fletcher, Robert Gordon, Steve Sheppard, and James Whitman. Other colleagues and friends responded with helpful comments in private conversations and in discussion groups at the Columbia Law School. In this regard I would like to thank, in particular, Jörg Arnold, David J. Cohen, David Heyd, Konrad Huber, Frank Lossy, Herbert Morris, Nancy Rosenblum, Kurt Seelmann, Jeremy Waldron, and Ernest Weinrib.

The November lectures are published in a slightly revised format under the same title in the May 2002 issue of the *Yale Law Journal*. I want to thank the *Journal* staff and, in particular, Brad Daniels, for expert editorial assistance.

Since 9/11, and in particular after 11/13 — when President Bush issued his order establishing military tribunals — I have been moved to reconsider and redraft all of my arguments. The problems of war and guilt have taken on a practical importance that I had originally conceived to be a matter largely of theoretical interest. In the arguments that I set before the reader in this book, the problems of guilt for treason and war crimes and the procedural issues posed by the military tribunals now bear heightened political significance. These have become problems of enormous practical relevance.

Several people have been of great value in my working through the original material in order to generate a book that deals with issues that will long remain with us in the "age of terrorism." Keith Levenberg provided expert editorial and research assistance. Lenge Hong was invaluable in editing the manuscript and preparing the index. Above all I am indebted to my editor at Princeton

University Press, Ian Malcolm, for appreciating the value of the project and working closely with me to find the proper path between philosophical inquiry and political relevance.

Unfortunately, those who have helped me must take the bad with the good. They constitute the collective from which my thinking and this book have emerged. May they forgive me for daring to stand alone to publish my unique understanding of the issues on which they all have valuably different points of view.

Romantics at War

CHAPTER ONE

War's Appeal

Sometime they'll give a war and nobody
will come.
— *Carl Sandburg*

W hen the first plane hit, we thought
it was an accident. We did not anticipate an attack. We could not
even muster fighter planes fast enough to protect the second World
Trade Center tower or the Pentagon. If the passengers on the
fourth hijacked jet had not been courageous, we might have suffered even more serious harm in Washington, D.C. But not only
our military was caught by surprise. Our minds were also asleep.

We had received all the clues necessary to know that we were
in danger. Islamic fundamentalist terrorists had already tried to
blow up the World Trade Center. Al Qaeda had attacked the bat-
tleship USS *Cole* and the American embassy in Nairobi. We were
put on notice that a dramatic attack was in the offing: We ignored it.

Experts rarely know what is going to happen tomorrow. The
sovietologists did not foresee the collapse of the Communist em-
pire in 1989. The market watchers — with few exceptions — did
not expect the NASDAQ crash that hit investors in March 2000.
September 11 was no more visible to the eye than these other
world-shaking events.

But I am less concerned with the ability of military experts to predict specific events than with our general ability to think clearly about the aftermath, about the life-and-death questions that have tormented us since we sat stunned in front of our television sets. We may have been unprepared for that morning, but there is no reason to muddle the meaning of that event and to accept our military and legal responses without serious reflection. We must ask ourselves how we justify our use of force to the rest of the world and, more importantly, to ourselves. Is this war? Are we engaged in self-defense, in the pursuit of justice, in establishing a "new world order?" Who is the enemy? These are not easy questions.

I write in an effort to bring some clarity to these issues. This is a book about going to war, about war's appeal to us and to our enemy, about honor, about crimes that are committed in the name of war, and about the guilt of those who collectively commit crimes. In the face of a military attack, we all see our lives and our futures on the line. Without a firm understanding of the miliary actions taken in our name, we cannot be at ease; we cannot allow others to risk their lives and allow our opponents to die without knowing why.

Let us think first about the language we use. One word is on everybody's lips — terrorism — but what does it mean? The concept eludes easy definition. Were the American revolutionaries not terrorists? Did they not fight without wearing uniforms? Did they not conduct unorthodox raids against English regulars marching in uniform? Were we engaged in an act of terror when we dropped the atomic bomb on Hiroshima? There are too many questions and too few easy answers.

We know that terrorism is about violence. But there is good violence and bad violence. Is every violent crime an act of terror? Hardly. It is not clear, when we use the word today, whether we mean to refer to haphazard violence — something like the terror that descended on the French with Robespierre and the guillotine — or we mean to talk about terror as an instrument of national policy, with clear objectives of intimidating and manipulating civilian populations. Dropping the A-bomb in Japan was not haphazard, but it may have had the purpose of scaring the public into a posture of surrender. It is not clear whether the use of violence is worse when it is helter-skelter (à la Charles Manson) or when its purpose is to intimidate.

Fighting terrorism is not like going to war against Germany or Japan. We knew what Germany was, where it was. Not only do we not know where the terrorists are; we would not know them if we saw them. We are fighting with the most modern instruments, but we are flying in the dark.

War and Justice

If the use of the word "terrorist" is problematic, what about "war"? We have been in a state of armed conflict with Al Qaeda and the Taliban in Afghanistan, but does this conflict amount to a "war"? Not every shootout at the OK Corral qualifies. Perhaps the United States is just acting like the sheriff bringing the culprits to justice. From the very beginning, President George W. Bush and his administration used the language of both war and justice — as though these two ways of thinking about violence were compatible. Bush has said repeatedly that the attack was "an act of war." That makes it sound like Pearl Harbor. Yet the early mantra of the war was: "We have to bring them to justice." That makes it sound like the prosecution of Timothy McVeigh.

War and justice are radically different ideas. War is about pursuing and protecting our national interests — in this case, the security of our own territory. We have the right to go to war without having any cause greater than survival. So why do we hear so much talk about justice?

The Pentagon initially labeled the military campaign "Infinite Justice," and from the beginning of the military campaign the focus was on Osama bin Laden as the master criminal, the ringleader of the whole operation. The bombing of Afghanistan — and the relentless search of the caves in Tora Bora — had the style of an episode in the hit television series *Law and Order*. Are

we serious? Is bombing a foreign country merely a case of doing justice by more violent means? If so, it is justice by violent
reprisal.

Justice is about giving every person his or her due, about re-
storing moral order in the universe. Seeking to correct the balance leads to thinking about the interests of victims and the importance of reintegrating them into society. The government must
prosecute criminals in order to do justice for the victims. The
Latin Americans have bequeathed to the international community
the term *impunidad* (impunity) to capture the particular corruption of governments that fail to prosecute. Abandoned victims, it
is argued, suffer twice: first from the crime, and second from the
failure of others to express solidarity with them by hunting down
the culprits and punishing them.

The search for justice leads to the moral equation of an "eye
for an eye"—the biblical principle of comparing the numbers of
victims who have suffered with the number of offenders to be
punished. If we lost three thousand people in the collapse of the
World Trade Center, the theory goes, those responsible for the
attacks should also lose three thousand lives.

Justifying war demands less of our moral sensitivities. Abraham Lincoln insisted on war against the eleven rebellious states
not because the Union was a righteous cause but simply because
it *existed*. The logic was simple: The Union was and it must be.
As president he was committed to preserving the United States as
a single nation. This was not a cause of rectitude but of survival.
Later in the war, with the Proclamation of January 1, 1863, which
liberated the slaves still under the control of the Confederacy, the
"great emancipator" began to think of the Civil War as a moral
cause. But even emancipation had a military purpose: the slaves
so liberated would rise up as a fifth column and fight their former
overlords. Other wars of national unity, fought at roughly the
same time in Germany and slightly later in Italy, made no claim
to being causes of justice at all. These were wars fought to realize
the needs of the nation. The yearning of the culture to consoli-

date under a single government was all that was required to go to war. Lincoln was clear about the difference between a pragmatic war to preserve the Union and a moral war to abolish slavery. Would that we were so clear today.

To make an arrest, the police are not entitled to send in B-52s and target population centers just to eliminate the offender's base of operations. European police will not even enter a foreign country, except in "hot pursuit" — on the trail of a fleeing suspect. The claim that the United States is the sheriff of the world, entitled to use its armies as a means of law enforcement, verges on megalomania.

If this is justice, then we should be focused on the individual culprits. If this is war, then individuals are beside the point. No one cared about the Japanese pilots who returned safely from the attack on Pearl Harbor. They were not criminals but rather agents of an enemy power. They were not personally "guilty" for the attack, nor were their commanders, who acted in the name of the Japanese nation. The same principle arguably applies to the minions of the organized terrorist movement. They follow orders within the chain of command, even though in this case their sponsors and organizers may be as diffuse as the World Wide Web.

The worst part of the conceptual morass attendant on the war in Afghanistan is the accompanying silence on the issues that matter. The bombing was well managed but the arguments of justification are treated at best as disposable rhetoric. Words may not be laser-directed missiles but they have an explosive power of their own. Describing the conflict as war or justice lays a verbal mine that could be a treacherous obstacle in the future.

In Afghanistan the future came fast. A few months after the bombing began, the United States military forces began capturing enemy fighters, whom they shipped back to the Guantánamo Bay base in Cuba. Once again the Bush administration refused to choose between justice and war. Yet at this phase of the war it was not *both*; it was *neither*. Not war, not justice. Had it been war, the military would have been obligated to treat the detainees as prisoners of war and accord them the protections of the Geneva conventions. The camp conditions were probably not substandard, but the military insisted on interrogating the detainees, and this was not likely to be successul with prisoners recognized as POWs. Under international treaty provisions, prisoners of war are required to disclose only their name, rank, and serial number.

If this is not war but the pursuit of justice — a criminal prosecution — the provisions of the Bill of Rights bearing on a fair trial should apply in Guantánamo as they do in the United States; some experts argue to the contrary, but there is little law on the subject. If the Fifth and Sixth Amendments apply to the detainees, then as detainees they are entitled to representation by counsel. Either way, the interrogations would have been practically impossible. Thus the Bush administration began in late September 2001 by being committed to both military principles and the criteria of justice, and by the beginning of 2002, it appeared devoted to neither. (Eventually the government conceded that the Geneva Conventions applied to the Taliban but not to Al Qaeda. Still, it refused to draw the necessary conclusion and treat Taliban fighters as POWs.)

This conceptual confusion creates a dangerous situation, one that will not be resolved without considerable intellectual battle. We need to rethink the basic concepts of our jurisprudence of war and assess which of these concepts can survive and apply in a world beset with nontraditional threats from agents we call "terrorists."

The conflict in Afghanistan was certainly an "international armed conflict." And perhaps that is all that is required to say that it is a war. Some international lawyers object to calling it a war because Al Qaeda is not an organized state recognized by other states. But this form of legal recognition was discarded a long time ago as a requirement of war. The Civil War was a war in the fullest sense even though no one recognized the Confederacy as a state. After the Battle of Bull Run, the Union and Confederate armies exchanged prisoners. Recognition of these reciprocal duties has made war respectable in the history of international armed conflict. War is supposed to be civilized behavior. That is why we have the Hague and the Geneva Conventions laying down the basic rights and duties of all nations at war.

Captured "terrorists" frequently want to be treated as POWs. It is a coveted status. It confers legitimacy and ensures that the detention cannot last longer than the war itself. When hostilities cease they are entitled to go home. Timothy McVeigh wanted to be treated as a POW, but he was not taken seriously. The captured Palestinian fighters in Israel also claim that they are entitled to POW status, but the Israeli government insists on treating them as criminals subject to prosecution for their crimes. At the same time, the Israeli military targets suspected terrorists for assassination, a justified procedure if this is an armed conflict between two combative states. Everyone — governments and rebels alike — wants to have it both ways. It is no wonder that we are in a conceptual morass.

There is much to be said for recognizing the battle against the elusive enemy of terrorists as a "war." For many, this word breeds fear; it sounds too bellicose and dangerous. "Justice" sounds like a more humanitarian objective. But this is an illusion based on a misconception of the nature of war. In an international armed conflict we pursue particular policy objectives that can be achieved only by employing the lamentable means of destruction and death. It is bad enough to think of war as politics by other means. But to think of war as justice by other means runs the risk of imitating the holy mission of the enemy. Suppose the terrorists of September 11 credibly pledged never to attack again. Would we have any justification for harming a single soul? Yes — as punishment in the pursuit of justice. No — as action in pursuit of our military interests. Yes — for the sake of the victims. No — if the objective is safeguarding our security. This shows that the aims of war can be more merciful than the imperatives of seeking moral order.

Those now stuck in the idiom of justice argue that if the United States has killed more civilians in Afghanistan than the civilian losses it suffered on September 11, then the war cannot be justified. This argument is just as misleading as demanding an eye for an eye for every American lost. A war of self-defense does not seek to right the moral equation. It responds rather to fear. It seeks not revenge but safety. The purpose of neutralizing and disabling the enemy is solely to prevent future attacks and to restore the conditions of peacetime commerce.

A whole set of interconnected ideas beg for clarification. We want to know what a terrorist is, what war is, and what kind of groups can enter into war. These elusive concepts will continue to nag at us. I will attempt to make some sense of these ideas and provide some verbal tools for thinking clearly about American policies in the wake of September 11, but I cannot promise too much. We must live with a certain ambiguity.

To put our quandaries in an historical context, I shall argue that those sympathetic to war in our time are heirs to the Romantic tradition. We are the children of William Wordsworth's and Johann Gottlieb Fichte's ardor in resisting Napoleon. We think and feel in the moral currents still surging from John Brown's attack on Harpers Ferry and from Abraham Lincoln's conceiving of the United States as a single "nation under God" that must "long endure." We have come to think of our nation as an actor in a drama of good and evil—of the forces of freedom pitted against an "Axis of Evil."

The revival of Romantic sensibilities in the United States challenges the prevailing liberal orthodoxy in our liberal arts colleges, in the law schools, in the courts, and in the media. Liberal principles, drawn from Aristotle and Kant, support the commitment to abstract justice—an idea that should prevail in our courts but arguably should have only an incidental role in our foreign policy. In the age of terrorism we are torn between our Romantic and liberal selves, and this explains why we fluctuate in our thinking about war and justice.

The Romantic sensibility carries implications for the issues of our time. The flames and fears of war lead us to neglect constitutional principles in contemplating trials of our opponents. We are confused about issues of loyalty and the problem of treason against the nation. The open recognition of our Romantic sentiments will enable us to understand, I argue, our perception of collective action in the commission of war crimes and genocide. It accounts for our inclinations to think of groups and nations as guilty for their crimes. The notion of collective guilt — long an anathema of liberals — becomes plausible in the Romantic perspective on collective action.

As the argument develops we will see that there is no reason to treat collective guilt, as do many liberals, as the expression of a primitive morality. There is another side to the story — a humanistic interpretation that leads to the mitigation of punishment in cases like those of Adolf Eichmann and Slobodan Milosevic. And yet within the Romantic tradition, there lies a great danger. If we take this alternative vision too seriously we encounter problems signaled by the words "national character," "original sin," and "authenticity," and ultimately the problem of enforcing a moral order against those who, in full Romantic flowering, sincerely and violently act out their aberrant hatreds.

We are engaged, therefore, in a quest to reach a deeper understanding of our conflicted selves, of grasping how we are simultaneously drawn and repelled by war, how we believe passionately that the government is doing the right thing to the point that we implicitly subscribe to emergency maneuvers that are arguably in violation of the Constitution. We are undertaking a quest to understand a set of problems — the nature of war, honor, crime, and justice — in brief, the problems of glory and guilt in the age of terrorism. At the foundation of the inquiry, however, lies a pursuit for self-understanding, for grasping our existential condition in a time in which we seek, in Yeats's words, to avoid "anarchy . . . loosed upon the world" and to hold the center when "the worst are full of passionate intensity."

Rediscovering the Appeal of War

We thought the age of war was behind us.

After nuking Hiroshima, after napalming Vietnam, we had only distaste for the idea and the practice of war. As the twentieth century drew to a close we could think that it was the end of history — at least the history of wars that could change the map of civilization. After the collapse of the Soviet Union, wars seemed not only unnecessary but repulsive. The thought of dying for a noble cause, the pursuit of honor in the name of *patria*, brotherhood in arms — none of this appealed to us anymore. The disdain for war has accumulated slowly since the end of World War II. "I hate war and so does Eleanor," opined FDR in the oft-repeated lyrics of Pete Seeger. In the 1960s Tom Lehrer caught the mood of the war-weary. "We only want the world to know / That we support the status quo. . . . / So when in doubt, / Send the Marines!" War had become taboo — or at least, so we might have thought.

A shift in our attitudes toward war became evident even before September 11. If the post–World War II and Vietnam eras found expression in films like *Dr. Strangelove* and *Apocalypse Now*, the new spirit of patriotism became visible in Steven Spielberg's film *Saving Private Ryan* and in Tom Brokaw's bestseller *The Greatest Generation*. Slightly more than fifty years after the event, the invasion of Normandy became a focal point of nostalgia and renewed interest in the lives of heroes bound together in the brotherhood of battle. Consider that Joseph Ellis, best-selling historian and professor at Mount Holyoke College, made up stories of his heroic military adventures to please his students. It would have been unthinkable for a professor circa 1970 or 1980 to think that he could impress a university audience by pretending to have fought against the Vietcong. The post–September 11 call to arms came when many Americans were yearning to believe, once again, that our highest calling lay in going to war for freedom and the American way.

On September 10 I was attracted to publicity for a new series on HBO — *Band of Brothers* — based on Stephen Ambrose's novel of the same name. In the immediate aftermath of the attack, Hollywood speculated that no one would want to be reminded of war and death on the silver screen. Family comedies were to become standard fare. But marketing experts are no more reliable than the experts who feared the military might of the Soviet Union or who predicted an ever-rising Dow Jones. It turned out that some of the most prominent films of 2001 relied upon themes of honor and glorified combat. *Lord of the Rings* — nominated for an Academy Award as the best picture of the year — invokes all the themes of honor and glory in combat that we thought had become passé in our political culture. As projected onto the hobbits and their mythological world, these themes could speak to the American public longing for orientation in a time of danger. Writing in the *New York Times*, Stephen Holden noted this theme in the leading films of 2001, in production well before September 11, and asked: "What is it about films that lends them such an eerie (if vague) predictive quality?"

Whatever happened on September 11, it happened to us. And being there, we bring with us our urges for romantic adventure, our yearning for national honor, our willingness to expose ourselves to risk and to conquer the dangers by using force. For many, "patriotic" became the word that fit the new mood of pride and resistance. In that period of fifty years when we thought that "right-thinking people" had nothing but contempt for war, we — and particularly we members of the chattering class who fill the media, blanket the air waves, and teach the young — also rejected the mind-set that makes war attractive. Honor and patriotism took on negative connotations. They were the symbols of a macho culture better left behind. We also had disdain for the Romantic view of the world that tends to glorify the nation and war as an expression of patriotism. But now perhaps we can begin to recognize that our national honor matters to us and that there is no sin in being patriotic about the United States and its leadership in the world. It may be time as well to recognize the appeal of Romanticism as a factor that inspires both patriotism and a willingness to go to war for the sake of national interests.

How do we explain the revival of Romantic sensibilities in our time? Young Americans want to prove that they too can qualify as among the "greatest generations." The fear of war has dissipated. The contempt for military incompetence is forgotten. As a symbol of the fighting forces, Secretary of Defense Donald Rumsfeld shows himself to have true grit in his CNN briefings. There is even some Romantic regard for the exotic fighters in the kaffiyeh and flowing robes of Al Qaeda. In ambivalent identification with the aggressor, professorial and student panels meet to ponder why "they" hate us so much. "What have we done wrong?" they ponder in the inevitable distortion of blaming the victim. A young American named John Walker Lindh goes to fight for the Taliban and he is captured. Some clamor for his immediate execution. Others, including top officials in Washington, see him as one of us who went astray in his search for authenticity and religious truth.

Romantic sensibilities are at large again. The feelings that inspired the English poets from Wordworth, to Keats, to Byron flow once more through our veins.

Perhaps the half-life of historical influence is shorter than we think. Two and a half generations after the event, memory begins to distort. Nostalgia sets in. Fifty years after the end of the Civil War, we were ready once again for war on a grand scale, this time, in the words of Woodrow Wilson, "to make the world safe for democracy." We forgot the brutality of the killing fields in Gettysburg and Antietam and began to think of war as a means of social progress. Fifty years after the end of World War II, we began to cultivate nostalgia for the heroism of our men at Normandy. The grandchildren of those who died would celebrate not only the victory over fascism but the meaningfulness of combat. The values of brotherhood, courage, and honor overwhelm the prior sense that shooting at other human beings is irrational and barbaric.

Though we rarely use the word "honor," the virtue still appeals to us. We are familiar with the debate about whether the war against terrorism has any practical value. The critics argue, with good cause, that bombing poor Muslim countries only has the effect of inculcating hatred of the United States in a new generation. We might get rid of bin Laden and Mullah Omar but there will be many to take their place. The conclusion is: Don't fight back, except by political, financial, and educational means. Don't use military violence because it will only yield more terrorist violence in the future.

There may be a lot of truth in this criticism. There is no way knowing for sure whether the bombing of Afghanistan will have the long-term effect of reducing or increasing spontaneous outbursts of killing and mass destruction. And if some catastrophe of mass destruction befalls us in two decades, we will not be able to determine whether it would have happened, had we taken a more conciliatory route in late 2001.

The implication is that our military policies cannot be justified solely by their short-term success. As we failed to anticipate the attack of September 11, we are probably failing now to calculate accurately all the consequences, for good or for ill, of our actions.

If we are not sure that a military response is the right response, there must be other factors at work in our thinking. In fact, we are more sensitive to national honor than we are inclined to admit. To sit back and suffer attack, without responding in kind, is to accept a form of national humiliation. It is precisely the humiliation that comes to the minds of Muslims when they think of the Crusades and the Christian invasion of Jerusalem in the eleventh century.

Of course, we do not speak easily of honor. We think of it as the ethic of the Mafia or of Pashtun tribesmen who claim that their honor requires that their wives wear burkas. But this concept that rarely speaks its name (at least in the West) may be driving, in part, the wars being fought at the beginning of the twenty-first century. Israelis and Palestinians, Indians and Pakistanis, Americans and Afghanis — we are all sensitive to our image of strength and military prowess. We cannot think rationally about the costs and benefits of going to war because *not* going to war in response to a military attack is to sacrifice our national honor. And honor has its imperatives that are hardly measured in conventional trade-offs. We might dress up this argument by claiming that honor and strength are great values in the Arab world, and therefore we can gain influence in that part of the world only by profiling our power. As bin Laden put it in one of his videotapes, "When people see a strong horse and a weak horse, by nature they will like the strong horse."

Sociologist David Mandelbaum describes the use of the word *izzat* in Arabic and Persian culture: "It is a word often heard in men's talk, particularly when the talk is about conflict, rivalry, and struggle. It crops up as a kind of final explanation for motivation, whether for acts of aggression or beneficence." The same Arabic word, meaning roughly "honor" is used in Turkish and thus signals a widespread reliance on this value we share with Islamic cultures.

But we should not think that we are much different on this score from our opponents. We care as much about honor as they do. As the Egyptians and Palestinians have felt recurrent national disgrace in losing one war after another to Israel, we would suffer debilitating humiliation by simply absorbing the catastrophe of military attack without a military response. All the arguments about counterproductivity, about producing more terrorists in the future, pale in comparison with this incessant drive to maintain our role as a superpower on the stage of world politics.

But adhering to an ethic of honor should give us second thoughts. Taking the blow on September 11 without a military response would be like suffering a slap in the face and not responding with a challenge to fight. If honor requires the use of bombs and missiles, then we are implicitly endorsing a dueling culture. Indeed, it may be true that though the behavior of *individuals* has evolved toward ways of coping with conflict on the basis of needs and interests, the values that move *nations* are rooted in the past.

One is reminded of the views expressed by the late eighteenth-century German philosopher Immanuel Kant on the possibility of excusing a homicide committed in a duel. If someone kills another in a duel is he guilty of a felony? The slayer can say on his behalf, "My opponent agreed to the duel. It was either kill or be killed." In the ideal world, Kant reasoned, dueling would be abolished and the killing would be homicide. The culture of honor was, in his opinion, an atavistic throwback, but the law had nonetheless to recognize that honor matters to people as they are. If they wish to duel, therefore, their wishes must be respected. The survivor should not be prosecuted for homicide—at least as long as the culture of honor and of dueling still influence the minds of those who take up arms and march the prescribed number of paces.

We could say the same about the culture of violence in international affairs. Honor and strength go hand in hand. The culture of dueling lives on. Now it is called war.

The peculiar appeal of military violence brings to bear the Romantic view of the world that prevailed in Europe in the early nineteenth century, when the resistance against Napoleon and the affirmation of national identity filled the minds of poets, theologians, and even lawyers. Though Wordsworth initially subscribed to the universal pretension of the French Revolution, later he could think only of the glory of English soldiers joining with the Spanish to resist the march of Napoleon. Johann Gottlieb Fichte found his national fervor as an outgrowth of a version of Kantian philosophy, a version centering on the self and its capacity to define the world according to its inherent impulses. Like Lord Byron, who took his Romanticism seriously and devoted his fortune and ultimately his life to the cause of the Greeks in their fight for independence against the Turks, Fichte too became a man of action. According to legend he organized his own ragtag band of soldiers in Berlin to fight off Napoleon's armies. His "militia" included Friedrich Schleiermacher, the famous theologian who found a way to God in his Romantic indulgence in sentiment, and Friedrich Carl von Savigny, the legal philosopher who rejected the French Civil Code and insisted that Germany take its own path in the development of legal institutions.

The Romantics were thinkers who felt compelled to translate their thoughts into actions. And the actions often took the form of armed conflict. In the nineteenth century the outstanding example was Byron, who suffered a premature death from an illness contracted as he was preparing with Greek troops for battle on the island of Missolonghi. On the American side, we overflowed at midcentury with Romantics willing to fight, some of these a little more crazy than others. John Brown captured the life of action in his raid on Harpers Ferry, and later luminaries like Ralph Waldo Emerson and Henry David Thoreau wrote admiringly of his Romantic sacrifice for the nation.

Another good example on the American side was Francis Lieber, the immigrant philosopher, schooled in the idealism of his Kantian teachers, who joyfully left his classroom in a small South Carolina college to join German liberals as they fought in the uprising of 1848. He returned to the United States, became a professor at Columbia College in New York City, and devoted himself to writing the first codified law of war. He was a zealous defender of the Union cause and believed fiercely in Lincoln's Romantic creed that Americans were a single nation that had to live and die together.

In the beginning of the twentieth century, the appeals of Romantic war took center stage. As Barbara Ehrenreich describes the popular reaction to World War I, the outbreak of hostilities in 1914 unleashed "a veritable frenzy of enthusiasm . . . not for killing or loot . . . but for something far more uplifting and worthy." Romantics have not had an easy time articulating what is so "uplifting and worthy" about war; they simply know it when they feel it.

The Spanish Civil War had a similar appeal in the period between the World Wars. Thousands of Americans, craving adventure, formed the Abraham Lincoln Brigade and left en masse to fight alongside other starry-eyed volunteers against General Franco's forces in Spain. Those who knew of Byron's escapades in Greece could not but feel the historical parallel. The escape of the quotidian, the pursuit of glory, fighting for a just cause — this is Romantic war at its best.

Romanticism and Its Opposites

A good way to situate the contested concept of Romanticism in intellectual history is to see it as one pole in a larger set of oppositional concepts. On the one hand, we have stability, order, universality, and the boredom of the predictable and domestic. On the other hand, we have revolt, disorder, partiality, and the intense flames of lust and creativity. This is, of course, the way Romantics might describe the sentiments that move them.

The Romantic movement is, after all, about feeling. The English poets rallied around Wordsworth's dictum that poetry is "the spontaneous overflow of powerful feelings." The triumph of emotion is evident as well in the rise of Romantic music, the surge of Beethoven's symphonies in the concert halls of Europe. As lovers of emotion in the arts, we are children of the Romantics, but we easily forget the distinguished and respectable positions against which the Romantics were reacting.

Romanticism has many antonyms. In the context of music, the "Romantic" is opposed to the classical, represented by Haydn and Mozart, with, as one analyst put it, their "concern for musical form with a greater emphasis on concise melodic expression and clarity of instrumental color." Romantic music became associated with national self-expression. Johann Sebastian Bach wrote in the spirit of universal Christianity, but the Romantic music of the nineteenth century became identifiable as national music. Beethoven and Brahms saw themselves as German composers, and Chopin's music is considered Polish. In the world of painting, the contrast is between the schools of Vermeer and Rembrandt, on the classical side, and the expressive and expansionist forms of the French impressionists, notably Delacroix, on the Romantic wing. In the realm of theology, the Catholic Church stood for orthodoxy and the rational defense of religious doctrine. Protestant theologians like Georg Hamann and Friedrich Schleiermacher broke new ground by appealing to the world of feeling as the premise of religious experience. Lawyers debated whether the Civil Code imposed by Napoleon in 1804 could become the model for all of humanity. In 1814 Savigny wrote his famous tract favoring the independent national development of legal cultures and, in particular, German law. He coined the famous expression *Zeitgeist* — spirit of the times — that has become synonymous with the Romantic resistance to universal culture.

The American analogue to Savigny might well have been Oliver Wendell Holmes Jr., who cultivated the common law tradition with a literary flair then novel in legal studies. As a veteran of the Civil War, wounded three times in battle, he was skeptical about whether right and wrong could be so clearly discerned that men should lay down their lives in battle. He became part of the pragmatic movement that took hold a decade after Appomattox and brought his philosophy of experience into the law, both as scholar and as judge on the Supreme Court. "The life of the law has not been logic but experience," he wrote famously in 1881. As legal scholar Anne Dailey writes in a new interpretation of Holmes, the judge echoed great Romantic themes. Like Emerson, he was willing to flirt with ideas of the infinite and the profound. Thus he celebrated the profundity of legal thought in *The Path of the Law*: "[Through the remote aspects of the law of universal interest, you can] connect your subject with the universe and catch an echo of the infinite, a glimpse of its unfathomable process, a hint of the universal law."

For poets, musicians, theologians — and yes, lawyers — the experience of the culturally embedded self becomes a path to truth. The world outside is understood as a reflection of the world within.

If we have to single out one figure to represent the alternative to this reliance on "leaps of feeling," it would be Immanuel Kant, whose philosophy distinguishes rigorously between the realm of reason and the world of sensual impulse. Though he was later misinterpreted by Fichte and other Romantics, Kant is the leading Enlightenment expositor of faith in reason. Reason, a quality shared by all human beings, illuminates the path to objective truth. The slightest contamination of reason by sensual impulses destroys reason's impartiality. The world of sensual impulse can lead, according to Kant, only to subjective judgments, with their "truth" limited to the person whose feelings are in play.

The notion of humanity, as Kant understood it, is based on the universality of reason. Human beings share the capacity to enter the world of pure reason and there discover the moral law that should govern their behavior. Only when they enter this world of reason — only when their wills free themselves of sensual input — only then can human beings claim to act "morally." The essential point is that all of humanity is grounded in a single universal source of dignity — namely, the capacity to reason. Reason is not always available to us in our thinking about right and wrong, for we are subject to the incessant demands of our senses and our desires. To the extent that human beings can enter the realm of reason, however, they can become like God and the angels, who, according to Kant, live exclusively in a world of intelligence uncontaminated by sensual distractions.

The most difficult point to grasp in Kantian thinking is that reason inhabits a dimension beyond the five senses. We have to think about reason the way we think about a transcendental God. We can touch and feel neither God nor reason. The way to approach the Kantian realm is not to try to invoke one's capacity to feel but just the opposite: to abstract oneself entirely from the world of sensual impulse. Herein lies the fundamental cleavage with the Romantic worldview: Kant fled from sensuality in order to embrace reason as the path to truth, while the Romantics embraced nature, sensual impulses, the inner world of feeling as the lamp of truth.

There is much to be said for the Kantian view of the world. Kant bequeathed to us the idea of human dignity—a quality shared by all human beings, regardless of culture, nation, history, race, or gender. Though the concept has not gotten much play in American legal thought, the notion of human dignity lies at the foundation of postwar European jurisprudence. The German Constitution of 1949 declares boldly in its first article: "Human dignity is inviolable." And it continues: The primary duty of the state is to "protect and promote" human dignity.

Since the Second World War there has been an explosion of advocacy in favor of human rights—the rights that belong to all people simply because they are human. This entire movement trades on the Kantian idea that a single principle of dignity unites all members of the species.

This concept of universal dignity is as close as we can get in a secular world to the biblical idea that all human beings are created in the image of God. Being made in God's image is, after all, the basis for thinking that we share some feature that makes us distinctively human. For both adherents of the Bible and devotees of Kant, the notion of universal human value carries important implications. In the Book of Genesis the prohibition against homicide is derived from our being made in God's image. "He who sheds the blood of man, by man shall his blood be shed," for we are made "in the image of God" (Gen. 9:6). Kant takes the same stance in favor of treating human life as an absolute.

As Kant was writing far to the east in Königsberg, the *philosophes* in Paris were preaching ideas that led to the crowning slogan of the French Revolution—*liberté, egalité, fraternité*. Thomas Jefferson, too, was a child of the same set of Enlightenment values. Without the influence of those who advocated the ultimate equality of all human beings, he would never have coined the immortal lines of the Declaration of Independence: "We hold these truths to be self-evident, that all men are created equal, that they are endowed by their Creator with certain inalienable rights, among these life, liberty, and the pursuit of happiness."

These claims constitute the foundations of our legal culture. Our commitment to individual rights and to equality before the law would not be possible had the values of the Enlightenment not triumphed in American culture. Yet these are precisely the values against which the Romantics rebelled.

This, then, is the fundamental and enduring conflict between the universalism of Kantian morality and the Romanticism of the poets, theologians, and lawyers who cultivate the self and the particular, the uniqueness of their national experience. Of course, as in any wholesale description of intellectual trends, there are, at the retail level, many exceptions and nuanced middle positions. Of interest in this study is not the proper classification of every well-known figure but the articulation of a way of looking at the world that is more closely associated with the Romantics than with any other self-identified collection of writers and artists.

The tension between the Romantic and universalist outlooks is captured in the careers of two critical words — honor and dignity. Honor is critical to the Romantic, dignity to the Kantian universalist. Honor is associated with appearance to others, in the way we fulfill our roles on the stage of social interaction. Dignity is intrinsic to the human condition. Everyone has it merely by virtue of being born. As the secular analogue to "being made in God's image," the Kantian value of dignity adheres to criminals and nobles alike. You can lose your honor but not your intrinsic dignity. Though you can act in an undignified way, your intrinsic worth, acquired at birth, is never extinguished.

The important implication of linking humanity and dignity is that nations have no inherent dignity. Their consolation is that they have honor — depending on how they act in the international arena. Nations have roles to play — they are like soldiers, lawyers, and politicians who fill parts on their respective stages. Nations can experience glory and grandeur as well as humiliation. But speaking about the dignity of nations is mixing incompatible vocabularies.

To be reminded of the different associations of honor and dignity, think of the usage some generations ago when we spoke of women "losing their honor" by, say, becoming pregnant out of wedlock. Being a man or a woman in this culture was to play a certain kind of role defined by social conventions. It had nothing to do with intrinsic dignity, which was certainly not lost by going one's own way in matters of sex and morality.

Expansionist and Reductionist Thinking

At the core of the Romantic sensibility lies a way of looking at the world, a mode of thinking that I will call expansionist as opposed to reductionist. To understand this distinction, think about the world that is assumed in our daily conversations. Relative to this fuzzy baseline of conventional understanding, one can either expand on the conventional perceptions of the world around us or reduce these impressions to a set of agreed-upon units — like persons, drives, atoms, or elements in the periodic table. Reductionism is the more common vice. Strict empiricists seek to reduce scientific laws to observable data and nothing more. A good example is Hume's analysis of causation as the recurrent concatenation of events. If B is observed to follow A on a regular basis, then it follows, supposedly, that A causes B. But this way of looking at causation fails adequately to account for the factor that Kant termed the relationship of "necessity," an assumption that we make in order to account for the world we perceive.

Expansionists seek abstract entities to account for things we observe. They follow Kant and Plato in their willingness to posit entities that exist beyond the five senses. At one level we grasp reality in the world of the senses but our minds can roam beyond that which we touch and see and expand the range of our available concepts. In politics, the expansionist move is to find a clash of great ideas in seemingly earthly conflicts. By contrast, the reductionist seeks to localize the dispute and keep it close to the ground.

The expansionist Theodore Parker saw in every political dispute bearing on slavery a struggle between the Slave Power and the Freedom Power. The reductionist would see two individuals at odds about their immediate interests. The expansionist dwells on a grain of sand and like William Blake reaches out to the mysteries of the universe. The reductionist looks at a grain of sand and finds a chemical composition.

On the lighter side, a cartoon in the *New York Times* invoked this distinction in a satire of Al Gore's imagined comment on President Bush's 2002 State of the Union address. Addressing the linking of Iraq, Iran, and North Korea as a single compact of enemies, Gore is described as saying, "Now we're at war, we need a well-read wonk in the White House. I've read Ahmed Rashid. . . . Where others see 'evil axes,' I see the nuances of political stratega." The expansionist sees a mythological struggle between good and evil. The reductionist liberal "policy wonk" understands the nuances of the situation.

In a leap of imagination, the expansionist thinks about grand struggles. But beyond this, we don't know how much more the Romantic is willing to claim. The quest recalls Hamlet's protest to his friend: "There are more things in heaven and earth, Horatio, than are dreamt of in your philosophy." The element of "more" eludes definition. The Romantic yearns for the infinite and the profound. But as Isaiah Berlin reminds us, *la profondeur* represents a depth without limit. The deeper the probe, the more elusive the target.

The reductionist seeks to bring reality down to its component parts. The actions of groups become the sum total of individual actions. If Romantics express the expansionist impulse, individualists incline toward reductionism, seeing the world as consisting of units—in particular, of human beings acting as "sovereign" entities. The terms "struggle" and "movement" and "nation under God" resonate in the veins of the engaged Romantic. The reductionist replaces the expansionist self with the causal language of incentives and drives. If Romantic theologian Theodore

Parker saw the Civil War as the acting out of great ideas on the stage of history, an economically minded scholar like Richard Posner would prefer to think about the respective advantages of abolition and slavery.

Ironically, reductionism facilitates universalization. If the world consists fundamentally of individual persons, it is possible to generalize about these individuals wherever they happen to be, whatever language they speak, or whatever religion they may happen to profess. The reductionist impulse engenders the universalist spirit of the Enlightenment. Its language stresses rights, dignity, equality — all the values that constitute the foundations of the modern liberal state. Indeed they might call themselves "liberals," as do many philosophers in the spirit of the Enlightenment. I am wary of that label because of its associations with economic liberalism and the "L" word in contemporary political conversations. But for want of a better term I will use it to refer to the universalist individualistic worldview at odds against the Romantic temperament.

The great moral philosophers of our time have all been liberal individualists. The list includes John Rawls, Ronald Dworkin, Amartya Sen, Joseph Raz, Thomas Nagel, and Bruce Ackerman. They may quarrel with economists such as Richard Posner and Milton Friedman, but the economists — with their theories of consumer sovereignty and free choice — simply represent another branch of the liberal tradition.

Lost in the contemporary debate is an understanding of the passions that drove the Romantic reaction to the Enlightenment and that continue to influence the way we think, albeit quietly and without proper recognition. We fail to appreciate the appeal of partiality and respect the demands of emotion. We are disinclined to acknowledge nations as actors in history or to understand the way they become guilty for their crimes.

The Romantics haunt us from the grave. Their spirit lives on, in part, in everyone torn by the conflicting sentiments of equality and loyalty, impartiality and solidarity, universality and commitment to those whom we love. We live in the world but we need a home. And the Romantic spirit dwells in these yearnings for partiality and solidarity. The Romantics influence our thinking and yet we have failed to take their measure. We must retrieve them from the recesses of our culture and assess them as they actually shape our assumptions about politics, law, and war.

Irreconcilable Conflicts

The language we teach our children, the
bedtime stories we tell them . . . are as
good a way of satisfying our national
obligations as a declaration of readiness to
die for the sake of the nation.
— *Yael Tamir*

Is the conflict between liberal individu-
alism and Romanticism the kind that lends itself to a solution?
Could both sides just sit down and negotiate, compromise, and
split the difference? Here, interestingly, it depends on whom you
ask. If you put the question to a child of the Enlightenment, the
answer is, of course, that there must be some way to accommo-
date the Romantic hostility to the Enlightenment within a broad-
ened conception of Enlightenment values. This seems to be the
ambition of Nancy Rosenblum in her book *Another Liberalism*,
which begins with a provocative account of the Romantic attraction to war and culminates in an effort to reduce Romantic
yearning to another version of personal autonomy and other liberal values. Many followers of John Rawls fend off charges by
communitarian critics by arguing that the need to be embedded
in a community is simply another good — like wealth and liberty — that shapes the selection of the principles of justice.

If you ask a Romantic whether accommodation is possible, the
answer must be no — for at least in Isaiah Berlin's magisterial account of the movement, the Romantic break with the Enlightenment was meant to be radical and irreconcilable. Standing in op-

position was an essential part of the movement. Defiance became important in itself. For the liberal, alternative worldviews are simply another opportunity for tolerance and inclusion. For the Romantic, alternative visions generate a meaning-filled drama of opposition and struggle.

There are numerous contrasts between the Romantic and the liberal ways of thinking, but in Berlin's elegant account, the basic point of distinction lies in their approach to solving problems. The Kantian approach to the world treats reason as the universal solvent. All questions find a rational solution in the structured worlds of physics, ethics, or logic. Culture, language, history, and religion pose no barriers to the rational deliberation of all human beings about their differences.

Three propositions capture the universalist and rationalist spirit of the Enlightenment: First, all genuine questions can be answered — either by us or by those wiser than us. Second, these answers are ultimately knowable — again, not necessarily by us but perhaps by those who will come after us. And third, these answers are compatible with each other in the sense that they constitute a coherent and consistent view of the world. Bernard Fontenelle, a representative figure of the period, regarded the geometer as the ideal. Only a sense of geometric harmony could express the kind of consistency in politics and morals that reason required.

We might think of the invention of the metric system and its adoption in France in 1795 as the symbolic scientific achievement of the age. The idea that all weights and measures would translate neatly into one another offered the correct picture of a harmonious universe. Everything we touch and see can be reduced to variations on the single unit of measurement — the meter — which stands in a precise arithmetic relationship to the circumference of the Earth. The meter, in turn, generates the units of weight and volume that tie together this rational system for gauging the world around us. The standard meter, today located in the French National Archives, is the perfect symbol of the rationalist impulse to order the world in logically compatible units.

If the "meter bar" is my preferred symbol of the Enlightenment, then allow me to take the number π as the insignia of the
Romantics. The beauty of π is that it cannot be definitely pinned
down. The attempt to express the ratio of a circle's radius to its
circumference leads to an infinite extension of numbers — 3.14159
. . . ad infinitum. The deeper one probes, the stronger the sense of
an unreachable limit. The interlocking order of nature breaks
down. The radius and the circumference have no common denominator. This simple fact, known to the Greeks, was but the
first crack in the rational geometric structure. Eventually, mathematicians used their systems to expand our sense of available reality. They invented imaginary numbers based on the nonexistent
square roots of negative integers. The most dramatic break came
during the Romantic era when Nikolai Lobachevsky and Janos
Bolyai dropped the necessity of conforming geometric premises to
the observable world. There was no need to assume that parallel
lines could never intersect, not even in infinity. In this contingent
world, the geometrician could begin with any set of premises that
promised to generate elegant theorems. With the anchor of a
shared world lifted, there was no limit to the imaginary worlds to
which mathematicians might journey. Elegance and simplicity replaced truth as the criteria of genius. Romanticism had entered
the world of precise calculation.

The late eighteenth- and early nineteenth-century surges of Romantic thought — say Hamann's theological reflections or Delacroix's paintings — were more likely to originate not with geometric reflections but with the passions of the self. Wordsworth
thought of his poetry as an opening of the self to an identification
with nature, with the nation, and with higher spirits beyond. The
non-Euclidian geometricians, contemporaries of late Romantics,
shared the yearning to disengage from the world as it is. For enlightened rationalists the subject stands apart from the object of
contemplation but for the Romantic the distance between the "I"
and the "it" becomes blurred. The diverse subjectivities of the
new geometricians, as well as those of the poets and the theo-

logians, defined points of view irreconcilable with the Enlightenment spirit. The expansionist self takes over and the perceived
world becomes dependent on personal vision and imagination. In
the field of music the contrast is stated differently, but still we
have on the one hand the classical harmonies of Bach and Haydn
not located in any particular national culture, and on the other
hand the nineteenth-century outpouring of Beethoven and
Chopin, which become identifiable as the musical languages of
particular cultures.

To speak of these broad movements of the Enlightenment and
the accompanying Romantic reaction, we must abstract from particular writers and appreciate "the family resemblance" among
writers who may diverge on many points. Ludwig Wittgenstein
coined the phrase "family resemblance" to explain this phenomenon of imprecise generalization. In a family of some twenty blood
relatives, each person will resemble some in some respects and
others in other respects. For example, A might have the same
color hair as B, C, and D and the same shaped nose as C, D, and
E. E in turn might be tall like B and C while the others are
shorter. No one will resemble everyone in every dimension and
yet we can still see that the group constitutes a single family.

The Romantic movement is similar. Wordsworth and Fichte may
think similarly on the issue of nationhood, though they arrive at
these conclusions by different paths. Herder and Rousseau might
concur on their approach to language but differ on many points
from kindred Romantic spirits. Together they constitute a family
of ideas because of the complex intersections within the group.

There are also some intriguing crossover figures. For most purposes Rousseau is a Romantic. With his high regard for the primitive and the natural, he stands front and center in Berlin's account as a founder of the Romantic movement. Yet Rousseau
relied upon the theory of a hypothetical social contract and the
principle of testing legitimacy by "the consent of the governed,"
both mainstays of liberal thinking in our time. Kant is considered
the leading thinker of the Enlightenment and yet he offered argu-

ments about the centrality of the self that Fichte and other Romantics could expand and adapt to their special purposes. In the world of ideas, it is hard to find "pure" representatives of any collective movement. All categories pale in the face of rich and original thought. Yet to keep our mind on the broader agenda, we have a great deal to gain by accepting a certain amount of imprecision in stating the grand contrast between these two movements that continue to compete for loyalty in the contemporary mind.

Our concern is not whether the Enlightened or the Romantic thinker should gain the upper hand, whether one of their positions is right or wrong. There is no neutral way to choose between the cerebral appeal of universal rationality and the siren of passionate subjectivity. We are caught, as the Romantics would say, in an ongoing struggle between two conflicting worldviews. Whether we can resolve this struggle depends ultimately on whether we come down in favor of the Rationalists or the Romantics. Without prejudging that question, we have much to learn by opening our minds to the Romantic alternative. At stake is appreciating the way in which Romantic views percolate through our culture and influence our attitudes toward nationhood, honor, and war.

Language and Difference

The notion of irreconcilable difference lies at the heart of our inquiry and there is no doubt that it is an idea that enlightened liberals have trouble grasping. Accommodation is the key to liberal thinking. Whatever the value, it can be reduced to a value that is absorbed within the liberal system of thought. If the issue is the need for communal association, that can be rendered compatible, as Will Kymlicka argues, with John Rawls's approach to the fundamental values that we all share. If the question is the imperative of loyalty to our friends and nations, that too, as Josiah Royce claims, is subject to universalization. The notion of the rupture, the unbridgeable gap, the partial and discontinuous — these ideas have little purchase in the work of Rawls, Dworkin, Ackerman, or the entire camp of American Kantians. We confront an idea that itself breaks the mold of the dominant mode of thought.

One key to the great divide between liberals and Romantics is their respective attitudes toward language. The spirit of universalism requires indifference to the role of language as the factor dividing the world into irreconcilable spheres. From the writings of Augustine to the hip linguistics of Steven Pinker, there has always been a tendency to think that all human beings dwell in a universal preverbal conceptual world. They acquire language to name the thoughts and images they have stocked in their minds. In Pinker's lexicon, this language of images is called "Mentalese" and its presumably the same in all human beings. It is expressed poetically in the Book of Genesis, where the animals pass before Adam and the words uttered to describe them become their names (Gen. 2:19).

This attitude is carried forward in the modern liberal attitude toward language. Language is thought to be something like a computer program. Whether you use Microsoft Word or WordPerfect, the message is the same. The same attitude prevails in thinking about the medium of French or Chinese. The factor of language carries no significance in the liberal paradigm. It is but a veil that covers the universal human being, a communicating agent with a Chomskian universal grammar. It is hardly accidental that the philosophy of liberalism, as I have described it here, is largely an English-language phenomenon. It is a characteristic belief of those who speak and think in the world's hegemonic language that language is largely irrelevant. In fact, the concept of "liberalism" as it is used in these philosophic discussions, is itself a feature of the English language. The word "liberal" as used in Europe carries largely economic connotations. A liberal follows, for example, Friedrich Hayek's principles of free-market economics.

From the very beginning Romantics rebelled against this conception of language as a background condition that has no constitutive function in the definition of personality. Johann Gottfried Herder was the strongest proponent of the view that the self evolves in the acquisition of language and that therefore there is no way of thinking of a universal person apart from his or her roots in a particular language. For Herder and his followers this attitude toward language provided a natural basis for a nonchauvinistic conception of nationalism. Every culture must seek to thrive on the basis of its own language, and every person has the right to its distinctive form of authentic expression. Being oneself, being authentic, requires the cultivation of one's native language, whatever it happens to be.

Wordsworth captured this sentiment for the English language:

> We must be free or die, who speak the tongue
> That Shakespeare spoke: the faith and morals hold
> Which Milton held. — In everything we are sprung
> Of Earth's first blood, have titles manifold.

Languages have their imperative. Whether English, German, or Navajo, they are entitled to survive. There is no common denominator beyond language that we could adopt in lieu of the tongue in which we feel free and authentic.

Perhaps one could have it both ways; perhaps the Enlightened universalists could be right and the Herderians too, but this would require that all languages translate readily into all others. The world could have been constructed that way — the way the different dialects of Chinese all read the same characters but pronounce them differently. Cantonese and Mandarin approach this kind of one-to-one mapping, but even there, there are differences in the written combinations of characters. Other languages testify to the incredible diversity of the spoken word. Hebrew and English, Hungarian and French — these and the other six thousand currently used languages represent distinctive worlds, each with its own way of packaging reality and guiding the perceptions of its native speakers. The universal pretensions of liberal thought break down in the face of irreconcilable linguistic differences.

The idea that all languages translate into English dies hard. At some level, we of the hegemonic language are inclined to think that we possess the world's universal linguistic solvent. The problem is that we are not even aware of the cultural particularities that we foist on other countries. This is nowhere more evident than in the current drafting for treaties and documents on international human rights and criminal liability. The proposed International Criminal Court will supposedly hear its cases and conduct proceedings in the six official languages of the United Nations—Spanish, French, Russian, Arabic, Chinese, and English. Yet the official negotiations all occurred in English, and the texts contain impossible-to-translate terms that are familiar to American lawyers but appear arcane and mysterious to lawyers from non-English-speaking countries.

Two examples make the point. "Fairness" and "reasonableness" are as American as McDonald's but while the term "Big Mac" translates easily, these terms do not. The notions of "fair play"and a "fair trial" run through the discourse of lawyers: President Bush's November 2001 order to establish military tribunals, a legal move subject to harsh criticism, sought to reassure the world that the suspects would receive a "full and fair trial." The only problem is that most of the world does not understand the term "fair trial." Even our European colleagues are likely to confuse a fair trial with a just trial (*un process juste, un processo justo*). In a just trial, the outcome squares with the culpability and desert of the offender. In a fair trial, the key is not the outcome but the way the game is played. In the context of the military tribunals, one can see the difference. If the deck is stacked against the suspect by using military judges, bypassing the jury system, and eliminating the right to an independent civilian appeal, the claims of a fair trial are dubious, whether "justice" is done or not.

The same problem adheres to the notion of reasonableness—a

pervasive term in American law. Just think of the common expressions in our language—beyond a reasonable doubt, reasonable care, reasonable person, reasonable time. I am not sure that American lawyers could function without invoking the idea of reasonableness at least once every few sentences of argument. Yet most of the lawyers of the world do not know what we are talking about. Even if their language contains a word for the Kantian idea of reason—by no means obvious in Arabic and Chinese— the word does not enter into the lexicon of the local lawyers. Germans have the word *Vernunft*—the word that Kant used in speaking about pure reason. But German lawyers rarely couple this word in the phrases so familiar to English-speaking lawyers.

The English version of the statute establishing the International Criminal Court, of which I will have much to say later, uses the terms "fairness" and "reasonable" dozens of times. The only way that our colleagues from other linguistic families can understand the meaning of these terms is to imitate the speech patterns of English speakers. Whether they like it or not, Anglophone lawyers impose their worldview on the legal treaties of our time.

The French had similar pretensions in the early nineteenth century. They assumed that French was the language of civilization, that the *Code civil* was the right legal way for the entire world. The German Romantics dissented. Savigny said, No, Germany must follow its own cultural path. The English Romantics, following Wordsworth, joined the anti-French reaction. Byron died in the name of national autonomy—in his case, the Greeks. This was action in the spirit of the Romantic creed: Each culture, bound together by language and history, should be able to realize its own destiny.

Among modern philosophers, the Romantic position on language finds unexpected support in Wittgenstein's championing each language as a distinctive way of life. He implicitly concurred with Herder that the self takes shape in the learning of language. There is no preexisting private language, no Mentalese, that each individual has at birth and then, supposedly, translates into the public language. Twins can develop their own language in their private interaction, but the individual standing apart from society cannot, per Wittgenstein, learn to speak. This position on language generates a strong critique of universalistic ideas, for without a common denominator of thought — prior to particular languages — there is no basis for supposing that all human beings constitute a single community. The world's peoples are irreconcilably split into linguistic villages.

Individuals and Collectives

My analysis of language underscores the importance of the words "individual" and "collective" in clarifying the faith of the Romantic. In speaking a language, individuals express themselves and also testify ineluctably to their membership in a collective. What does this mean exactly and how else might these terms be interpreted?

Romantics and liberal individualists both focus on individuals, but in different ways. Romantics cultivate the individual as a source of value. The unique feelings of the poet, the private vision of the painter, the existentialist quandary of the theologian — these are elevated in Romantic thought to ultimate points of reference. Genius is celebrated as the supreme virtue. For liberals, individuals are at their best when they are the man in the street, one like the other. Their self-replication can occur at the base level of their preferences, their libidos, their aggressive impulses, or at the higher level of abstract reason.

Liberals from Adam Smith to Immanuel Kant all thought about individuals as created in much the same form. It should not surprise us, then, that the crowning moral achievement of the eighteenth-century Enlightenment was Thomas Jefferson's effort to bring all individuals under a single formula of moral equality. The claim "all men are created equal" is surely right — as one view of the cathedral. We are indeed all made in the image of each other, but the Romantics insist on a different perspective on individuality — on creative sentiment as a lamp radiating illumination to infinity.

The Romantic conception of the individual as an expandable source of spirit explains the easy transition in Romantic thinking from the individual self to the nation. The nation bears the factors that constitute each individual — the language, the history, the culture, the bond between geography and self. As the extrapolation from the Romantic self, the nation forms intentions, acts, achieves greatness, suffers defeat, commits crimes, and bears guilt for its wrongdoing. We find variations on this theme in Romantic ideas ranging from Herder's views on the characteristic cultural expression of every nation to the political principle expressed in Rousseau's *volonté generale*, or general will. The general will — as opposed to the aggregated wills of all individuals in the society — expresses the will of the nation as such. It is not to be found simply by asking individuals to vote their preferences. It is found, at a deeper level, by probing the spirit of the entire nation (however vague this may sound to contemporary liberals).

Not surprisingly, Romantics are drawn to movements, to crusades, and finally to armed conflict. They are prone not to petty bar fights but to mass engagements under a flag proclaiming their collective identity. For Wordsworth, the 1809 Convention of Cintra, allying British and Spanish troops against Napoleon, was an ecstatic moment bestowing upon English soldiers a chance for heroic greatness. In these battles on the field of honor, they can see great ideas at work. They can see the meaning of national existence and the ennobling effects of human conflict. By identifying with a nation or a cause they can achieve transcendence of the self. Their lives are at once merged with the fate of the group and ennobled by linkage with a virtuous idea or a sense of historical destiny. This is Romantic war at its most seductive.

The term "individuals" can be given either a liberal or a Romantic interpretation; the same is true of collectives such as society and the nation. Rousseau guides us through this distinction by expounding two interpretations of the popular will—the aggregative and associative senses of the term. In the aggregative sense, the popular will (*la volonté de tous*) is the sum total of individual wills in the society. This liberal version of the popular will resembles the economic idea of the whole society's preferences, which are found by adding up all the preferences of individuals in society.

The associative sense of the popular will (*la volonté generale*) is expressed by the society as a single entity abstracted from the individuals who constitute it. As Rousseau wrote: "The general will studies only the common interest." To believe in the nation as an actor is to accept the idea of the popular will in the associative sense. Admittedly, it is difficult to know when one sense or the other is intended. When we discuss the will of "We the People," for example, we could mean the popular will in either the aggregative or the associative sense. Bruce Ackerman, as I read him, thinks of "We the People" acting in an aggregative sense. In my view, the will of the American people (at least since the Civil War) has been understood associatively as the spirit of a unified, organic nation.

Understanding Collective Guilt

The recurrent claim of this book is that Romantic sentiments generate certain characteristic attitudes toward war. The followers of Wordsworth and Fichte are inclined to think of the nation—in particular, *their* nations—both as expansions of their individual selves and as distinctive agents in history. In the common dimension of Romantic thinking the nation acts as a character in the drama of war and reconciliation. This means that the nation has intentions and engages in actions in execution of those intentions. If the nation can act, it can commit crimes as well as achieve greatness. When the nation engages in criminal behavior it must stand accountable for its crimes. It is appropriate, then, to speak of the nation as collectively guilty for its crimes. Of course, not all Romantic enthusiasts do or would make this claim and it is not easy to pinpoint any single writer who makes the argument exactly as I do. Their concerns were elsewhere, but they generated a body of expansionist thought that cohered as a way of viewing the world. In this worldview, at odds with the principles of the Enlightenment, collective guilt becomes a plausible extension of the self and the nation.

This is at least the outline of the argument. But the Romantic, we should recall, is typically engaged in defining his position *in opposition* to a liberal orthodoxy. Universalist and tolerant, the liberal will always seek to absorb the criticism and move on. And yet on this issue — collective guilt — the liberal draws the line. There is something about the combination of the two words — "collective" and "guilt" — that sets the liberals' teeth on edge. In a 1948 article, written in the heat of controversy about German and Japanese guilt for the war, H. D. Lewis globally condemned all conceptions of "collective responsibility" as "barbarous." But surely there are many situations in which a number of actors participate in causing a harm and no one would think twice — at least not in the law — of affixing collective responsibility of the group for having caused the harm. What H. D. Lewis must have had in mind is attributing guilt to someone simply because he was a member of a group of which some other members committed a crime. The evil, in his critique, is sometimes called "guilt by association" or "collective punishment." Membership in a group — the German or American nation — becomes the basis for transferring the guilt of some to others and imposing punishment on the group regardless of the guilt of its individual members.

The fact is that there are many ways to think about collective guilt, some of which might be barbarous — for instance, leveling and killing a whole village because one identified resident killed a soldier in the occupying force. But there are other approaches to the concept that morally sensitive observers should welcome as a more nuanced approach to the proper balance of blame between the community and the individual. Recognizing collective guilt in Germany could have served to mitigate the punishment of Eichmann. Remaining sensitive to collective guilt in Serbia would be a proper antidote to the tendency in the International Tribunal in the Hague to treat Milosevic as the symbol of genocidal evil in the region.

A sensitive approach to collective guilt challenges the degree to which individuals act in ways that are totally independent of the collectives and the nations in which their personalities are rooted. I have no simpleminded determinist thesis in mind but rather a challenge to the excessive individualism of the showcase trials of international criminal justice. Sometimes a cigar is a cigar, but sometimes, to follow Freud, a cigar stands for something more. Similarly, sometimes a criminal is simply an individual acting alone, but sometimes he or she acts in a way that invokes the presence of a state, a nation, or some other collective entity. The challenge, which we will address later in this book, is articulating a vision of collective guilt that requires a distribution of guilt among responsible parties. The nation, I argue, is one of these parties. There will, then, be difficult problems to assay, such as whether the collective guilt of the nation is associative or aggregative, or if the nation is guilty, whether it follows that particular individuals are also guilty. These questions await a more certain clarification of nations as actors in history — actors whom we can consider seriously as bearers of glory or of guilt.

Lawyers as Liberals

Without reflecting about it too much, most lay people instinctively take the idea of collective guilt seriously. They might be willing to attribute this kind of associative guilt to Americans for slavery and the destruction of Native American culture, to Germans for the Holocaust, to South Africans for apartheid, and to other nations for their respective acts of indecency. Yet I sense that I am already on controversial ground, and I can anticipate the objection: No, no, the word "guilt" is not the right word. Perhaps we should say that *individual* Germans were guilty for Auschwitz, or that we Americans are responsible for the great sin in our founding, or perhaps we could say that South Africans — or perhaps only white South Africans — should feel ashamed for their policies of segregation. Individual guilt, collective responsibility, collective shame all appear to be acceptable concepts — and yet as soon as the word "collective" is joined with the notion of "guilt," the battle lines are drawn.

Among those who react most strongly to the idea of collective guilt we can expect to find the lawyers. The legal culture — and particularly, the American legal culture — leans strongly toward the liberal culture of individual rights and the protection of personal freedom. Mary Ann Glendon wrote an influential book complaining that Americans, in contrast to Continental European lawyers, speak incessantly of rights, and never of duties. This may be true but an even more egregious shortcoming of the legal culture is its preoccupation with individuals and their actions.

The liberal (or reductionist) bias pervades everything lawyers say and do. Our concepts are geared to individuals, their rights and responsibilities. Corporations are reduced to persons under the Fourteenth Amendment. Countries become individuals under international law. At its earliest stages, as noted international law scholar George Schwarzenberger wrote, the "monarch and state were for all practical purposes treated as identical in most European countries." We notice this in the early law of treason, which treated the desire to kill the king as equivalent to betrayal of the nation. We even affirm corporate criminal liability as though the complex organism of the corporation could be reduced to a single actor liable for committing a crime. The polycentric collective as a subject is basically foreign to the legal way of thinking. The generalization holds in our legal system as well as in the civil law tradition: Collective entities, their actions, their responsibility, and their guilt — these are ideas that run afoul of the methodological commitments of the legal mind.

One common-law exception is the law of conspiracy, which seems to address the peculiar danger represented by collective criminal action. Criminal organizations pose a heightened danger in their collective interdependence and reciprocal support, a danger that exceeds the aggregative threat of the individuals constituting the conspiracy. The idea that agreements to commit a criminal act could be punishable violates the principles of individual culpability that govern Continental criminal jurisprudence. And yet in Europe as well as in the United States there is a growing tendency to fashion the criminal law to counteract the perception of "organized" threats to societies — particularly in the cases of the IRA, the Mafia, terrorists like the Baader-Meinhof gang in the 1970s, and now Al Qaeda.

Legal studies suffer as well from the bias toward methodological individualism. For the last several generations, the leading thinkers in American law have tried to reduce law to a social science, and the social sciences, as we understand them, are governed by something like Newtonian laws of regularity and predictability. If there is a science of law, it would have to resemble economics or psychology.

In recent years, Western philosophers and theoretical law professors have argued at length about the merits of theories of rights as compared with utilitarian theories for maximizing the welfare of society. This quarrel turns out to be an in-house dispute among the liberals. Both Immanuel Kant and Jeremy Bentham — as well as their contemporary analogues, Ronald Dworkin and Richard Posner — are members of the same liberal family, perhaps feuding relatives, but nonetheless closer to each other than they are to the Romantics with their commitment to irreconcilable differences.

In American universities dominated by the classical, universal conception of law, the study of comparative law has suffered, for if all human beings are alike and all advanced legal cultures are ultimately akin, what is the point of taking seriously the particular traditions of France and Germany, Islam and Judaism? The law, as we know it in Blackstone and under the Due Process Clause, rests on reason, a standard suitable for all of humanity.

In comparative law, there would be much to learn from the Romantics — and especially from their anti-universalist bias and their taking language seriously as a factor dividing societies and rendering cultures unique and irreducible to a single mode of life. The fascination with the unusual and different became an important part of the early stages of Romantic thinking. And language was seen as a symptom of the exotic. Montesquieu startled French society in the early eighteenth century by making it aware, in his *Persian Letters*, of the phenomenon that some people now call "difference." Would that we saw more of this orientation today in the study of law.

The appalling monolingualism of American law professors and students is only part of the problem. Even in comparative legal studies, there seems to be virtually no attention paid to the way in which syntax and semantics guide legal thought. In fact, no one quite knows the answer to the riddle of language and legal thought. Surely, the claims of linguist Benjamin Lee Whorf are overdrawn: The particularities of language do not determine legal conclusions. Yet it is equally hard to accept the hypothesis that language is a neutral factor in assessing the ways Americans and Chinese think about legal problems. The liberal mind understandably ignores language, because the assumption is that all people reason and express their intuitions in the same universal framework. Some even believe in a preverbal language like the "Mentalese" proposed by Pinker.

There is something pitiful about the modern American law school and its self-limiting focus on American law as written in the English language. The professors speak about "the law" and "the Constitution" as though their parochial documents were understood and celebrated all over the world. They remind one of medieval theologians who mistook their religion for the single truth worth studying. The condition of European law faculties is not much better. Germans read Germans, and the French read the French.

A Romantic invasion of the law schools would open the law to the conflict that in fact exists among the legal cultures of the world, to the beauty of the exotic and the different, to the relevance of language, to a self-conscious concern about nationhood and, yes, to a willingness to think seriously about collective crimes and collective guilt.

But the situation is not that simple. The fascinating fact is that despite their liberal facade, the law has always nurtured an undercurrent of corporatist thinking and a covert appreciation for the idea of nationhood and the possibility of collective guilt. The deeper we dig into the law, the more examples of collective thinking come to the surface. A good example is the Second Amendment to the U.S. Constitution, which protects "the right of the people to keep and bear arms." Libertarians interpret this provision as a guarantee of the right of each and every Bernhard Goetz to pack a .38 on the New York subway. Yet historical research into the meaning of "bearing arms" suggests that this term is reserved for the description of organized groups, armies and militias, carrying weapons. Hunters don't "bear arms." And it is a few degrees off to describe Goetz as having "borne" arms on the day he shot four victims on the subway. The right to bear arms is arguably a collective right, properly reserved to organized militias, for as the language of the amendment underscores: "a well-regulated militia [is] necessary to the security of a free State." This is, of course, a highly contested area. I mean to suggest only that a collective understanding of the Amendment might be the best reading.

This is but one example of collective thinking that might account for legal provisions that are typically interpreted as the source of individual rights. The field of international criminal law, the rapidly developing body of principles governing war crimes, genocide, and similar offenses, rests on an intersection of individualist and collectivist thinking. Here we can witness the nations of the world coming into their own as organic actors — providing the backdrop for the criminal prosecutions of all the individuals standing seemingly alone in the dock.

CHAPTER THREE

Collective Crime

The punishment of war criminals should be
an act of international justice, not the
satisfaction of a thirst for revenge.
— *Hans Kelsen*

Traditionally, international law ad-
dressed the behavior of states. The state is a collective reduced to
a person, a sovereign, a single entity that can take its place alongside the other sovereigns in the law of nations. As all human
beings are created equal, all states are equal subjects in international law. Traditionally, in the way we thought about international relations, the only players were states; individual human
beings — the plural subjects constituting the state — did not count.
Since the Nuremberg proceedings, however, treaty-makers and international criminal courts have emphasized the responsibility of
individuals for crimes against the law of nations. Human rights
lawyers seem to assume that this development is a salutary transition toward the proper criteria of responsibility for aggression,
genocide, crimes against humanity, and war crimes. In the Rome
Statute of July 1998 — defining both the procedures and the substantive law of the proposed International Criminal Court — the
critical assumption appears in article 25(3): "The Court shall
have jurisdiction over natural [as opposed to legal] persons."

The formal emphasis on the potential liability of all natural
persons and only natural persons departs from some traditional

principles of law. For example, heads of state were not traditionally subject to criminal prosecution unless they were first removed from office. We note in the indictment and trial of Slobodan Milosevic, former president of Yugoslavia, that international criminal responsibility now encompasses heads of state as well as citizens, commanders as well as foot soldiers. They are all "natural persons."

The implication of punishing only human beings is that legal entities such as corporations and political parties are exempt from liability under the Rome Statute. If there is a reason for this rigorous commitment to personal liability, it must be based on a theory of guilt. If only individuals can "really" act and be guilty, then of course only individuals — and not legal persons — can be subject to conviction and punishment.

But to paraphrase Hamlet's mother after she sees herself portrayed in the play within the play: One has the feeling that the ladies and gentlemen in Rome did "protest too much." The facade of individual criminal responsibility obscures basic truths about the crimes that now constitute the core of international criminal law. The four crimes over which the court has jurisdiction — aggression, crimes of war, crimes against humanity, and genocide — are deeds that by their very nature are committed by groups and typically against individuals as members of groups. Whatever the pretense of liberal international lawyers, the crimes of concern to the international community are collective crimes. It is true that as a formal matter only individuals are prosecuted, but they are prosecuted for crimes committed by and in the name of the groups they represent. Once the collective nature of these crimes comes into proper focus, once we overcome the liberal bias that has prevailed since Nuremberg, we should be able to see the influence of collective action in domestic criminal law as well.

In order to make out the case for collective action and collective guilt in international criminal law, I must do the rather conventional things that lawyers do — such as reading the Rome Statute in the context of its history and its purposes. My point is to show that although the orthodox view stresses individual responsibility, the heart of international criminal law remains collectivist in nature.

War and the Law of War

We learned in the early twenty-first century that the concept of "war" itself is among the most ambiguous terms. In the traditional model of war, which is probably honored more in the breach than in actual examples, the sovereigns of different states — typically monarchs — declared war against each other. Then after the official declaration, the sovereigns sent armies into the field to fight each other, as though they were engaged in a jousting match. The battlefield was like a Roman arena where gladiators fought to the death. In the battle, there was honor, there were rules of combat, and there was a decisive victory by one side or the other.

The First World War seems to conform, more or less, to this model. In late June 1914, after months of tension among the states of central Europe, a young man in Sarajevo, a member of the Serbian nationalist movement Black Hand, shot and killed the Archduke Franz Ferdinand, heir to the throne of Austria-Hungary. On the assumption that Black Hand acted for the nation and that the government was responsible, Austria demanded that the Serbian government prosecute the responsible parties. It threatened war if Serbia failed to comply. Serbia tried to negotiate but Austria, not satisfied, and desiring to promote its hegemony in the Balkans, declared war one month later. There followed a chain reaction of bellicose movements, declarations, and counter-declarations of war. Russia mobilized in solidarity with Serbia; this led to Austria's declaring war against Russia. Because of treaty commitments Germany sided with Austria and declared against Russia. Three days later France, recognizing a treaty obligation to support Russia, joined the fray with its own verbal affirmation of the state of war. This partial listing is enough to make the point that war arises, traditionally, not from an attack but from a statement by the contending states that they intend to enter into a state of armed conflict.

This self-conscious proclamation of the imminent onset of hostilities carries great weight in international law because by common understanding the state of war brings into being an alternative order of rights and duties. Routine and obviously criminal behavior — killing, battery, deprivation of liberty, destroying property, arson, theft — becomes legal and even meritorious in the course of military battle. This body of rules that legitimates conduct otherwise subject to punishment is called *jus in bello*, or law-in-war. This order has its own internal logic and tradition. The state of war establishes a distinctive structure of norms and norm creation. A peaceful legal order based on a constitution recognizes citizens who have many rights against the state and, in the American legal culture at least, few duties of service toward the state and community. The U.S. Constitution speaks of rights but never mentions the duties of citizens. The legal order of war is just the opposite. It replaces the citizen with the soldier, a subject of the military organization who has many duties and few rights. The trade-off for this servile status is immunity from prosecution for violent acts committed in furtherance of military goals.

The declaration of war, therefore, is of critical importance in shifting from one legal order to the other. And yet the practice of declaring war is slowly disappearing from the practice of international diplomacy. The United States has not declared war against any nation since 1941 and the onset of World War II. The common practice today is either for the president to act on his own in execution of an alleged "police action" or for Congress to pass a joint resolution instructing the president to use all necessary force to repel the military forces of some foreign county engaged in seemingly aggressive actions. It was in this way that we legitimated our use of force in Korea, Vietnam, Iraq, and finally Afghanistan.

The demise of declarations of war seems to suggest that the justification of war is solely a matter of internal constitutional law. We have to make sure that the president is not exceeding the office's defined powers as commander in chief of the armed forces and intruding upon Congress's exclusive power "to declare war." In the last sixty years we have witnessed a gradual erosion of the legislative war power and the augmentation of the powers supposedly implied in the office of commander in chief. Lost in this transition is the international significance of the declaration of war. The official announcement of intended hostilities served the critical purpose, as between states, of signaling a transformation of the applicable legal order from the rules of peace to the rules of war.

In the absence of declarations of war, the beginning of war has come to rest more and more on the occurrence of an aggressive attack. Thus the Civil War began when South Carolina forces lobbed shells on a Union installation, Fort Sumter, in the middle of Charleston harbor. World War II began after Germany invaded Poland, and it came to the United States with the surprise aerial bombardment of the U.S. Navy in Pearl Harbor. President Bush labeled the attack of September 11 "an act of war" and thus took it to be equivalent to an official statement of intention to go to war.

The difficulty with the attack-as-declaration understanding of initiating warfare is that there are problems answering the twin questions: Who is attacking and who is being attacked? Bombing targets and firing shells are speech acts, and the problem is always: Who is saying what? What would Khrushchev have been saying if he allowed one of his ships to sail past the American quarantine of Cuba in 1962? Would that have been an attack against the United States and all of its allies?

The truth is that you never know exactly what the attacker is saying. The context confers meaning, but the contexts for aggressor and victim might be different. And the symbolism of the act lends itself to multiple refractions. Apparently, many Islamic fundamentalists take the presence of American bases in Saudi Arabia to be an invasion of Dar el Islam, including regions far away from their base. When the West applies its lens to this same situation, we understandably see our own presence as less threatening.

The attack of September 11 was ambiguous on both counts. We did not know who was attacking and what kind of declaration it was supposed to be. There was similar confusion after the agent of Black Hand killed the archduke in Sarajevo. Was this the action of a single individual, or an organization, or the entire Serbian state? Similarly, though it seemed a safe bet that the nineteen hijackers were acting on behalf of someone, we did not know how to describe the concentric circles of responsibility. Even if, as initially suspected, a gang called Al Qaeda turned out to be sponsors, we did not know how many states to include within the ambit of the enemy — states that supported Al Qaeda (Afghanistan), those that tolerated and indirectly nourished it (Pakistan, Saudi Arabia?), or finally all those that pursued parallel policies of preparing for aggressive war. In his State of the Union speech on January 29, 2002, President Bush extended the circle of enemy countries as far as Iran, Iraq, and North Korea: At least one of these probably had nothing to do with the attacks of September 11.

There is always ambiguity on the other side of the equation as well: How do we circumscribe the identity of the party attacked? In the great case of 2001, was it just the two towers, or was it New York, the United States, or all of the West? How did the added strike on the Pentagon change our perceptions? I recall that on September 11, I was in Toronto teaching an intensive two-week course to Canadian law students. The subject of the class bore on questions of war and guilt and therefore I felt it appropriate to ask the students a few hours after the Twin Towers went down, "Who was the attack directed against? Do you feel targeted?" To my partial surprise they did not feel under attack. Though most of them expressed solidarity with New Yorkers, they did not feel personally under the gun.

Most citizens of the United States responded with a greater sense of personal identification with the thousands of victims and bereft families. In the end the sense of national identification matters.

Declaring war by attacking is always ambiguous. We never know precisely who the attacker and its allies are, and we never know the precise contours of the precise intention expressed in the surprise devastation. Yet we do know that war is a collective activity. A single assassin, acting alone, cannot effectuate the kind of attack that will signal entry into a state of war.

The collective entities that enter into war have traditionally been states but they were not always so. The American Civil War counts as a war even though the Confederacy was never recognized as a state. The 1995 decision by the Court of Appeals for the Second Circuit in *Kadic v. Karadzic* recognized that the Bosnian Serbs under the leadership of Radovan Karadzic constituted an organized force equivalent to a state for purposes of international law. De facto war requires coordinated action, a chain of command, a sense of organization and, above all, a consciousness on the part of the individuals engaged in military action that they are acting as part of the collective effort.

It has become increasingly evident that the concept of war serves one function in domestic law (e.g., German or American law) and a totally different function in international law. The term "war" appears in the Constitution and the Bill of Rights five times in provisions as diverse as the definition of treason (waging war) to a prohibition on the states from engaging in war (unless in imminent danger). Engaging in war is regarded as a particularly dangerous activity that requires special constitutional scrutiny. This remains true even if Congress has gradually abandoned its function of declaring war in the case of military conflicts.

In international agreements, the term "armed conflict" has gradually replaced the term "war" as the term of relevance. For example, the Rome Statute defining the International Criminal Court uses the word primarily in expressions like "war crimes" and "the necessities of war." Whether war crimes are possible, however, does not depend on whether a state of war exists. The critical question is whether the alleged crime occurs in the course of an "armed conflict," typically international but not always.

The use of the term "armed conflict" moves the focus of the ICC away from the behavior of states toward the actions of armed individuals. Two gangs on the streets of Los Angeles engage in armed conflict. Indeed any shootout between two gun-toting brawlers would satisfy that definition, but these cases are presumably not of "concern to the international community" — one of the conditions laid down by the Rome Statute for the Court to take jurisdiction over a dispute. Of course we don't quite know what is of concern to the international community and why, but one can be sure that purely local conflicts between individuals or between gangs would not rise to the required level of international significance.

The indispensable condition for getting beyond the purely local and acquiring international valence would seem to be organized activity — collective action. We can validate this thesis by taking a closer look at the four crimes that are subject to prosecution in the International Criminal Court. Let us consider aggression, war crimes, crimes against humanity, and genocide, both as they are officially defined in the Rome statute and as they operate in practice as crimes signaling collective responsibility.

Aggression

This is the one crime of the four that still eludes formal definition, and yet it is absolutely central in structuring the law of war. An act of aggression will, when defined, constitute a crime under international law. And yet we have difficulty knowing how much intrusion, how much interference is necessary to constitute an act of aggression. Was it enough for Serbia (or Black Hand) to kill the archduke? Was it sufficient for Egypt to amass troops on the

Israeli border and close the Suez Canal? There are obviously many forms of intrusion that fall short of marching troops across the border.

The United Nations General Assembly tried to define "aggression" in 1974, but the definition fails to deal with the nuances of intrusion. The Resolution relies on "armed force by a State against the sovereignty, territorial integrity or political independence of another State" but then goes on to say that "a blockage of the ports or coasts of a State by the armed forces of any other State" would be sufficient. Under this definition it looks as though during the Cuban Missile Crisis of 1962, the United States committed aggression by blockading the shipping lanes to Cuba, while the United States regarded the Soviet installation of long-range missiles in Cuba as the relevant act of aggression.

It is not surprising that the United Nations has yet to exhaust the subtleties of this concept. Defining what it means "to cross the line" has always troubled lawyers — not only in the case of war but in the more humble area of defining the law of trespass. What about shining brights into your neighbor's living room? Does that trespass upon his property? The spectrum runs from slight intrusion — leaves from your tree blowing onto your neighbor's property — to actual physical occupation. The precise line between mine and thine baffles the logic of lawyers. No wonder the international community cannot define the kind of aggression that constitutes a crime "of concern to the international community."

But we can be sure at least that the intrusion must be the coordinated effort of an organized armed force. If a single Arab-American tourist throws rocks at Israeli military installations, that is an act of vandalism but not an act of aggression. The group dimension of aggression carries with it the suggestion of recurrent and committed battle with aims of conquest or at least of settling some political dispute.

As the law of war has evolved, the traditional grounds for "just wars" have fallen by the wayside. A religious community or a nation can no longer justify a war in international terms by appealing to the truth of its religion or its constitutional principles. Jihad might appeal to believers but it has no status as a justification for war. Nor does imposing the principle of equality on others — however passionately the West may believe in it — justify going to war. It would not have been justified to invade South Africa in order to put an end to apartheid and it would not have been justified to invade Afghanistan solely to terminate the brutal suppression of women.

The legitimation of going to war is regulated by a body of law called *jus ad bellum*. These are rules external to the war itself that determine whether the war is lawful or unlawful. These rules are to be distinguished sharply from what we earlier termed *jus in bello* — the rules, internal to the war, that define the permissible limits of combat.

This basic distinction provides the architecture of the law of war, and it is critical for understanding the role of aggression in defining the limits of lawful war. As religious wars, punitive wars, and wars of expansion have become unlawful, one clear category of legitimate warfare remains, and that is the inherent authority of states to invoke collective self-defense against aggression. I refer to this authority as inherent on the assumption that all states have the right to survive on their territory. The basic principle of international order is that the established order, whether morally right or wrong, carries legitimacy. Aggression destabilizes the existing order.

The Charter of the United Nations, article 51, is the benchmark for all discussions of this issue: "Nothing in the present Charter shall impair the inherent right of individual or collective self-defense if an armed attack occurs against a Member of the United Nations." The use of the terms "individual" and "collective" self-defense require some clarification. With this distinction, the Charter means to refer to each state defending itself *individually*, or, as part of a regional security pact, *collectively*. But when a state defends itself against aggression, its invocation of self-defense is collective in another sense. Individual persons have the right to use self-defense when they are threatened with an imminent attack against their person or their other vital interests. By analogy, nations have the authority to invoke collective self-defense (in this specific sense) when they are attacked as nations. The picture here is of two collectivities in conflict.

Suppose that one nation commits aggression against another. Everyone in the targeted group is subject to being killed and therefore enjoys a right to repel the aggression. The modern law of war has restricted this reciprocal relationship to combatants. Only combatants are subject, under the Geneva Convention, to being killed, and therefore only combatants enjoy this collective right to use force. To avoid ambiguity, we will use the term "collective self-defense" to refer to the shared right of individuals to use defensive force.

To conclude, we should note the tight conceptual connection between the crime of aggressive war and the collective right of self-defense. The former triggers the latter, and without aggression (or at least "armed attack"), there is no right to use force in response.

War Crimes

War crimes exist at the frontier between two legal orders. On the one hand, the alternative legal order called "war" suppresses the identity of the individual soldier and insulates him or her from criminal liability; on the other hand, the international legal order now holds individuals accountable for certain forms of immoral and indecent treatment of the enemy. When an individual commits a war crime, he or she breaks out, at least in part, from the collective order of war and emerges as an individual guilty of violating prohibitions adopted in the international legal community.

The Rome Statute lists over fifty distinct war crimes. With all the subparts and variations, there are probably close to a hundred distinct charges possible. It would be tedious to list and discuss all of them but a sample will be sufficient to support my thesis that these crimes, like aggression, reflect the participation of a collective organization.

The three basic categories that govern the laws of war are combatants, civilians, and prisoners. The second and third categories of people are protected against intentional harms and the spill-over effects of war. The very idea of the "civilian" presupposes that there is some collective called the "army" that fights for the state. The members of the army are distinguished by their uniform or some other insignia. This is necessary, as we shall see, to apply the principle of collective self-defense. The idea of the "prisoner" similarly confirms the possibility of having previously fought in the army.

The practice of taking and caring for prisoners testifies to the collective nature of armed confrontation. Maintaining prison camps requires a level of administrative organization and geographical permanence lacking in informal bands. John Brown conducted a raid, but he was not prepared to establish prison camps. Also, the proper treatment of prisoners, coupled with the expectation of reciprocal proper treatment, makes it clear that war entails repeated engagements, including confrontations among different individual soldiers on both sides.

The important point is that war creates an alternative identity. The person who goes to war ceases being a citizen and becomes a soldier in a chain of command. As Rousseau emphasized, in his alternative identity, the soldier is a mere servant of the state. He is not an autonomous agent, motivated by enmity for the enemy. As Rousseau conceived of war, the only actors were the states pitted against each other.

The principle of taking prisoners with the corresponding right of combatants to surrender without being killed lies at the foundation of the law of war. Terrorists do not take prisoners. They take hostages whom they are prepared to mistreat for their purposes. Robber bands and vandals do not take prisoners. They kill, loot, and move on. It is not surprising, then, that one of the fundamental war crimes prohibited by the 1907 Hague Convention and the Rome Statute is "declaring that no quarter will be given." "No quarter" means that all prisoners will be killed; safe surrender is no longer possible. The mere declaration of "no quarter" is a crime, for it breaches the foundational understanding of modern war that limits military engagement to actual combatants.

The prohibition against "declaring that no quarter will be given" testifies to the collective nature of the conflict at stake. It would hardly constitute a crime for a single soldier, separated from his unit, to shout out "I will take no prisoners." The declared intention to kill prisoners must come from a collective army unit and express the will of the collective. The same analysis applies other specific war crimes such as "pillaging a town" and "intentionally using starvation of civilians as a method of warfare." These are crimes that by their nature must be orchestrated by the military command, even though they are executed by discrete individuals.

It is true that many crimes listed in the Rome Statute look like they could be committed by individuals acting alone. For example, as to "persons protected by the Geneva Conventions," that is, civilians and prisoners, it is a war crime to engage in "wilful killing" or "torture" or to conduct "biological experiments." There is nothing about these acts that requires collective participation by an entire army, let alone an entire nation. Yet it is clear that many, such as those mentioned above and many others, do not lend themselves, conceptually, to commission by individuals acting alone. The statutory language contains no suggestion that there is a distinction between the two categories, and therefore it is fair to read into the statutory scheme a principle of collective action in all offenses. Individuals who kill civilian prisoners do not, by virtue of that action alone, commit a war crime.

It is by no means easy to mark out the distinctions between

individual crimes, war crimes, and actions within the proper scope of military action. I want to illustrate this problem by focusing on two hypothetical cases. Both arise during the German occupation of Poland. In one case a Pole kills German soldiers, and in the other, a German officer kills a Pole.

The first case is inspired by an incident that actually occurred in France and is discussed in Marcel Ophuls's film *The Sorrow and the Pity*. Let us imagine German troops marching toward Warsaw after the Polish government has surrendered and ordered the army to lay down its arms. Suppose a farmer, standing by himself in the fields, sees the troops marching down the road in formation. He rushes to his barn, takes his rifle up to a window in the hayloft, and shoots at the soldiers as they pass. He kills three soldiers. Does the legitimating effect of warfare encompass these killings that would otherwise be murder under Polish law or under German martial law?

One naturally has some sympathy for the Polish farmer defending his homeland. In his influential book, *Just and Unjust Wars*, Michael Walzer expresses sympathy for members of the French resistance who, disguised as farmers with their guns hidden behind their hoes, shot and killed passing German soldiers. But to return to our hypothetical, if the German soldiers had, as a military action, killed the farmer as they passed by, they would be clearly guilty of a war crime in violation of the Geneva Conventions and the Rome Statute. They would have engaged in "a wilful killing of a person protected by the Geneva Conventions." Extending this shield to the farmer against the dangers of warfare entails duties on his part. He is not entitled to think of himself as a free agent acting on behalf of the Polish army.

This seems to be true whether or not the government had already surrendered. According to Francis Lieber, who drafted the first code of the laws of war in 1863, the principle of obligatory self-restraint applies to resistance fighters: "If, however, the people of a country, or any portion of the same, already occupied by an army, rise against it, they are violators of the laws of war, and are not entitled to their protection." Absent the protection of the law of war and the right of collective self-defense, the farmer is guilty of murder, either under Polish law or German martial law. If he acts independently of the army, his situation falls outside the collective activity that defines the law of war and reverts to a case to be tried under domestic law.

But let us suppose that the government has not yet surrendered and the Polish army is still engaged in resistance: Could not the farmer invoke the general right of self-defense against external aggression? The answer is no. The Polish army has a collective right of self-defense against the German army, and individual Poles — as well as individual Germans — enjoy a personal right of self-defense if they are actually attacked. Collective self-defense is broader than individual self-defense, because if one army attacks another army, all combatants on one side are per se aggressors against the soldiers on the other side. Membership in the group aggressing makes them liable to be killed in response, and membership in the group under attack gives each member the right to act in collective self-defense. The farmer acting alone, however, cannot pretend that he is a stand-in for the Polish army. He cannot invoke the collective right of self-defense and would have to rely, instead, on his own individual right to defend himself against an imminent attack directed personally at him. The problem is that there is no imminent attack against him. The German soldiers marching down the road present no threat to his personal security.

This case is so difficult because we assume that the German invasion of Poland is illegitimate. Our sympathies are on the side of the Polish farmer, yet these sympathies have no bearing on the legal analysis of the case. Recall the architectonic distinction between the right to go to war (*jus ad bellum*) and the law as applied in the course of war (*jus in bello*). The United Nations Charter regulates the former; the Geneva Conventions and the Rome Statute address the latter.

The remarkable premise of international law is that these two spheres of law have nothing to do with each other. Apartheid is now regarded as a crime against humanity. But that crime on the part of South Africa would not justify a military invasion to put an end to racial oppression. That is, a violation of the internal law of war has no bearing on the external question as to whether the war is justified. Similarly, Germany's having waged aggressive war in violation of *jus ad bellum* cannot legitimate an action — like the killing of the German soldiers — that would otherwise be a crime. The correct result under international law — as hard as it might be to swallow — is that the farmer is guilty of murder under domestic law.

The critical point is that the farmer acting alone, or even a group of partisans acting alone — however appealing their cause — cannot claim the rights of warfare, including the right of collective self-defense. This is the critical line between terrorism and warfare. Terrorists such as Timothy McVeigh cannot claim the rights of war for the simple reason that they are not engaged in an armed conflict between organized military forces. The crucial point in this argument is demarcating the boundary between collective actions covered by the law of war and individual crimes punishable under domestic law. The Polish farmer falls on the side of individual action governed by domestic law.

A more difficult case arises if we imagine that it is nighttime, and a German officer seeking relaxation dons civilian clothes and goes to a local bar. There are also Poles in the bar. Having had too much to drink, a Pole exchanges harsh words with the German officer, who takes a knife lying on the bar and kills the Polish citizen. I want to assume that this is an intentional killing and would be classified as the most serious form of criminal homicide under local law, be it Polish or German law. The question is whether the killing also becomes a war crime subject to prosecution in an international tribunal.

Again we encounter the provision of the Rome Statute, based on the 1949 Geneva Convention, defining war crimes to include any "wilful killing" of local civilians. True, the Rome Statute also qualifies the definition of war crimes so that the International Criminal Court should take jurisdiction over war crimes "in particular when committed as part of a plan or policy or as part of a large-scale commission of such crimes." This language implies that the solitary soldier killing a solitary Pole in a bar would not be committing a crime of high priority for prosecution. But the theoretical question remains whether the killer's identity as an occupying soldier and the victim's identity as a local resident are sufficient to take the crime beyond the realm of national jurisdiction and make it of concern to the international community.

There is, admittedly, some controversy on this point. There are some thoughtful advocates of human rights who argue that every crime committed by an occupying soldier against a civilian is a war crime. I learned much from an extended conversation with Antonio Cassesse, a professor of international law in Florence, Italy, and a former judge on the International Criminal Tribunal for Yugoslavia. Cassesse took the position that in my hypothetical case, the German officer was guilty of a war crime. If this is true, then a whole range of local crimes committed by occupying troops would have to be tried not at home but in the Hague. These would include every homicide, every theft, every rape, and in the language of the statute, every "outrage against personal dignity" — however unrelated these acts might be to military operations and the war effort. It is difficult to find a serious discussion of the issue in the literature on international criminal law, and therefore I take Cassesse's to be representative of an entire school of human rights advocates who wish to promote the importance of international criminal tribunals.

I find this view hard to accept, and to explain my opposition, I turn to a familiar problem in American law, namely distinguishing between the behavior of state officials that comes within the province of the federal courts and those that are purely local and remain within the competence of the states. The basic rule is that the federal courts have jurisdiction only in cases of "state action," that is, action by state officials. But not every action taken by an employee of the state is regarded as state action. There is room in the law for the purely personal, for activities undertaken off-duty, on vacation, after hours in the private realm. The phrase used by the courts is "under color of state law." That is, the state official must be acting in the name of the state, displaying as he or she acts the power and the authority of the state. "The acts of a state officer in the ambit of his personal pursuits," the courts say, "are not acts under color of state law."

The analogous concept in our hypothetical case would be: Under color of the occupation. Killing, rape, and other outrageous action taken in the name of the occupying power, uses of force that invoke the collective entity behind the occupation, should be regarded as under the color of the occupation and therefore subject to prosecution as war crimes in an international tribunal.

If this is true, then it follows that the homicide in the bar does not constitute a war crime. The German officer is not acting in his role as a soldier. The dispute is purely personal. He should be prosecuted either by a Polish court or in a German court-martial. Admittedly, there is a practical problem whether an impartial trial of a German officer could be expected in either a Polish court or a German military tribunal. And in fact the United States has faced serious diplomatic problems under circumstances much less extreme. When American soldiers commit personal crimes against local civilians abroad, there has been a great deal of controversy about whether a court-martial is a reliable procedure satisfying the victims' need to see that justice is done. The end result in most countries where the United States has bases has been to cede jurisdiction to the local courts.

In view of these practical difficulties, one can understand the appeal of a neutral international tribunal. Yet these procedural questions do not address the question of principle, namely whether every action of an occupying soldier, no matter how personal and how private, is an action of the military itself and therefore properly classified as a war crime. I want to insist that at some point the collective gives way to the personal and private. The limitation inherent in federal supervision over the states in the United States should apply, by analogy, to international supervision of domestic justice. This question will and should continue to trouble us. We cannot avoid searching for this limit, because the theory of war crimes is based implicitly on collective action, and at some point, the element of collectivity wears so thin that the action must be regarded as purely personal.

To summarize the results of the two hypothetical cases, both the farmer and the officer are liable for homicide under local law. The farmer may not invoke the collective right of self-defense as a stand-in for the Polish army. This is solitary action, not group action. The choice in the second case is between domestic law and international law, and again because the officer acts as a private individual, in his personal capacity, he is liable for homicide and not for a war crime. In both cases, the individual acts on his own, not as an agent of the collective, and therefore the only applicable law is the domestic law regulating individual behavior. Both the law of war, as a factor suppressing the individuality of soldiers, and the law of war crimes presuppose collective action.

Thus we have encountered two cases that support the general thesis that crimes in the international arena require both collective action and individual execution. And yet one can scour the literature of international law, without results, for recognition of this elementary point. The international lawyers are so pleased about the extension of individual responsibility to the behavior of "natural individuals" that they have forgotten about the way the definition of "offense" implicates collective action. The great danger of ignoring the collective component of every international crime is that we think of these crimes of killing, rape, and cruelty just as we think of individual crimes against domestic law. And yet, as we have seen, the offender must act in the name of "under the color of" the collective—the army or the nation. The liberal paradigm has become so strong in legal thinking that it forces from the radar screens of lawyers the possibility that the nation of the offender is also implicated in these crimes that are of concern to the international community.

Before leaving the subject of war crimes, we should note that after World War II, "grave breaches of the Geneva conventions" became federal offenses under U.S. law — but only under the condition that the perpetrator is a member of the U.S. armed forces or the victim is an American citizen. The name of the offense was changed to "war crimes" in 1997. This means that if Al Qaeda was guilty of a war crime by orchestrating the mass killing of civilians on September 11, 2001, it also committed a crime under federal law.

Crimes Against Humanity

When we turn from war crimes to the third category, crimes against humanity, the collective nature of the required action is apparent on the face of the statute. The specific acts must be "part of a widespread or systematic attack directed against any civilian population." Of course, it might be technically possible for a single individual, without the aid of an organization, to carry out a "widespread and systematic attack." Perhaps the Unabomber, Ted Kaczynski, came close to meeting this standard by sending out his letter bombs to different people on different occasions. Yet the Rome Statute makes it clear that individuals acting alone cannot commit crimes against humanity. The "widespread or systematic" attack must be "pursuant to or in furtherance of a State or organizational policy to commit such attack." The words could not be clearer; in my view the phrase "organizational policy" merely brings to the surface a requirement implicit in all the offenses that fall within the competence of the International Criminal Court.

As in the case of war crimes, the Rome statute breaks down the general offense into many specific variations, such as murder, enslavement, torture, rape, and sexual slavery. The defect of the definition is that it falls short of the precise definition usually required under the principle that a statute must give "fair warning" to the public about the acts that might be treated as criminal. The listing of specific offenses closes with a catch-all phrase: Also punished as a crime against humanity will be "other inhumane acts of a similar character intentionally causing great suffering, or serious injury to body or to mental or physical health." Basically, this means that anything the court regards as bad will be punished as an international war crime.

The drafters of the statute disengaged the offense from its origins in a problem posed in the Nuremberg trial. There was no offense in international law that covered Germany's indecent treatment of its own citizens. The killing of Polish Jews was a violation of international duties toward Poland, but the killing of German Jews did not violate any duty to any other state. Thus the prosecution conceptualized the idea of a duty to all of humanity.

Since then the notion of a crime against humanity has become something of a loose cannon in the world's jurisprudence. A new doctrine has spread around the world that has led to such curious legal phenomena as Belgium seeking to prosecute Ariel Sharon, the prime minister of Israel, for having committed crimes against humanity some twenty years before when, as defensive minister during the Lebanese war, he stood by and allowed Christian Phalangist groups to kill Palestinians in the massacre at Sabra and Shatila. The new doctrine is called "universal jurisdiction" and it means that states that adopt this principle can prosecute war crimes and crimes against humanity wherever they are committed. The United States has not participated in this fashionable extension of judicial power, but its soldiers and political figures could well be subject to the claims of other countries.

Belgium, Germany, Canada and a few other states have become so audacious as to think that they can judge war crimes and crimes against humanity whenever and wherever they occur. This practice has a destabilizing effect on international cooperation because when it claims jurisdiction, a state like Belgium ignores the capacity of another state to pass judgment on its own criminals. In fact, Israel set up a commission to assess Sharon's behavior in Sabra and Shatila and concluded that although there were mistakes made, he was only "indirectly" and not criminally responsible for the killings committed by others. Belgium ignored this finding. This creates an extremely dangerous situation, because the principle of the Fifth Amendment that no "person be subject for the same offence to be twice put in jeopardy of life or limb" does not apply in these cases of universal jurisdiction. If Sharon had been tried and acquitted, he would still have been subject to prosecution in Germany or Canada. He could twice have been put in "jeopardy of life or limb." He would not have had "a day in court" leading to a definitive judgment that he was not guilty and was free to go about his business.

For my purposes, however, the worst part of this tendency toward universal jurisdiction is the belief that if Sharon had been guilty of a crime against humanity, he could be judged and sentenced in abstraction from the nation in whose name he acted as military commander. Belgium was not in a position to judge or even to think about the complicity of the entire Israeli nation in any crime that Sharon might have committed and therefore Belgium had a commitment to thinking of him as an individual acting alone. This way of looking at his conduct distorts the crime as it is understood in international law, where equal emphasis is directed to "the State or organizational policy" that expresses itself in the alleged offense.

At the international level, few of these problems arise. First, the Rome statute recognizes the principle of deference to local justice. The ICC will act only if the local courts are, for political reasons, "unable or unwilling" to prosecute. Second, an international tribunal has the competence as well as the perspective to assess the role of the collective entity, the army, or the nation that provides the framework and the apparent authority for the defendant's actions.

Genocide

The fourth crime, genocide, appears, at least on the surface of its defining language, to be subject to commission at the hands of a single person acting outside of organizational influences and structures. All the Genocide Convention — and now the ICC Statute — requires is that the individual engage in one of five specified acts, ranging from homicide to coerced assimilation of children, against members of a "national, ethnical, racial, or religious group." The purpose of the action must be to inflict harm on members of the group with the "intent to destroy, in whole or in part," the group "as such." It looks like a single individual, acting alone, could have this intention. Consider the follow hypothetical case.

A sinophobe is walking down the street in New York. He is looking for Chinese victims and he kills the first two Chinese simply because they are Chinese (or look Chinese). It is not implausible to describe his goals as intending to destroy part of the Chinese people. Technically, he has committed genocide. He has killed Chinese with the intent to eliminate this national group "in part." Is there a sensible construction of the Statute that would avoid this counterintuitive result? I think there is.

One could quarrel whether two victims would be enough to constitute destruction of a people "in part." But apart from this, there is a more basic question about whether this kind of application of the statute misses the point of genocide altogether.

The first thing to note about the Statute is that it addresses serious and persistent group conflict. The limitation of its scope to a "national, ethnical, racial, or religious group" reminds us of similar limitations in the definition of hate crimes in the United States. Genocide and hate crimes both represent aggravated forms of their underlying offenses. That is, genocide is punished more severely than simple homicide and certainly more than the forms of cultural genocide specified in the Rome Statute, namely forced abortions or the coerced "transferring of children" to a cultural milieu other than their own.

Genocide and hate crimes are punished more severely because they claim two victims, the individual and the group. The group's suffering lies primarily in the actor's intention. There are few cases in history of one nation's actually eliminating another. The Nazis may have intended to kill the entire Jewish people but their crime, horrible as it was, did not go beyond a murderous attempt. The same feature marks cultural genocide: Forcing children to go to school in a language other than their own may harm the children by uprooting them from their cultural framework but rarely does a government succeed in assimilating entire cultures. There the criminal stigma of genocide as defined by the Rome Statute lies not in the typical harm that occurs but in the supposed wickedness of the intention.

In the field of hate crimes, the element of intention or bias plays an equally critical role. These statutes in the United States provide aggravated penalties if the offender commits an assault or other crime of violence with an intent to harm a member of a protected group "as such." That is, it must be the purpose — and not just the side effect of the crime — to inflict harm on the white, or black, Jew, Christian, or Muslim.

In both genocide and hate crimes, there is considerable controversy about deciding which groups get protected and which do not. In the United Nations debate leading to the adoption of the Genocide Convention in 1948, there was a proposal to protect politically defined groups. But for rather obvious reasons the Soviet Union led a campaign to eliminate this ground from the offense, and the General Assembly complied. Yet apparently the Spanish variation of the Convention did include the category of political persecution and thus provided a basis for charging Pinochet with genocide for systematically eliminating political opponents after he took power in Chile.

It is hard to understand why women are not protected under the genocide statute and only episodically under the hate crime laws. One would think that the Taliban's suppression of women in Afghanistan, particularly barring them from education, would be just as bad as coercing abortions or seeking forcibly to assimilate minority children. Apartheid is a crime against humanity, but forcing women to wear burkas when they go out in public seems to escape scrutiny. All of this smacks a bit of moral arbitrariness.

For liberal individualists, it is particularly difficult to explain why some groups are protected and others not. Suppose that someone hates baldheaded people and decides to kill the first bald man he meets on the street. He acts with the kind of bias toward bald people that if exercised toward blacks would render his offense a hate crime. If we look just at the behavior of the individual and his sentiment of hatred, there seems to be no difference between hating bald men and hating Chinese people. Yet hate-crime statutes do not include idiosyncratic hatreds that might be just as virulent as racial or religious hatred.

The liberal account of protecting certain groups and not others stresses the element of efficiency. If there are not enough beneficiaries to warrant the investment of legal resources, we should not do it. This supposedly explains the legislative disposition to protect Chinese people but not bald men. But there are few indications that efficiency considerations account either for the contours of genocide or for hate-crime legislation. If the issues were numbers, one would expect a different outcome on the protection of women or political opponents.

The better account of both genocide and hate crimes is that the attack is understood in the society as an expression of collective conflict. Both the offender and the victim are merely representatives of groups that are engaged in ongoing hostilities. Genocide has the particular feature that the historical paradigms stand not merely for bias but for the ambition to eliminate the hated group. Only when the conflict is collective can we say that the victim and other members of the group are exposed to continuing danger, a danger that persists even if the particular offender is caught and imprisoned. This kind of conflict exists among "national, ethnical, racial, and religious group[s]." It exists sometimes between politically defined groups. And in the extreme the mistreatment of women bears the same characteristic of collective oppression. But it does not exist between the hirsute and the bald, or between students and teachers. Some crimes are individual events; others bear the dangers of collective action.

Proof of this thesis is found in the willingness of the international community to treat killing as genocide simply because the offender and the victim belong to hostile, embattled groups, whether or not these groups meet the technical definitions of the law. The leading example is the conflict between the Hutus and Tutsis, a conflict that has generated numerous prosecutions for genocide, both in the special tribunal established for Rwanda and in the Belgian courts under a theory of universal jurisdiction for genocide committed abroad. The differences between the Hutus and Tutsis are not national, not racial, and not religious, and nor are they ethnic. The difference derives from historically rooted social and economic factors. The Tutsis owned land or cattle. The Hutus were originally peasant farmers. Their separate identities took hold, under encouragement by the Belgian colonialists. When Hutus rose up to slaughter their rival group, neither the United Nations nor the international community at large had qualms about applying the crime of genocide to the Hutus' persecution of their rival group.

The reason that the international community can respond so clearly to collective persecution in Rwanda is that the motivating force behind the law is not the letter of the 1948 treaty defining genocide but rather an historical paradigm of organized killing to eliminate a *genos* (Greek for "race" or "class") from the human species. Rafael Lemkin, a Polish Jew obviously influenced by the Holocaust, invented the word in 1944 as the opening move in a campaign to subject group-based hate campaigns to international stigma. Lemkin emphasized the "nation" and its culture as the interests that would be protected by a new crime of genocide. The great evil of killing off a nation, he argued, was not simply the murder of large numbers of people but the resulting "loss of its future contributions to the world." Lemkin's words recall the Romantic conception of nationhood and the role of meaning in national self-expression in language, literature, and law.

I have shown that the international crimes within the jurisdiction of the proposed International Criminal Court are collective in nature. Crimes of aggression, war crimes, crimes against humanity, and genocide are the consequence of embattled and violent hostility expressed by one group of people against another. Individuals act, but at the same time, the nation or collective also acts and expresses itself in the action. True, we hold individuals accountable for these crimes, but the formal structure of liability should not camouflage the collective personality inherent in the crime. The individual offenders are liable because they are members of the hostile groups that engage in unlawful aggression, commit "widespread or systematic" cruelty, and perpetuate harms with a design to eliminate opposing cultures. They are not like the criminals and victims as we know them in the domestic scene, where both criminal and victim are seen as autonomous individuals.

The relationship of Romantic thought to the belief in collective action is surely not a simple equation of cause and effect. The idea of collective action predates, by far, the literary and artistic period we label Romantic. The notion of the collective, as we shall see later in the argument, has roots in Greek and biblical thought. My point is to demonstrate that our conventional liberal, individualistic ways of thinking about criminal liability simply do not account for the sentiments that actually shape the operative contours of international criminal law. The mind of the law may speak in the language of liberal individualism, but its heart lies in the disfavored ideas of collective action and collective guilt. The spirit of the Romantic is with us, even if her voice is muted and too often scorned.

CHAPTER FOUR

The Guilt of Nations

What magic is in the pronoun "my" that
should justify us in overturning the
decisions of impartial truth?
— *William Godwin*

We have concluded without too much
difficulty that armies act, governments act, nations act. Collectives act. Perhaps this is a rather elementary conclusion. We could
have reached it intuitively — without the pyrotechnics about the
proper interpretation of the nature of war and the Rome Statute.
Once I was in a conversation about this topic with Bernard Williams, in which my astute interlocutor responded, "Of course,
there is a difference between collective and individual action. Just
think of this sentence 'The Fifth Army feinted toward the Rhine
and then fell to looting and raping.'" It was a brilliant example,
for when we hear that single sentence we intuit the difference. We
know that it was the army as whole that feinted a move toward
the Rhine but individual soldiers who began to commit crimes.

But our conclusion goes beyond this important insight. The
claim is that the crimes covered by the Rome Statute display two
dimensions of action — individual and collective at the same time.
Williams's example clarifies that actions can be individual or collective in nature. My view is that they can be both at once, and
that we must recognize and differentiate between the individual
and collective dimensions when we prosecute suspects like Eich-

mann, Milosevic, and the Hutu nuns convicted in Belgium for genocide in Rwanda.

The great danger of ordinary criminal prosecutions is that we succumb to a search for scapegoats. Recalling the ritual detailed in the Book of Leviticus, we load our loathing for the crime onto to the suspect and send him, metaphorically, into the desert to die, thereby extinguishing our collective sin for having allowed the crime to occur. The criminal process is one of the best means ever devised to facilitate this cleansing of the collective soul. I am not speaking of the cleansing of the offender's soul, but of our own, the society's shared sense of guilt in allowing one of its members to become a victim of crime. The criminal process enables us to believe that the suspect alone bears guilt for the crime, that the suspect alone should be punished — and even more to the point, that we, the righteous ones, are entitled to inflict that punishment.

Perhaps we are getting ahead of the story, for all we have established is that collectives engage in action. It is too soon to jump to the conclusion that criminal trials are an elaborate ritual for blaming a single individual and escaping blame ourselves. This is a fair objection, but the reader should be *en garde*. Bolder intellectual propositions await. We can expect to be engaged and destabilized in our liberal assumptions about individuals as the sole bearers of guilt and responsibility.

The question that confronts us now is how we make the transition from collective action to collective guilt. To focus on this question, let us take a variation of Bernard Williams's example: "The Fifth Army declared that no quarter would be given; they killed all prisoners and began pillaging the town." This sentence describes three distinct war crimes: the declaration, the killing, and the pillaging. A proper investigation would isolate some individuals who actually carried out these acts, but the problem is whether in the commission of the war crime, the Fifth Army also acts, commits the crime, and renders itself guilty of the crime. This is a practical test of the problem of collective guilt.

The declaration that no quarter be given must be articulated by someone, and the only person who can do so with proper authority is the commanding officer. He or she acts under color of authority, in the name of the entire army, and in this sense the army is implicated in the action. The problem with regard to the theory of collective guilt is whether the individual soldiers in the unit are also responsible for the declaration simply by virtue of their being soldiers in the army. This question is not exactly the same as whether the Fifth Army is accountable, and we shall have to turn in due course to the problem whether collective guilt necessarily implies that each and every member of the collective is also guilty. I will eventually take the position that an entire nation might be guilty without implying that each citizen, each national, is also guilty. The United States might have been guilty of supporting slavery but it would be illogical to infer that every citizen, every abolitionist, was also guilty in the same way.

As collective action, the killing of civilians differs from the declaration that no quarter be given. Numbers of soldiers carry out the killings, we may suppose, in a coordinated fashion. They may or not may not be acting on the basis of an order from their commander in the field. They act intentionally, but liberal individualists have long insisted that these intentions be individualized. Each soldier has his or her own intention. In recent years, however, some leading philosophers, notably Margaret Gilbert and John Searle, have argued that the soldiers' intention in this case is singular: They share a collective intention to kill.

Collective intentions arise when each participants thinks, "We are doing this together." We are taking a walk, playing a musical composition, or voting to pass a bill in a legislature. When one of the four passengers ready to fight on United Airlines 93 used the now famous expression "Let's roll" to signal their defensive attack against the hijackers, they were acting with a collective intention. Each had the sense: We are in this together. This strikes me as a better account than the individualist claim that each of four passengers acted autonomously, with a separate and private intention. There is nothing about the separateness of our bodies that requires us to think of all collective actions as nothing more than the sum total of individual actions.

In the hypothetical case posed above, the killing of prisoners might be a series of individual killings, but the more plausible scenario is that the soldiers act with a collective intention, a shared understanding, that they are engaged in a common enterprise. The individuals are guilty for their individualized actions but it is hard to escape the conclusion that they are all collectively guilty for the crime as well. Admittedly, there is a problem in holding bystanders guilty for the actions of the soldiers who actually carry out the deed with their own hands.

But one wonders whether there are ever total bystanders who can say that they are totally innocent of collective wrongdoing. An instructive example is the way, with a home video camera turning, a group of police officers stood by as four of their number beat Rodney King with their batons in a San Fernando Valley parking lot. The four officers who took an active part in the beating clearly exercised a collective intention to pummel their victim. The twenty-odd officers who stood by provided at least emotional support. Though they were not prosecuted, they were not totally innocent either. The incident was widely seen as an indictment of the Los Angeles police force as a whole. In the minds of the public the LAPD bore collective guilt for having created the environment in which a racially motivated beating could easily occur.

It is not necessary for criminal guilt to affirm that every participant intentionally causes harm. There are many variations of criminal liability that depend not on intentional but on negligent or reckless action. It is relatively easy to find every member of a group accountable on grounds of negligence or recklessness for creating and tolerating an environment in which there is high risk that some people will start using killing or, as in the Rodney King affair, using excessive force. The entire group is accountable for the high-risk environment. Think of a protest by the Ku Klux Klan in which all the participants participate in burning crosses and chanting epithets at blacks living in the community. Even if they resolve ahead of time not to get violent, one of them might break ranks and assault the victim. It would be difficult to deny the responsibility of the whole group for this departure from their plan. They create a high risk of violence, and whatever their intentions, they are responsible on grounds of recklessness for the outcome.

Although the law of war crimes nominally requires intentional conduct, this is not true in practice. In a case arising out of the Japanese occupation of the Philippines in World War II, the U.S. Supreme Court affirmed the conviction of the general in charge of the occupation, Tomoyuki Yamashita, on the ground that he negligently allowed his men to run wild and commit atrocities on the civilian population. The same principle readily extends to an entire group of people who tolerate a climate favorable to actions in violation of the laws of war.

In speaking about a group of soldiers killing civilians, we are drawn to describing the activity as "they killed" rather than "it killed." The choice of singular or plural reflects our consciousness about whether the primary actors are a collection of individuals or a single entity. Recall the switch at the time of the Civil War in our thinking about the United States. The antebellum locution was, "The United States were"; postbellum it became, "The United States was." This switch in usage obviously reflected a growing consciousness that the United States existed as a single nation indivisible.

The use of collective nouns has the appeal in some situations of dispensing with the need for proof. In the mood of solidarity that prevailed after September 11, 2001, the *New York Times* ran a special section entitled "A Nation Challenged." And if some people someplace in the United States did not feel challenged? The general description of the nation is not so easily refuted. Similarly, CNN repeatedly used captions of the form "America Under Attack," "America Mourns," or "America Fights Back." If the phrase had been of the form "*Americans* Mourn," which would have been more descriptive of particular attitudes, CNN would actually have had to report on the specific individuals who were mourning.

In our hypothetical case of the soldiers killing prisoners, it seems more natural to describe the activity with the plural pronoun "they." It is not clear, however, how much turns on these linguistic points. There is some unavoidable variance between British and American usage. Americans are more likely to use collective nouns. For example, the British would say, "The jury were undecided." Americans say, "The jury was undecided." The thought is presumably the same.

Some verbs like "pillaging" point clearly to collective activity. We noted this earlier about the act of "bearing" arms. The same could be said about "waging war," or "legislating" or "winning the Superbowl." Only armies wage war, only legislatures legislate and only teams win Superbowls. "Pillaging" is among these verbs. A single soldier who is stealing jewelry is not pillaging. He is stealing. There is no good definition of "pillaging" in the literature, but we can assume that the activity is akin to plundering or despoiling. It is the systematic theft and destruction of property.

In these cases of collective verbs, collective responsibility comes first; individual responsibility comes afterward. Congress is responsible for the bill. Individual congressmen and -women bear, at most, derivative responsibility.

One recurrent question troubles us: What about the dissenters? What about those who oppose the action or openly resist? Are they guilty as well? One way to approach this problem is to distinguish among various types of guilt as they may be used in talking about individual and collective guilt. To aid in this effort we turn to two authors — one a philosopher and the other a novelist — whose works illuminate the various dimensions of guilt.

Two Authors: Two Approaches to Collective Guilt

The philosopher Karl Jaspers spent the war years in Germany and then after the war moved to Basel where he reflected on the currents of opinion charging Germany with war guilt. He wrote his classic work *The Question of German Guilt* in this period when there was a widespread tendency to regard the Germans as collectively guilty, in particular, for the mass murder of Jews, Poles, and Gypsies. There was considerable talk about collective punishment in the form of permanent limitations on the future development of German society. One of these forms of collective punishment would have been the implementation of the Morgenthau plan, which would have forced Germany to maintain an agricultural economy. In retrospect, few current writers have kind things to say about the scheme hatched by Secretary of the Treasury Henry Morgenthau. But at the time it seemed plausible as a recognition of Germany's collective guilt and the danger Germany would pose if it once again developed an economy capable of supporting an armaments industry.

Writing with ideas like this swirling about him, Jaspers comes out in favor of collective guilt but opposed to the idea of German guilt as an instantiation of the idea. To reach this nuanced conclusion, he situated the problem in a larger framework of four kinds of guilt: criminal, moral, political, and metaphysical.

Criminal guilt is the most familiar of the four. And indeed the notion of guilt, as we use it today, stands in close association with the concepts of crime and punishment. The term for guilt translates readily across Western languages (*culpabilité* in French, *Schuld* in German, *vina* in Russian, *bünösség* in Hungarian, *ashma* in Hebrew). "Guilt" does not appear in the law of contracts, property, or accidents. It is used uniquely in criminal law. We see this in the familiar common-law institutions of guilty pleas and guilty verdicts. The notion of "innocence" as expressed in the "presumption of innocence" means innocence from crime. Someone who defends against charges of breach of contract is a few degrees off if he or she asserts a claim of "innocence." The term is part of a complex of ideas, including guilt and punishment, framed by criminal law.

It would be difficult to formulate the notion of crime without implying a conception of guilt in the action. This is a good argument in itself for recognizing that crimes based on collective action imply collective guilt. Yet there is always a nagging concern about the unfair treatment of dissenters and those who are simply passive bystanders to the behavior of those bent on committing the crime. What should we say about those less involved? That they have a lesser degree of guilt or perhaps that they are to be charged with a different kind of guilt. Jaspers enriches the debate by suggesting moral, political, and metaphysical guilt as alternatives.

Moral guilt may coincide with criminal guilt, but it need not do so. As Jaspers uses the term, the realm of morality focuses our attention on the inner quality of the deed, but not in the way we are accustomed to thinking today. Jaspers would say that those who act under duress or personal necessity, namely those who are said today to be morally excused, are still guilty — as long as they could have avoided the act. Thus Dudley and Stephens — the famous sailors shipwrecked at sea who killed and consumed a cabin boy to fend off their own death from starvation — made themselves morally guilty, even though many commentators today would say that they should have been excused under the law. No one blames them for submitting to overwhelming pressure, but they could have exercised heroic capacities to abstain from cannibalism and risk death by starvation. Their failure to do so was enough for them to be morally guilty. In 1884 an English court found them legally guilty, sentenced them to death, and then the Crown commuted the sentence to six months in prison.

Jaspers places both political and metaphysical guilt beyond the moral category of the avoidable. They attach even in cases of living under dictatorships where it is not humanly possible to avoid the inhuman actions of those in charge. Political guilt is borne by each person in a political community merely by virtue of being there and being governed. As Jaspers disarmingly puts it: *"Es ist jedes Menschen Mitverantwortung wie er regiert wird"* (Everybody is co-responsible for the way he is governed.) According to this view, the citizens of Stalinist Russia and fascist Germany were politically responsible for the actions of their leaders. They were co-responsible, along with the dictatorial parties, for their political life. (The shocking version of this claim for Americans would be that Africans brought to the United States in chains were politically guilty for the existence of slavery!) It is not clear whether this shared guilt derives from the unrealized ability to overthrow the dictator or whether it follows simply from the fact that as Jaspers put it, this is the political realm in which *"ich mein Dasein habe"* (my existence is lived out). In the latter theory, political guilt derives from identification with the society and from being there at the time of the crime.

Jaspers's argument for political guilt based on personal history resembles Freud's account of why we bear responsibility for the evil impulses of our dreams: "Unless the content of the dream . . . is inspired by alien spirits, it is part of my own being." For the sake of effective therapy, we must accept our dreams as our own. This argument appeals to our desire for authenticity and coherence in our personalities. The same demands of consistency require us to recognize that we are part of the culture that has nourished us. The theme of alienation runs throughout both Freud and Jaspers. We should not treat our dreams as alien to us, and we should not be aliens in our own land. This is the best way to understand Jaspers's claim that we accept co-responsibility and political guilt for the way we are governed.

Jaspers thinks of metaphysical guilt as arising from solidarity with other human beings. The failure to attempt a rescue even with no prospect of success generates this form of existential guilt. "We did not go into the streets when our Jewish friends were led away; we did not scream until we too were destroyed. . . . We are guilty of being alive." Metaphysical guilt goes beyond all other forms of guilt. As Jaspers argues, "Someplace between human beings there is room for the unconditional proposition that either we live together or we do not live at all."

These propositions bring to mind a Talmudic analysis of sacrificing one to save many. As the case is put, a Jewish village is surrounded by an enemy force. The enemy says, "Give us one of you as a hostage, or we kill everyone in the village." The rabbis reflecting on this hypothetical case concluded that the duty of the villagers under these circumstances is to die together rather than arbitrarily designate one of their number as a hostage. This example illustrates Jaspers's point that there are some situations in which the solidarity of human beings requires them to endure the same fate. But suppose the villagers remain passive as the enemy troops enter the city and arbitrarily pick a hostage. If they resist, they will all be killed. But by failing to resist, failing to die, they become, as Jaspers claims, metaphysically guilty for the death of their compatriot.

The problem is where the duty of solidarity ends. Claims of metaphysical guilt are presumably limited to a particular cultural situation and therefore stop short of the universal guilt advocated by Father Zosima in Dostoyevsky's *The Brothers Karamazov*. If everyone is guilty for everything, then everyone is also innocent. The distinction loses its bite.

These arguments for political and metaphysical guilt offer a qualified defense of collective guilt. Jaspers defends the idea that some groups can be charged with political or metaphysical guilt, but he takes a strong stand against the idea that nations as such can bear guilt of this sort. He denies the guilt of the German people (as opposed to Hitler and his party) for the war and the Holocaust on the ground that the German nation has no clear contours. There is no way of knowing who is included and who is not, who is at the core of the nation and who is at the periphery. He does not deny that some people possess more or less of certain national characteristics, but nationality is a scalar—not a categorical—concept. It is not like being male or female, but more like being tall or short. You can have more or less German-ness in your sense of identity, but there is no fixed level in this variable identification that defines someone as a German in his heart. There are many different Germans; no single identity can be reduced to a composite German. As he writes, "An entire nation [*Volk*] cannot be reduced to a single individual. A nation cannot suffer heroic tragedy. It cannot be a criminal; it cannot act morally or immorally. Only individuals in the nation can do these things."

But if the nation is a scalar concept, why is not the army treated in the same way? Perhaps because you have to join the army; you are born into the nation. But still you could identify more or less with the army. You could be more or less a soldier as you are more or less a member of your national community.

The element of self-identification raises the larger question of how the subjective experience of feeling guilt should enter into the analysis of collective guilt. For some illumination on this point we turn to a different author, a contempory novelist, an accidental philosopher, Philip Roth.

In his recent novel *The Human Stain*, Roth provides us with a rich study in collective action and collective guilt. Coleman Silk, a high-ranking professor and dean at Athena College, refers to two persistently absent students as "spooks." Unbeknownst to him, the missing students are African Americans. The remark takes on racial overtones, and it is widely publicized as a bigoted reference to blacks. The entire campus turns against Silk, drives him out of his job, and additionally taunts him with charges of sexual exploitation for dating a woman much younger than himself. His death in an automobile accident breaks the mood of hostility and causes people to reconsider their knee-jerk responses. At his funeral service, a black professor named Herb Keble, Silk's first hire at the university, takes the podium and confesses his cowardice in failing to defend Silk. His language is important: "I stand before you to censure myself for having failed my friend and patron, and to do what I can . . . to begin to attempt to right the wrong, the grievous, the contemptible wrong, that was done to him by Athena College."

Keble confesses not only his personal guilt but the collective guilt of the entire community. He discovers something about himself — that he was cowardly and disloyal toward a friend — and he feels guilty. But he also senses that everyone around him shares the same weakness of character. He adds that the mistreatment of Silk "remains a blight on the integrity of this institution to this day." He points the finger at them at the same time that he indicts himself.

The liberal response to this argument is that Keble is only accusing other individuals of complicity in his wrongdoing, but in fact he is doing more than that. He claims that the whole college community is guilty. They provided reciprocal emotional support for their persecution of Silk; they acted as a group in the sense that their intentions, attitudes, and actions were all self-consciously interdependent. The group consciousness deprives them of their ordinary capacities for compassion. Simply standing in a one-to-one relationship, no one would have been hostile toward Silk for an understandable mischoice of word.

To say that the entire college is guilty is not to suppose that there is a separate being someplace called "The College" and that this being feels guilty. It is rather to trade implicitly on a well-established philosophical argument about collective intentions and collective actions. As John Searle argues about intentions, we can — in a reciprocal understanding of what we are doing — share an intention. We might have this form of "we-intention" in taking a walk together, playing in a quartet, or sitting in the legislature and passing a law. If we can have the consciousness of acting and intending as a group, we can surely tender feelings as a group. These feelings might be hostility, contempt, or, as in Herb Keble's example, feelings of guilt for a wrong we committed together.

Collective guilt of the college might have been possible, but

Keble did not establish it by generalizing from his own feelings. His argument trades on a confusion between feeling guilty and being guilty. The steps in the inference go like this:

1. I feel guilty;
2. Therefore I am guilty.
3. The rest of the college has the same reason to feel guilty as I do;
4. Therefore, the whole college is guilty.

A giant hole in the argument arises from his assumption that the others feel the way he does and that he can make the same weak inference from their feelings to their state of guilt.

The better argument for Athena's guilt would follow the progression from action, to collective intention, to collective guilt. There is little doubt that the college acted collectively in shunning Silk. They each did it with knowledge that they were acting together. It was not the case that each said to him- or herself, "I will do this, and others will do it too." They thought in the manner of "we-intentions" — that is, "We will do this together." Now to say that the college acted does not require that every single person was aware of what was going on. There might have been a person or two holed up in the library who never heard of the affair, but a few holdouts do not diminish the collective nature of the college's action. The fans can cheer collectively even if there is a dissenter sitting in the audience with his hands over his ears. The important point is that the college acted as a body with a sense of shared identity among the participants. They all thought implicitly: "If you are one of us, you will treat Silk in the way we do." That is, the college acted not just with an aggregative will but with an associative will that expressed its identity at that moment in time.

There is little difficulty in characterizing the action toward Silk as wrong and therefore an inappropriate basis for blame and for describing the college community as guilty. The action toward Silk was intolerant, an expression of self-righteous political correctness. They did not give him a fair chance to explain himself.

This happens all the time in the groups in which we live. Intolerant collectives turn against their perceived deviants and torment them to the point of misery.

To take the step from collective wrongdoing to collective guilt, we need a theory of culpability, some ground for saying that the members of Athena College bore more than just responsibility for having participated in the collective act. The ground of culpability would be negligence or recklessness. Recall that we discussed this possibility above in the example of the Ku Klux Klan tolerating a high-risk environment of violence. Here the risk speaks to the moral error of those hounding Silk. Each member of the community could have corrected his biased judgment about Silk but did not. They were willing to run the risk of error when it would have been easy to sit down with Silk, talk to him, and revise their judgment.

The fictitious case of Coleman Silk at Athena College illuminates the general problem of collective guilt. Other cases — say, anti-Semitism in Europe — entail the same kind of group and conformist behavior in situations in which self-correction would not be difficult. Athena typifies the "banality of evil" made famous by Hannah Arendt's account of Eichmann in Jerusalem. The group members follow each other like sheep until something happens to shock them into awareness of their wrongdoing. But at any moment they could have turned to each other and said, "Let's think about what we are doing here." They had the capacity all along to understand their brutality and intolerance, but they could not bring themselves to see it. This is the paradigmatic case of being aguilty and not feeling it until the finality of a death awakens the normal human capacity for empathy.

Later I shall offer a more detailed account of guilt as the failure to correct inclinations to do evil and suggest that in these cases of "group think" that inhibit correct behavior, the collective and the individual are both to blame and the culpability for wrongdoing should be distributed between them. The argument, it turns out, has practical significance for the sentencing of offenders who are caught in an environment in which self-correction requires heroic efforts.

The Nation As Collective

To make the transition from the guilt of small groups like colleges to the guilt of nations, we need a different methodology. There must be some way to single out the nation as the primary bearer of the guilt for actions committed by subgroups within it — groups like the army, a dominant political party, or a social movement that, like the intolerant members of the Athena community, allow themselves to descend into collective sin or criminality.

The problem is essentially one of attribution. Imagine a large circle with several small circles within it. Within each of the small circles there are several x's representing individuals. The small circles stand for subgroups within the society: families, colleges, professional organizations, clubs, armies, units within the armies, and the like. The large circle stands for the nation defined historically by its language, sometimes by its religion, often by its historical struggle for survival and independence. Some x's within one of the smaller circles, say the army, commit some great wrong but with the knowledge and spiritual support, to varying degrees, of everyone in the nation defined by the outer circle. The problem is attributing the guilt for this action. Should the target of the attribution be the smaller circle, namely the army, or the larger circle, the nation?

We have to ask ourselves what in our social and political lives makes the nation take on reality as an entity with a life of its own. This is the conception of the nation that one finds in Romantic writers from Wordsworth to Herder. What could make it appeal to us today? The solidarity of the nation appears particularly strong in the face of an attack — at the time of suffering. Witness the language used to describe the September 11 attack. The victims were not the government, not the culture, not just the people, but the American *nation*. By using the term nation in its post–September 11 supplement entitled "A Nation Challenged" the *New York Times* meant to say that something more is at risk than our tall buildings, the security of our borders, or even our population. The nation is attacked, and everything is at risk: the collective American experiment, the future, and the unique vision of democracy and freedom.

The same idiom presented itself to Abraham Lincoln in the Gettysburg Address, November 19, 1863. The *nation* was at war testing whether this *nation* or any *nation* conceived in liberty and dedicated to equality "can long endure." The concept of the nation enabled Lincoln to transcend the particularities of North and South. As he recognized in his Second Inaugural Address five months later, "both [sides] read the same Bible and pray[ed] to the same God" and both were part of the nation that suffered for the offense of slavery. God gave "to both North and South this terrible war as the woe due to those by whom the offense came." The entire nation suffered for its offense in founding a republic on the basis of slavery.

The contours of the nation become high profile—they stand out relative to subgroups like religions, political parties, and other organizations—when, because of their historical situation, people become particularly conscious of their language, their historical legacy, and their belonging to a particular experiment in culture and government. Admittedly, the people constituting a self-conscious collecive might exist as the subnational or supernational level. The Québécois constitute a nation strongly identified with their language, their *Code civil*, and their sense of historical oppression. Jews constitute a nation—both within Israel and in their diaspora. (The concept of "diaspora" itself testifies to the existence of a home and a nation). Since the establishment of the state of Israel, Palestinians have become a nation, with an identity now separate from the rest of the Arab world.

The sense of the nation as an actor in history differs from culture to culture. Since the Civil War, Americans have experienced a strong sense of the nation as the bearer of the American commitment to liberty and equality. The French have long had a heightened consciousness of their nation in history, as revealed by a remarkable claim by Charles de Gaulle engraved on a monument near the Champs Elysées in Paris: *Il y a un pacte vingt fois séculaire entre la gloire de la France et la liberté du monde* (There has been a pact for the last twenty centuries between the grandeur of France and the liberty of the world).

One sees in this boasting by de Gaulle the great danger of taking nationalism too seriously. The feeling of national identity, cultivated by Herder and other Romantics, stresses the equal value of all languages, all cultures. Each bears the spark of civilization. We should cultivate our own language, seek harmony with those who share the same birthright, and do all this not because our nation is better than others — but simply because it is ours. It is constitutive of who we are. This, I believe, is the way Lincoln thought of the American nation — at least most of the time.

And yet there is always a tendency to slide from the equal respect of all nations into a sense of superiority and mission in history. Americans succumbed to this arrogance as they expanded westward under the doctrine of "Manifest Destiny." Lincoln sometimes slipped toward a glorification of the Americans as the New Israel. In a speech at Trenton, New Jersey, in 1861, Lincoln referred to America at war as "his [God's] almost chosen people." Shortly thereafter "In God We Trust" began to appear on coinage of the United States. It is almost impossible to go to war without the feeling that one's own nation, because of its intrinsic greatness, has a special place in the sun.

The fear of negative nationalism has always led liberals to be suspicious of claims like those of de Gaulle and Lincoln. If all human beings are created equal, there is no reason to think one national constellation is superior to another. Of course, nations often claim this intrinsic moral advantage. Jews think of themselves as a "light unto the nations." Americans seem to share the idea that they stand for unique principles of justice. Russians claim a special quality of soul—*dusha*—absent in other European cultures. But these groupings of men and women called "nations" seem to enlightened liberals to be merely contingent, accidental forms that will pass away as humanity matures.

Skepticism about the nation and other such collectives naturally provides a foundation for a general critique of collective guilt. The Enlightenment strikes back and the time to launch the attack is when the critic catches a whiff of national superiority.

In *The Question of German Guilt*, Jaspers has another card to play in his hand against the proponents of national guilt. He turns the table on Germany's accusers by pointing out that the historical paradigm for collective guilt had always been anti-Semitism. Those who charge guilt for the Holocaust should not slip in the very error that anti-Semites had made since the beginning of Church history. It was and is irrational, he claims, to hold Jews liable in eternity because two thousand years ago a specific set of Jews in Jerusalem collaborated with the Romans in crucifying a man who was later anointed as the Messiah. There is no doubt that the hatred of Jews had its roots, in part, in centuries of calumny against the so-called Christ-killers. If we now understand this kind of undifferentiated indictment of a nation as irrational and bigoted, he argues, we should not repeat the mistake by charging all Germans with the crime of the Holocaust.

Rhetorically and logically, Jaspers's point compels our attention. To ascribe irreducible national guilt to the Germans is to repeat the intellectual indecency of anti-Semitism. Implicit in the charge, however, is an assumption that national guilt is necessarily passed by birth to the next generation. Might it not be possible, however, to think of all compatriots living in Germany at the time of the Nazis as collectively guilty, but of Germans, born after the war, as free from the charge?

Surely, when the notion of collective guilt extends across generations and taints the unborn, it becomes a problematic idea, hardly compatible with our professed respect for individuality and particularly for the Jeffersonian principle that "all men are created equal." They cannot be born equal if some are tainted by the sins of their parents. The only way to salvage the concept of collective guilt, then, is to develop a conception of guilt that could attach to the nation without implying the nation's guilt is passed to particular individuals in the next generation. As our inquiry proceeds, we cannot ignore Jaspers's challenge to avoid versions of collective guilt that partake of the vice of anti-Semitism.

One way to avoid abuse of the concept of guilt is to rely instead on the notion of responsibility. In at least two familiar contexts, the notions of collective responsibility seem to be unproblematic. The first is the notion of collective debt or disability deriving from the behavior of past generations. There are many details and complexities in the debate about compensating Aborigines for expropriated lands or the descendants of slaves for their ancestors' captivity. The easiest case is the sort that occurred in Australia when the Supreme Court decided that the Meriam peoples, who had been living continuously on the Murray Islands from before the arrival of the English settlers, had good title to their lands when the province of Queensland expropriated them on the false theory that they were abandoned lands owned by no one. The tribe is still in existence and therefore title to the land could be and indeed was returned to the collective heirs of its original owners.

Compensating individuals for wrongs committed against their ancestors hundreds of years ago becomes more problematic. Several generations after the event we encounter problems identifying the heirs of both the perpetrators and the victims. Also, a lot depends on whether the heirs sue in their own names for their ongoing loss or on grounds of an inherited claim possessed by their ancestors. The Meriam people sued for the ongoing deprivation of their land. But the children of slaves may have no complaints about their own lives except that a great injustice was done to their forebears. Reducing the ancient wrong to a claim converts it into an item of property that can pass, as do other forms of property, from generatation to generation.

There is a problem, however, in determining who is entitled to receive the inheritance. If there is no tribe that can claim a collective right, then individuals must assert a share of the inherited right based on their blood lines. As individuals, however, they have a dubious moral right to be enriched simply because someone in the past was harmed — someone in their blood line whom they never knew. In this situation, the individuals are likely to buttress their claim by asserting that some collective — most African Americans descended from slaves — still exists to acquire an interest analogous to the collective tribal claims of the Meriam peoples.

Compensation for historical injustices requires some way to trace the continuity of perpetrators and victims. For the descendants of the victims to sue, as a class, the descendants of the perpetrators, as a class, one has to assume that the collective (e.g., all Australians, Americans, or Germans) counts as the bearer of rights and duties. That is, some theory of collective responsibility must come into play. If the individuals involved can be reliably assigned to specific classes of perpetrators and victims, then the problem of the debt's passing from generation to generation is no more problematic than the principle of state succession in international law. If states are responsible for the debts incurred by prior regimes, then the same principles apply to alleged duties to make compensation for past acts of wrongdoing.

More difficult issues arise in considering inherited disabilities. A good example is Article 9 of the Japanese Constitution, which states that the "Japanese People forever renounce war as a sovereign right of the nation" and prohibits the Japanese from maintaining "land, sea, and air forces." In practice, this provision is interpreted to permit a small force for purposes of self-defense. But the self-inflicted mark of Cain is inescapable. From now until eternity, the Japanese bear a disability not recognized, as far as I know, in the constitution of any other country. The current generation may feel no responsbility for the war, but surely General MacArthur had responsibility and probably guilt in mind when he imposed that provision on the Japanese Constitution. Entrenching disabilities of this sort in a constitution seems to say to the world: "There is a bad seed here in this nation, and it is replanted in the soil of each successive generation." The irony of the Japanese situation is that apart from this provision in the Constitution, Japan has had difficulty recognizing a need to make amends for its behavior in World War II. Until recently, it resisted apologizing appropriately to the Chinese or the Koreans. Its military self-restraint stands out as nearly its sole recognition of wartime guilt.

In these contexts at least, it is plausible to think of the nation as the entity that bears collective responsibility for the crimes of its subjects and citizens. It does not follow that subgroups are not also responsible, but if some collective entities are to be held accountable, then the nation is among them.

This argument does not resolve the question whether the appropriate word in this context is "responsibility" or "guilt." There is much more required to resolve that issue, and the place to begin is with an exploration of how individuals become guilty for war crimes. If we can understand how and when individuals are guilty for violations of the law, we can then address the problem of collective guilt for war crimes.

CHAPTER FIVE

Individuals at War

They that can give up essential liberty to
obtain a little temporary safety deserve
neither liberty nor safety.
— *Benjamin Franklin*

Entering military service brings a cur-
tain down upon one's prior life. The citizen disappears behind the
curtain, undergoes basic training, and reemerges as soldier. The
soldier becomes an agent bound in service to the state and the nation. As a good soldier, he or she obeys the officers in command.
Thinking less about right or wrong, surrendering to the moral
judgment of the commander, enables the phalanx of soldiers to
respond in military situations with discipline and efficiency.
Destroying property, wounding, and killing in the name of the
war are no longer immoral acts. To paraphrase the unforgettable
line from *The Godfather*, killing the enemy "is not personal." In
Clausewitz's famous phrase, "it is politics by other means." This
is the view that long prevailed.

Since the end of World War II we have begun to see individual
personalities reemerging from the command structure. That is,
the citizen loses his or her individuality by entering the command
structure and then reclaims it by acting contrary to the mores and
norms of military duty. The soldier is still part of the collective, as
we argued earlier, but since the Nuremberg trials we have wit-

nessed the soldier who is both an agent of the state and a morally responsible individual. Thus war and crime begin to intersect and overlap. The reassertion of the soldier as criminal is a phenomenon that requires our attention and understanding.

Whether they are eventually accused of war crimes or not, soldiers in post-Nuremberg military duty must be constantly on guard against acting on unlawful orders. While they could traditionally shift responsibility to their commanders, they can no longer do so. If they are aware that the order is "unlawful"—if the order, for example, is to enter the hamlet and kill all the women and children—they are duty bound to resist. If they do not, they can be held accountable for a war crime. The standard is still very deferential to the command structure, for the recipient of the order must be *aware* that the order is unlawful. According to American law, it is not enough that any reasonable soldier realize the illegal state of affairs. The particular soldier accused must understand that he or she is acting contrary to the law.

The Rome Statute has expanded even this emphasis on individual responsibility. In principle, the statute says, reliance on orders cannot excuse the commission of one of the four crimes—aggression, war crimes, crimes against humanity, and genocide. Ignorance of its illegality might constitute an excuse but only under the limited condition that the order is not "manifestly unlawful." This means that the order appear unlawful to a reasonable person. In cases of orders to commit genocide and crimes against humanity—presumably the two worst crimes of the four—all orders are assumed always to be manifestly or obviously unlawful. In other words, there is no possible excuse based on ignorance for these two more egregious crimes. The only problem with this approach is that the contours of genocide and crimes against humanity are contested. No one quite knows when, under this vague standard, military action is or is not prohibited. There is no consensus, for example, about whether the attacks of September 11 constituted a crime against humanity. But if a court decided that they were so prohibited, and if they were committed under "orders," the orders would, under the Rome Statute, not prevent a finding of guilt and liability by the persons who followed them.

In some respects this concurrence of war and crime should appeal to Romantics. With their zeal for individual self-expression, Romantics should be attracted by the criminal's independence and authenticity. Committing a crime promises the recognition of the person as actor, as author of his or her own deed. But war has a similar appeal. The Romantic begins with an overflowing self, then craves unity with others in a communal movement, but the self still craves recognition. The crime redeems the suppressed individuality of the conformist soldier.

Of course, there are less drastic ways of reclaiming the self. The soldier could take the cowardly paths of desertion or faking injury. But the zeal expressed in disregarding the line between combatants and civilians has a special appeal. Killing, even killing too much, always carries the exhilaration of crushing the enemy. When former Senator Robert Kerrey and his unit entered a hamlet in Vietnam and killed the apparently unarmed civilians, they did not think of themselves as criminals but as enthusiastic soldiers. The same is true, no doubt, of all the abuses in the name of war. Even when the facts are blatant—an order to mow down a group of prisoners, for example—the soldier might know that he is committing a war crime but nonetheless feel that he is acting for the sake of military victory and the good of country.

These are the seductions of both war and crime.

For all that we pretend to hate the criminal, there must also remain in all of us some ambivalent respect for the person who breaks all taboos, who strikes out on his own, who changes the world in a moment of aggression. From a psychoanalytic point of view, the things we find disgusting—eating feces, copulating on buses—are the actions that attract us more than we wish to admit. Crime has a similar appeal. We condemn the aggressors so vehemently precisely because of our repressed temptation to do the same thing.

Hannah Arendt misses something important about the experience of being a complacent "good German" during the Third Reich. Her view is that those who stood idly by, quietly tolerating the horrors of the concentration camps, lost their quality of being citizens and became, as part of her idea of the "banality of evil," automatons without personal choice and engagement. Erik Erickson struck closer to the mark when he analyzed the German self-identification with Hitler as both an act of submission and vicarious aggression. By feeling one with Hitler as he denounced the father-figure Churchill, the complacent Germans realized one of the virtues of the Romantic movement — asserting themselves in a great act of iconoclasm. In Erickson's view, they became servants and rebels simultaneously, all accomplished by identification with the *Führer*'s rebellion against the symbol of paternal repression.

The war criminal is both servant and rebel. Service to the nation should direct our attention to collective guilt, but this has not been the practice of the courts. In Nuremberg and in all subsequent proceedings, the impulse is always to blame these acts of criminal aggression on the individual, not on the nation. The liberal premises of the law are flouted when the accent falls on collective guilt, on the German nation rather than on specific officers and officials charged with waging aggressive war and committing crimes against humanity.

The charges in Nuremberg brought into focus the international law of war as a basis for condemning aggressive violence and imposing criminal liability. But what precisely was this "law of war"? It became the basis for these monumental trials as well as for hundreds of other prosecutions against Japanese and German soldiers and officers, and yet there is great uncertainty about what is prohibited and what is not.

However earnestly we take the Hague and Geneva Conventions, we can find little guidance about how to proceed against suspected international terrorists or soldiers captured in foreign expeditions of the United States, including the bombing of Afghanistan in 2001. As of this writing the United States is holding nearly two hundred detainees on its military base in Guantánamo

Bay. It is unsure what to do with them. Are they prisoners of war? Are they suspects of criminal acts? Are they both at once? Whatever the specific fate of these men, the problems of reconciling war and crime will remain with us. If we are living in a new era of warfare, we need to rethink the basic questions of crime and guilt as they apply to our enemies.

The "Invasion" of June 1942

There is no better place to begin this inquiry than by pondering the implications of a little-known "invasion" of the United States by eight German spies in the summer of 1942. The story is worth reciting in some detail for these events that occurred sixty years ago have a direct bearing on understanding the law of war today and how we should think of terrorists who inhabit the growing gap between "soldiers embedded in the chain of command" and the "individual criminals out on their own."

The United States had been at war with Germany for six months but we thought that our borders were still secure. The incident that began in the early morning hours of June 13 brought home the vulnerability of the coastline, our last line of defense.

A young coast-guard patrolman, John Cullen, was walking on the beach at Amagansett Beach on Long Island and he noticed four men with a small boat. He approached them, and one of them, named George Dasch, apparently in flawless English, said that he was a fisherman from Southampton who had run aground. Without suspicion of wrongdoing, Cullen suggested that Dasch and the other three wait until daylight at the coast-guard station. Then he heard one of the other three say something in German to Dasch. At that point Dasch said that he did not have a fishing permit and offered Cullen $260 to pretend that he had seen nothing on the beach that morning. The American took the money and left.

The four Germans on the beach finished their job of burying

explosives and their German uniforms on the beach and then, in civilian clothes, caught a train to New York City. Each had about $80,000 in his pocket (almost a million dollars in current value). In the meantime the coast-guard man reported the incident and turned in the bribe money. But by the time a patrol reached the beach, the Germans had left.

A similar landing occurred four days later at Ponte Verde Beach in Florida. Among the four in that unit, three—John Kerling, Werner Thiel, and Herbert Hans Haupt—were destined to play major roles in the annals of American law. The four left for Jacksonville and took trains north. Haupt was a naturalized citizen of the United States and had lived in the vicinity of Chicago with his parents from the age of five to the time, as a young adult, when he returned, almost by chance—after a miserable experience in a monastery in Japan—to Germany. (One of the reasons the German high command chose these eight is that they could pass easily in the United States on the planned mission of sabotage.) Haupt went home to his parents. On June 23, Kerling and Thiel met with an old friend, Anthony Cramer, a naturalized American, at the Twin Oaks Inn on Lexington Avenue in Manhattan. They thought their meeting was secret but in fact the FBI was watching.

And how did the FBI get so far so fast in tracking the eight saboteurs? They might not have cracked the case at all if Dasch had not immediately begun to get cold feet. Like his fellow agent Ernest Peter Burger and the others, he had ties to the United States as well as to Germany. Dasch and Burger were alone together in New York City without any supervision from Nazi agents. They confessed their doubts to each other about the mission, and Dasch resolved to switch sides. He also suspected that after the incident on the beach, the authorities must be bearing down on him. He called the FBI office in New York under the alias of "Pastorious" and he said he had a story that warranted the attention of J. Edgar Hoover. Better to go to Washington, he thought, and speak to the top FBI officials in person. He left on June 18.

By this time the FBI was on the case. After Cullen's encounter on the beach, a search party found the buried explosives and the uniforms the saboteurs had left behind. The FBI had no idea where the men were but they were ready for Dasch's call on June 19. They told him to wait where he was and they would pick him up. They interrogated him for the next five days.

The FBI made a deal with Dasch. He agreed to supply all the information the FBI needed to round up the other seven, and they promised him that he would not be punished by more than six months in prison. Whether this deal would be honored remained to be seen.

The FBI arrested Kerling and Thiel after their meeting with Cramer, and they found and seized the other five by June 27. J. Edgar Hoover held a press conference and took full credit without mentioning Dasch's betrayal of the mission. A few days later Roosevelt penned a note to Francis Biddle, then attorney general, indicating that he wanted to try the eight in a court-martial. The president immediately saw the parallel to a famous incident that occurred during the American Revolution. Major John André, a British spy, crossed over into American territory in civilian clothes, met with Benedict Arnold, and was then captured with incriminating documents stuffed into his boots. He was hanged three days after his arrest.

Inspired by this example, the president immediately signed an executive order mandating a trial by military tribunal rather than court-martial. The key point in the order is that it covered cases occurring in wartime of enemy nationals who enter or attempt to enter the United States for purpose of sabotage, espionage, or other hostile acts against the American war effort. The order also denied any possible right of appeal, habeas corpus, or legal relief against the military tribunal.

The problem was: What would the charges be? That Americans were terrified by the landings does not automatically define a crime under federal law. It would have been ridiculous to charge them with entering the United States without a visa. And yet they had not really caused or threatened any harm by the time they were arrested. They had not yet "attempted" to commit sabotage or any other serious offense against persons or property.

In his note to Biddle indicating his resolve, Roosevelt confessed that he had not read the relevant statutes. If he had he would have found a provision in the Articles of War, enacted by Congress in 1920, that came close to addressing the behavior of the eight Germans: "Any person who in time of war shall be found lurking or acting as a spy in or about any of the fortifications, posts, quarters, or encampments of any of the armies of the United States, or elsewhere, shall be tried by a general court martial or by a military commission, and shall, on conviction thereof, suffer death." This was called Article 82 at the time and it is still on the books.

It was a bit of a stretch to apply this provision to the case of the saboteurs at hand because the suspected spies were not found "lurking" near a military facility. They had not yet done anything to further their mission of sabotage. But the statutory definition of spying was close enough to create a strong impression of a trial and conviction under the rule of law. It also authorized the death penalty and summary trial by military commission, both of which Roosevelt and Biddle strongly favored.

An assistant solicitor general named Oscar Cox suggested that the better charge would be Article 81 of the same Articles of War, which prohibited the curiously named action of "relieving the enemy." This crime was committed by someone who gives "arms, ammunition, supplies, money, or other thing, or holds correspondence with or gives intelligence to the enemy, either directly or indirectly." It is not clear exactly how the saboteurs violated that provision any more than the spying statute.

Because no statute seemed precisely to fit here, there was a lot of talk about a violation against the laws of war. No one ever specified or defined the international offense that the saboteurs had supposedly committed. There was no evidence that crossing enemy lines with a hostile intention was a well-defined, recognized crime in the law of nations. There was certainly no relevant treaty. The most it could possibly have been was a crime recognized in the practice of the courts and in the writings of scholars. But there was no evidence of that either. And even had their actions been a crime defined by customary practice, the government should have recognized a major problem of principle in relying on an unwritten offense never defined by statute. Customary criminal law had been taboo in the federal courts for more than a century. Only Congress was entitled to define crimes punishable in the United States, and though it had the authority to do so, Congress had not specified the acts that constitute crimes against the law of war.

Of all the crimes charged against the saboteurs, the only one that ultimately made any sense was a conspiracy to violate either Article 82 (spying) or Article 81 ("relieving the enemy") of the federal code. This charge was eventually added as the fourth charge — after "violation of the laws of war" and of the two written articles of the code, numbers 81 and 82.

Neither the presidential order nor the statutory provisions mentioned a fact that would later become critical in the deliberations of the Supreme Court, namely that the eight saboteurs left the beach in civilian clothes, and during the entire period they were at large, they maintained the deception that they were just like other Americans or tourists. They gave no indication that they were agents of the German *Wehrmacht*. Yet this was a key fact in the guiding precedent of Major André. It would take some legal ingenuity to highlight this fact and to account for its relevance.

From the outset Francis Biddle was concerned about the constitutionality of trying the eight suspects in any court except a civilian court — the regular state or federal court. He confesses in his memoirs that he did not know much about the law of war, but he was well schooled in American constitutional law, and there was one decision by the Supreme Court that nagged at his conscience.

Immediately after the Civil War the Union military command

sought to try one Lambdin P. Milligan, a resident of Indiana, for his actions on behalf of the Confederacy — in particular, his efforts to liberate Confederate soldiers in captivity. The Union army invoked a military tribunal, which convicted Milligan and sentenced him to death (the usual sentence in these tribunals). His lawyers applied for a writ of habeas corpus and appealed the denial to the Supreme Court. The Supreme Court reversed the conviction and Justice David Davis expressed the sentiment of the Court in some of the most compelling language ever devoted to the sanctity of the Constitution in times of war:

> The Constitution of the United States is a law for rulers and people, equally in war and in peace, and covers with the shield of its protection all classes of men, at all times, and under all circumstances. No doctrine, involving more pernicious consequences, was ever invented by the wit of man than that any of its provisions can be suspended during any of the great exigencies of government. Such a doctrine leads directly to anarchy or despotism.

In the aftermath of September 11 many were heard to argue that civil liberties should be compromised for the sake of security, that the Constitution must be compromised in the face of terrorist dangers. If they are so tempted, they should consult the powerful words of Justice Davis in 1866. His staunch defense of a Constitution firm in the face of fear responded in part to Lincoln's having suspended the writ of habeas corpus during the war. Lincoln refused to obey Justice Taney's judicial order to comply with the historic writ and then sought to justify his conduct with his famous rhetorical question put to Congress on July 4, 1861: "Are all the laws but one to go unexecuted, and the government itself go to pieces lest that one be violated?"

In other words, the principle of necessity justified the suspension of the basic guarantee of freedom against a tyrannical government — the historic writ for testing the legality of confinement. Despite my respect for Lincoln's courage and commitment to the nation, I cannot bring myself to accept this abuse of democratic principles. Who is to be the judge of the risk that the government will go to pieces? When is the situation sufficiently dangerous to compromise the Constitution for the sake of national security? True, as Justice Arthur Goldberg once said, "The Constitution is not a suicide pact." But there is many a logical mile between guaranteeing trials as prescribed by the Bill of Rights and imminent self-destruction of the nation. This is the point that the Supreme Court sought to make by reversing Milligan's conviction.

The 1866 Supreme Court ruling articulated a standard that had poignant relevance for the temptations faced by Roosevelt and Biddle. When the regular civilian courts are "open and their process unobstructed," there is no justification for circumventing them and invoking a military tribunal. The courts were functioning in 1942 as they were in 1866. No wonder Biddle was anxious about the legality of his proposed military tribunal. But Biddle was caught in a many-sided vise. Roosevelt made it clear that if necessary he would follow Lincoln's precedent and disregard the Constitution in the interest of national security as he understood it. He famously admonished Biddle: "I want one thing clearly understood, Francis, I won't give them up . . . to any marshal armed with a writ of *habeas corpus.*"

Milligan and Roosevelt's intransigence were not Biddle's only worries. If the eight saboteurs were combatants in the German military, they had a right to be treated as prisoners of war, and as a result, they would have been exempt not only from the military tribunal but from all forms of criminal prosecution. The immunity of POWs was well recognized in international law. In his influential and path-breaking code "General Order No. 100," drafted for the Union army in 1863, Lieber declares that prisoners of war are "public enemies," but then goes on to hold in Article 56 that "a prisoner of war is subject to no punishment for being a public enemy." The Geneva Convention of 1929 anchored this protection in a prestigious treaty. Neither Biddle nor, when push came to shove, Roosevelt was about to disregard an explicit provision of a binding treaty.

Thus the prosecution faced opposing dangers. They were caught between the Scylla of the *Milligan* case and the Charybdis of the Geneva Convention. Yet for everyone involved in this case, two basic truths seemed apparent. First, the saboteurs were going to be convicted and executed. And second, the lawyers would have to find an argument for rationalizing Roosevelt's resolve to react quickly and effectively to Hitler's intrusion into the mainland of the United States. The military tribunal, consisting of seven high-ranking military officers, met in secret and heard evidence on the four charges against the eight defendants. The big problem was the charge of a violation against the laws of war. This was defined as "going and appearing behind the lines in civilian dress for the purpose of committing or attempting to commit sabotage, espionage, and other hostile acts." Whether this was in fact a crime recognized in international law was very dubious.

On August 3 the tribunal found all the defendants guilty — presumably on all charges — and sentenced them to death by execution. The Supreme Court had given its imprimatur to the verdict even before the trial was over. In hastily arranged hearings on the defense's application for a writ of habeas corpus, the Court had heard argument about the constitutionality of the proceedings. The fact that the Court heard the case was itself a symbolic victory for civil liberties. Roosevelt's executive order — like the Bush order establishing military tribunals in 2001 — tried to ban review in the appellate courts. The Supreme Court asserted its right to review the constitutionality of the trial, regardless of FDR's desire to keep the case within the military. The justices decided, without dissent, to validate the trial, but they did not supply an opinion, a legal argument for resolving the twin challenges of *Milligan* and the Geneva Conventions. That would come later.

Biddle intervened with the president and asked for clemency for the two defendants who had turned state's evidence and supplied information that generated the convictions. The president commuted Dasch's sentence to thirty years imprisonment, and the term of Burger, who also testified for the prosecution, to life imprisonment. The other six, including the other American citizen, Hans Herbert Haupt, were executed five days after the verdict.

The more difficult part was generating an argument for justifying this swift retribution. Chief Justice Harlan Fiske Stone undertook the task of writing an opinion — perhaps one should say an apologetic — several months after the executions occurred. Lawyers sometimes treat judicial opinion as a window on the judge's decision-making process. That was surely not possible in this case. The most one could expect from the opinion was some clever legal maneuvering that would rationalize a fait accompli.

Chief Justice Stone's After-the-Fact Apologetic

When you read Chief Justice Stone's opinion, you get the feeling that the question whether to convict and execute the eight defendants was still unresolved. In fact, six of the defendants were dead and the other two were in long-term confinement. The purpose of the opinion was to explain to us — later generations of citizens — how all of this could be compatible with both constitutional and international law. We discuss Stone's argument in the present tense for he is speaking to us today about how it might be possible to justify military tribunals, particularly in the aftermath of September 11.

The way to read Stone's opinion is to keep in mind all the shoals on which the search for a justification could founder. The first danger is *Milligan*, ever on the mind of both prosecution and defense lawyers during the trial. Biddle had devised a clever argument for limiting and circumventing the authority of this 1866 case. He thought that the general proposition about deferring to the civilian court was not necessary for the decision; it was, as lawyers say, mere dictum — a tangential discussion of the law. It would have been sufficient, he thought, to point to an 1863 statute that required the preliminary approval of the charges by a Grand Jury. Perhaps. But Stone is less troubled by *Milligan* than the lawyers were at the time of trial. He dismisses the precedent on the ground that Milligan had been a civilian and therefore it made sense to insist that his trial take place in a regular civilian court. He "was a non-belligerent, not subject to the law of war." In contrast, the eight German suspects were agents of an enemy nation.

This argument disposes of one danger, only to expose another. The government escapes Scylla and collides with Charybdis. If Milligan was a noncombatant, that could not be true of the eight German military agents. As soldiers on a secret mission behind enemy lines they were, it seemed, belligerents and entitled to be treated as prisoners of war. As prisoners of war they should have been exempt from prosecution for conduct that would otherwise be criminal. This was at least a principle of customary international law. Francis Lieber had recognized this principle in his model code of 1863, in which he defined prisoners of war as "public enemies" and then concluded that "a prisoner of war is subject to no punishment for being a public enemy." The same principle of exemption is implicit in the Hague Convention of 1907 and the Geneva Convention of 1929. If applied to the eight German spies, they should have been treated as exempt not only from military tribunals but from all prosecution for their actions, which after all was simply the kind of thing all armies do to seek a military advantage.

At this point in the logic of the case, the Court focused on the striking fact of wearing civilian clothes. This fact proved to be persuasive in the example of Major John André whose conviction and hanging were, by common consensus, free from doubt both under international and constitutional law. As a British agent wearing civilian clothes, he crossed into the American zone and met with Benedict Arnold. Why was the legality of summarily executing this spy in "civvies" so obvious? Yet it was the first thing on Roosevelt's mind when he sought to express his outrage about the eight saboteurs passing, undetected, into the heartland of the country.

There are two elements in the André case: spying and civilian clothes. Francis Lieber kept these factors together when he formulated the following rule in 1863:

> Art. 83. Scouts, or single soldiers, if disguised in the dress of the country or in the uniform of the army hostile to their own, employed in obtaining information, if found within or lurking about the lines of the captor, are treated as spies, and suffer death.

The Hague Convention of 1907 improved on Lieber's stab at the problem by laying down criteria that explained the difference between the combatant and the spy or saboteur in civilian clothes. In order to be treated as a combatant entitled to POW status, the fighter had to do two things that the saboteurs did not do: He or she must "have a fixed distinctive emblem recognizable at a distance" and "carry arms openly." When an enemy agent moves about in disguise carrying concealed weapons, of course, both of these factors are absent, but notice that POW classification under the Hague Convention does not require an examination of the soldier's motives. It does not matter whether he crosses enemy lines in civilian clothes in order to meet a lover or to commit sabotage.

Stone reshapes these sources: The critical boundary should run between lawful and "unlawful" combatants. In his words (emphasis added):

> The spy who secretly and without uniform passes the military lines of a belligerent in time of war, seeking to gather military information and communicate it to the enemy, or an enemy combatant who without uniform comes secretly through the lines for the purpose of waging war by destruction of life or property, are familiar examples of belligerents who are generally deemed *not to be entitled to the status of prisoners of war,* but to be offenders against the law of war subject to trial and punishment by military tribunals.

True, in this formulation, the factors of civilian clothes and hostile purpose remain interwoven. But at least now there is a label to describe the status of the fighter in disguise. He or she is an "unlawful combatant." In the sentences immediately preceding the passage quoted above, the distinction and its legal implications are made clear:

> By universal agreement and practice, the law of war draws a distinction between . . . lawful and unlawful combatants. Lawful combatants are subject to capture and detention as prisoners of war by opposing military forces. Unlawful combatants are likewise subject to capture and detention, but in addition they are subject to trial and punishment by military tribunals for acts which render their belligerency unlawful.

This may have been "universal agreement and practice," but the distinction was never explicitly laid down in an international treaty or code of war, and in fact, so far as I can tell, Chief Justice Stone is the first person ever to use the phrase "unlawful combatant." The only problem with Stone's approach is that he continues to interweave the hostile purpose with the wearing of a disguise. (Recall that the Hague Convention had defined lawful combatancy on the basis solely of being part of the army, wearing the external sign, and carrying arms openly. The fourth factor is observing "the law and customs of war," a factor that unfortunately introduces a behavior characteristic in the analysis.)

To understand the position of the Hague Convention, we must consider the reasons for the distinction between combatants and noncombatants. This distinction ultimately serves the interests of civilians by separating them, in principle, from the field of battle. Yet there is also at play a subtle principle of reciprocity between combatants. We can reconstruct this distinction and also explain the persuasive attraction of Major John André's case by revisiting our earlier discussion of collective self-defense.

When two soldiers from opposing armies encounter each other on the front lines, they each acquire a privilege and expose themselves to an additional risk. The privilege is to be able to kill the opponent at will, whether the opponent is attacking, at rest, or even sleeping. The risk, however, is reciprocal: Each side is in danger of being killed just because each is wearing a certain uniform. Those who refuse to wear a uniform or a "distinctive emblem recognizable at a distance" do not expose themselves to this reciprocal risk. They claim the right to be aggressors in wartime without paying the price, and this they may not do. To become a lawful combatant, therefore, one must be part of the collective called the army and accept the burden of wearing a uniform or emblem and carrying arms openly. The unlawfulness derives from the deliberate refusal to share in the risks of warfare.

An important point to remember, however, is that becoming an unlawful combatant in this sense is not in itself a crime. There is nothing punishable about walking around in civilian clothes, even behind enemy lines. The crime consists in spying or sabotage or some other offense contemplated behind enemy lines.

Think about the distinction this way. Pharmacists are entitled to possess and to give to others certain narcotic and other restricted substances. If other people engage in the same actions they are guilty of a felony. But suppose that someone plays the role of a pharmacist, when in fact her license had been suspended for nonpayment of dues or some other independent reason. She keeps narcotics in her office and occasionally gives them to "patients." Is she guilty of a felony? The answer is yes. If her license is invalid, she is not entitled to the privileges of a pharmacist. She is, as it were, an "unlawful pharmacist." Only lawful pharmacists may keep narcotics with immunity from criminal prosecution.

To turn the argument around, think of unlawful combatants as combatants who have lost their license. The eight German saboteurs lost theirs as soon as they buried their uniforms and passed into U.S. territory in civilian clothes. Their failure to identify themselves as combatants was not a crime but it did result in a disqualification — the loss of POW status.

Neither Harlan Fiske Stone nor other legal thinkers much appreciated this critical distinction between a crime and a disqualification. This accounts for some of the confusion in his language.

He wrote, for example, that "unlawful combatants . . . are subject to trial and punishment by military tribunals for acts which render their belligerency unlawful." Strictly speaking, however, this is not true. The failure to qualify under the Hague Convention implied that they were unlawful combatants, but they could have been prosecuted for this disqualification only for the offenses of espionage and attempted sabotage. The proof of this proposition is that they were charged under Articles 81 and 82 of the Articles of War. These provisions are about "relieving the enemy" and spying. Neither mentions a requirement of wearing civilian clothes or being an unlawful combatant. It is simply a regrettable confusion that Chief Justice Stone reasoned that they were guilty for a violation of the laws of war.

Today, owing to the jurisprudential strides achieved by H.L.A. Hart in the early 1960s, we are much more aware of the distinction between a rule defining a crime (spying) and a norm generating the possibility of achieving a legal status (becoming a lawful combatant). The basic difference is that the violation of the first kind of rule generates liability and punishment. The breach of the second kind simply means the actor does not secure the legal result she desires. For example she tries to become a licensed pharmacist and fails. She tries to write a valid will and fails. She tries to enjoy the privileges of being a combatant and fails. Recalling our early discussion of individual and collective responsibility, there might be a case for saying that a spy expresses the will of a collective body; he or she acts not for personal gain but for sake of the nation. In contrast, the disqualification comes closer to being a personal failing. If an individual soldier fails to qualify as a combatant, this is because of something he or she failed to do. Perhaps a superior ordered the burying of uniforms on the Long Island beach, but still the failing is personal. The actions of the men on the beach did not disqualify their commanders from being considered lawful combatants.

If this distinction between two kinds of legal norms had been understood and applied in Stone's opinion, we would have a much better picture of the legal significance of crossing enemy lines in civilian clothing. As it is, we are saddled with Chief Justice Stone's language, which treats the violation of the laws of war both as the definition of the crime and the reason for disqualifying the combatants from their status as combatants.

Sometimes there is method in confusion, as illustrated by Stone's opinion. He claims that the conviction can rest entirely on the violation of the law of war. Never mind that there is no crime of spying or sabotage under international law. There is no reference to either in the Geneva Conventions or the Rome Statute establishing the International Criminal Court. Yet the Stone opinion concludes that the first charge alone — the violation of the law of war — can justify the military tribunal.

In reaching this conclusion Stone keeps his eye on the ready for another dangerous shoal. Defense counsel had argued that if the conviction was grounded in the violations of the Articles of War (relieving the enemy, spying), these charges would have brought to bear certain technical aspects of the procedures designed for courts-martial. Stone had to defend the radically simplified trial and appeal that the eight defendants actually received. This leads him to the extreme and unsupported conclusion that the law of war itself was all that was required to legitimate the executions.

Despite this dubious maneuver, Stone still faces yet another constitutional problem. What is the logical leap from a violation of the law of war to the invocation of a military tribunal? He could rely on the language of the two provisions in the Articles of War (Articles 81 and 82), both of which end with, "[the defendant] shall be tried by a general court-martial or by a military commission and on conviction shall be punished by death."

This is the only explicit congressional authorization for a military tribunal or commission (the two terms are used interchangeably) to be found at the time in the federal statutes. But Stone chooses not to go this route, thus avoiding the argument that these provisions entail certain procedural projections. As a result, he runs aground on the provisions of the Constitution (Article III, the Fifth and Sixth Amendments), which guarantee certain procedural protections, including a jury trial, in all criminal cases. No one could plausibly deny that these were criminal cases. Why was there no jury trial?

The most convincing ground for limiting the scope of the Constitution is history — that is, if certain practices were recognized as acceptable prior to the enactment of the Constitution and the Bill of Rights, the new foundation for the legal system incorporates rather than repeals the historical practice. This reasoning is applied in interpreting the constitutional concepts of "speech" for purposes of free speech, and "religion" for purposes of freedom of religion. It also comes into play in constructing the meaning of the phrase "criminal prosecution" in the Fifth and Sixth Amendments.

Courts-martial are exempt from the ordinary requirements of jury trials because first the practice of self-regulation in the military existed prior to the Constitution and further because the Fifth Amendment itself recognizes an exception for cases "arising in the land or naval forces, or in the Militia, when in actual service in time of War or public danger." Technically this language is addressed to only one clause in the Fifth Amendment, but it testifies to the attitude of special treatment toward cases arising within the military itself.

The best instantiation of the historical argument is the exemption of petty offenses, punishable by less than six months in jail, from the scope of the Fifth and Sixth Amendments. These offenses traditionally did not require a jury trial and the Constitution did not change that historic practice. The same applies, Stone claims, to the practice of trying spies by military tribunals or commissions.

Thus we having an opinion that winds its way among conflicting dangers. The *Milligan* case, requiring a trial in courts "open and functioning," is sidestepped because Milligan was never in the military. The principle of immunity for combatants is circumvented because the eight saboteur suspects were in fact in the military but they acted unlawfully by not wearing uniforms. The procedural requirements prescribed in the federal statute are ignored because the prosecution supposedly proceeded solely under the customary law of war. And finally, the constitutional protections for criminal trials are sidestepped because the drafters of the Constitution supposedly did not intend to alter the practice of trying spies like Major John André in military tribunals. On the whole it was a masterful job of legal maneuvering.

The great problem with this decision lies in part in the strange phenomenon of writing a justification for a decision four months after six of the eight defendants had been executed. One hopes that it never happens again. Even as to the much criticized decision of the Court in *Bush v. Gore*, the justices at least had their opinions ready at the time that they announced their decision.

The impact of this decision in the saboteurs' case reaches far beyond the lives of the men whose lives were directly affected. The language of Harlan Fiske Stone continues to haunt the law and politics of the United States, and the most controversial and misunderstood term in Stone's elegant dance around the Constitution is his use of the phrase "unlawful combatant." How and why this term is misunderstood requires that we move forward in time to the aftermath of September 11.

President Bush Proposes Military Tribunals

For ordinary citizens the critical day was September 11. For lawyers and civil libertarians the missiles fell again on November 13, 2001, the day President Bush issued an executive order authorizing military tribunals to try any of the terrorists or the Al Qaeda members who might be captured in the ongoing war. Bush was supposedly taking his resolve to bring "justice" to the enemy seriously. The only question was: What kind of justice would it be? The justice of a civilized nation or the quickly dispensed judgments of a bloodthirsty avenger?

The tribunals Bush had in mind would be much like the make-shift military panels devised in the prosecution of the eight German saboteurs. They would be staffed by military officers subject to command influence, the proceedings would be in secret, and they could use any evidence they thought relevant. Of course, there would be no jury. The judges could decide by a two-thirds vote to impose the death penalty. There would be no appeal except as the order amusingly says, "by me [meaning Bush] or the Secretary of Defense" if he, Bush, so decides. "The use of the phrase "by me" recalls the words of France's Louis XIV: "*L'état c'est moi* [The state is me]." In this case, *La justice c'est lui* (Justice is him). Justice has become personal in the hands of George W. Bush. If he were to die, it is not clear whether the review authority would pass to the vice president. The answer is unclear because the power to make the final decision is vested not in the office but in the person (the "me") of George W.

The most disturbing aspect of Bush's plan is the definition of the people who would be subject to his special brand of justice. The executive order draws a clear line between citizens and non-citizens; only foreigners are subject to the less-favorable procedures. And among foreigners the class that qualifies for summary trial consists of either members of Al Qaeda, someone who engaged in or assisted international terrorism against the United States, or anyone who has harbored an Al Qaeda member or an international terrorist. In addition, the president must decide personally that is "in the interests of the United States" to deviate from constitutional practice and proceed with one of these tribunals.

Notice how far we have drifted from the case of the eight saboteurs. They were all members of an army with which we were at war. They violated the law of war by entering the country without uniforms. The class of people subject to FDR's justice was severely limited and defined by the conditions of a declared war. The people whose life and death lie in the hands of George W. Bush include a large portion of the world's population, certainly the Muslim population. They are all foreigners and if they did anything to aid or abet an act of terrorism or to harbor a terrorist they fall within the teeth of *justice à la Bush*. John Walker Lindh, the American who fought for the Taliban, should fall within the scope of the order, but as a U.S. citizen, he has been accorded a civilian trial in federal court. If this kind of arbitrary distinction between citizens and foreigners does not violate the equal protection of the law, nothing does.

The extrapolation from the "German" enemy to all foreigners supporting terrorism reveals a desperate need to think about the post–September 11 danger to the United States in the language of collective responsibility. Some larger entity must stand behind the individual attacks, but this entity could never take the place in our sentiments or in our thoughts of the nation as collective agent. An organization like Al Qaeda or any other loosely knit network of international terrorists is hardly a nation that lives in history. There is no way of knowing who is a member of this network without first making a judgment about who is guilty of an act of terrorism — and that is precisely the question at stake in the summary proceeding before the military tribunal.

The circularity of using "terrorism" twice — first as the criterion of jurisdiction and second as the definition of the crime — should make one wonder whether justice is possible in tribunals so defined. The way I personally make sense of this corruption of American law is to compare the reaction to terrorism with European ways of the thinking. European countries — England, Germany, Italy, Spain — have long used special tribunals and special procedures to fight the IRA, the Baader-Meinhof gang, the Mafia, and the ETA. They are used to gearing the trial to the "type" of defendant. Our greatest temptation in the United States — faced by a new kind of threat — is to return to the ways of thinking characteristic of the "Old World."

Carl Schmitt, the National Socialist philosopher, explained the phenomenon well. We have one criminal law for "friends," namely for citizens, and another for "foes," namely the foreigners, the "terrorists." Even though John Walker Lindh is a traitor, he is one of us and therefore he gets a trial in federal court. To be fair to the Bush administration, however, we have to note that as of this writing it has not invoked a military tribunal. It could have against Zacharias Moussaoui, the suspected twentieth hijacker, but it did not. Perhaps it never will, but there is every reason to think that military tribunals are in store for the "foes" captured in Afghanistan and detained at Guantánamo Bay.

To me personally, it is shocking that any serious thinker about American law would even consider arguing that the Bush order is compatible with the basic principles of the U.S. Constitution. Yet we find two of our leading and supposedly liberal professors of Constitutional law making precisely these kinds of arguments. Harvard Law School's Laurence Tribe actually wrote in *The New Republic*: "In wartime, 'due process of law,' both linguistically and historically, permits trying unlawful combatants for violation of the laws of war, without a jury." The University of Chicago Law School's Cass Sunstein testified to the Senate Judiciary Committee that he would "assume, without discussing the point, that the order does not violate the Constitution." Both seem to think that Congress has plenary authority to enact exactly the kind of tribunals that the president has ordered. Congress could distinguish between citizens and foreigners; it could, in circular fashion, build "terrorism" into the definition of who is subject to summary justice; it could impose the death penalty without a jury trial. If these are the views of leading scholars, the country should think twice about the future of the Constitution.

The most appalling error that Tribe and Sunstein make is that they ignore the clear language of the Constitution (Article III, section 2, and the Sixth Amendment), which guarantees a jury trial in every criminal prosecution. There is no plausible way of denying that a proceeding against terrorists for their "crimes" is a criminal prosecution. There are three recognized exceptions to the constitutional guarantees, and they all fall under the principle that practices that existed at the time of the Constitution's enactment are necessary abolished. The first exception is court-martial jurisdiction, which allows the military services to discipline their own members. The second is the field of so-called petty offenses, punishable by less than six months in prison. These trials are historically exempt from the requirement of a jury trial. The third exception was recognized in Justice Stone's opinion in the saboteur case. "Unlawful combatants" — modeled after the historical example of Major John André — are subject to trial before a military tribunal.

The use of the phrase "unlawful combatant" was the original sin of the Supreme Court in the 1942 saboteurs' case. The phrase has become disconnected from its origins and now it passes freely from generation to generation, always acquiring new and broader meaning. Originally the concept was limited to combatants who were disqualified because they carried their arms secretly or failed to wear an emblem, as required by the Hague Convention. Tribe, Sunstein, and scores of lawyers now read the phrase to refer to anyone who commits a war crime. It follows in their loose logic that any supporter of attacks against civilian targets is an "unlawful combatant" and subject to trial before a military tribunal. Thus a minor exception to the Constitution, carved out to meet the exigencies of a minor German incursion in 1942, threatens to swallow the Sixth Amendment. The Constitution is in danger, and it is receiving less defense than it should from leading scholars in the field. There will be little point in defeating international terrorism if we lose our constitutional principles in the process.

CHAPTER SIX

Guilty Relations

If this be treason, make the most of it.
— *Patrick Henry*

The German "invasion" in 1942 failed because the men chosen for the mission were all of divided loyalties. They had spent time in the United States. Most of them spoke English well enough to pass as citizens. Yet the *Reich* trusted them without any supervision to remain loyal to Hitler on American soil. Dasch caved in almost immediately and supplied the FBI with the inside information necessary to arrest the other seven. He betrayed the mission, partly out of self-interest, partly because he may have felt some residual loyalty to the United States.

This is a typical case of treason as betrayal — not as a crime but as a psychological and moral phenomenon. When people suffer conflicting loyalties, they must choose, and often the choices are unstable because the alternative loyalty remains in the wings, always ready to play the decisive role in motivating the actor's conduct.

Treason poses a puzzle for Romantics, for in these cases of divided loyalties the surging self cannot easily identify with the nation. There are two nations competing for allegiance, and the individual is caught between them. Instead of the Romantic unity of self and nation, we encounter individuals at odds with the countries that make claims on them.

117

The traitor appears to stand alone alienated from family, community, and nation. In this light he or she appears to be the paradigmatic individual, acting alone, rejecting the demands of community — and in many cases this might be true. If we recognize the role of dual loyalties in cases of treason, however, then the role of the collective comes back into focus. In this alternative light the traitor is not alone but merely torn between two collectives, each demanding its voice in his actions.

One would think that there would be great sympathy for those who betray one country for another, but it in fact it is considered a crime of first magnitude, typically mentioned first in the criminal code and punishable by death. Nations demanding loyalty are jealous masters and they brook no wavering on the part of their nationals.

As originally conceived in English law, treason consisted in breaching a personal duty of fealty to the king. The statute of 1351, usually referred to as 25 Edward III, explicitly declares a wide range of acts to constitute treason against the king. Some phrases in this statute would be familiar to Americans, for they are found today in the American Constitution. One form of treason is to "be adherent to the King's enemies in his realm, giving to them aid and comfort in the realm." Another is to "levy war against our lord the King in his realm." But the characteristic and problematic phrase in the statute is a prong of the offense not found in the Constitution, namely "compass[ing] or imagin[ing] the death of our lord the King, or our lady his Queen."

The "compassing" clause suggests that treason is a crime of hostile thoughts. Merely to have the intention of killing the king seems to be enough to have committed the gravest crime in the realm. This way of thinking about crime flies in the face of the basic assumptions of criminal law, namely that crime and punishment are about causing harm — tangible harm like death and loss of property — to other people. But the feudal relationship to the king was different. It consisted in an internal breach of loyalty, of breaking faith in the heart.

The policy of punishing the intention to kill resembles Jesus' pronouncement in Matt. 5:28: "But I say to you that whoever looks at a woman to lust for her has already committed adultery with her in his heart." This is an illuminating comparison. Indeed, if we are to find an analogy to treason in the field of sin and crime, the place to look is not to homicide or theft but to adultery. The standard crimes prosecuted in the courts are universal. They protect anyone, citizen or stranger, against victimization. But adultery and treason presuppose a specific relationship. A man can commit adultery only against his wife, and a wife, only against her husband. Treason conforms to the same pattern. Only those owing allegiance to the king can commit treason against him. If a Frenchman yearns for the death of the English queen, it is not treason.

It is not surprising, then, that in the context of this special relationship, there might have been a tendency to think of the crime as committed in the heart. But it is one thing to conceptualize a sin (adultery) as occurring in the heart, and quite another to define a secular crime punishable by death in the same way. If the suspect does not confess (the Constitution requires confession in "open court"), the manner of proving treason in the heart can be problematic and prejudicial. Every disloyal statement ever made becomes proof. Every speculative thought about whether the country was doing the right thing in wartime becomes relevant. In one famous case a priest named Crohagan said in Portugal: "If I come upon the King I will kill him." He was convicted of treason in 1634.

Because of the potential for abuse, there has always been some resistance to defining treason exclusively as a crime of sentiment. The 1351 Statute provided, in the quaint idiom of the time, that the inner disloyalty must be "probably attainted of open deed." That is, the prosecution had to prove that some "open deed" occurred in public and that it confirmed the treasonous intention. Exactly what this requirement means has taxed the ingenuity of judges and scholars to the present day. There were always some who thought that speaking hateful words toward the king would be sufficient to constitute this "open deed." Crohagan was rightly convicted, they said. Other scholars argued that the "open deed" had to be action actually furthering the actor's treasonable ambitions. Because Crohagan's hostile statement did not make it more likely that he would succeed in regicide, the critics argue, he should not have been guilty of treason.

The analogy between adultery and treason may be helpful but it should not be exaggerated. Betrayal in an intimate relationship carries the stigma of immoral conduct. It is the breach of trust and, in the case of marriage, of solemn vows. Treason is also immoral — but only relative to a particular sovereign. It may be wrong from the standpoint of the king, but from the perspective of rebels disavowing the king's authority, treasonous actions appear to be more a virtue than a vice.

In the case of the adultery, the betrayed spouse has no authority to condemn the adulterer to death (leaving aside illegal acts of vengeance). Yet the king, as the bearer of legitimate authority, may judge and punish traitors. In this respect treason is like war. It speaks to the issue of the king's survival. The crime of the traitor is not that he violates some shared norm of right and wrong but rather that he threatens the survival of the established legal order. In prosecuting treason, the king invokes a principle of self-defense against internal enemies. In warfare the principle of self-defense is directed toward an external enemy.

Treason under the Constitution

The drafters of the Declaration of Independence had good reason to fear for their lives and therefore to conclude their document: "We mutually pledge to each other our Lives, our Fortunes, and our sacred Honor." They were all subject to charges of treason for having rebelled against King George III. Their coming so close to prosecution for a capital offense left the framers with a keen appreciation for appropriate contours of treason in a democratic state. They put specific limitations in the Constitution on the power of Congress to define and punish the crime.

In the first sentence of the constitutional definition, the drafters picked up two crimes from the English statute: "levying war against the United States," and "adhering to their Enemies, giving them Aid and Comfort." Implicitly, only those "owing allegiance to the United States" can commit treason by engaging in either of these offenses. This requirement was later made explicit in the first article of the United States Criminal Code, which defines treason as a crime and prescribes the death penalty as punishment. The implication is that those who have no connection to the United States cannot commit treason.

The drafters deliberately omitted the "compassing" charge from the permissible scope of treason. This was obviously a net that swept too wide and included too many whose guilt consisted of no more than dissent against the established order. In addition, they tightened the procedural requirements for conviction by requiring either the unlikely phenomenon of the defendant's confession in open court or "the Testimony of two Witnesses to the same overt act." These are unusual clauses to find in the founding charter of a government. They testify to the great anxiety that the framers felt about their personal exposure to these charges and the misuses of the crime by the English who, as recited in the Declaration of Independence, "transport[ed] us beyond Seas to be tried for pretended offences."

Issues of treason and disloyalty were of foremost importance to the infant American republic. Whether the thirteen colonies would succeed as a single governmental entity was far from clear. There was reason to fear the French, the Spanish, and the English, and the internal loyalties to these and other powers generated uncertainties about the future of the United States as defined in the new Constitution. Under John Adams, the Federalists had enacted the Alien and Sedition laws of 1798, which punished contemptuous speech about governmental officials. The government was quick to fear provocative speech and talk about disunion and rebellion.

The most famous treason trial of the period was against Aaron Burr in 1807. Thomas Jefferson, president from 1801 to 1809, regarded Burr as disloyal both to him and to the country. The personal fear arose from their deadlock in the election of 1800, where Burr, running for the vice presidency, received the same number of votes in the electoral college as did Jefferson. (This was possible before the enactment of the Twelfth Amendment). After the thirty-sixth ballot in the House, Jefferson finally won but not without residual doubts about whether Burr had been campaigning to defeat the head of his own ticket. For his part Burr came as close to a Romantic figure as we have in early American history. Had he been a literary personality, we would think of him by analogy to Wordsworth or Byron or Fichte.

In 1775 he took up arms, together with his friend James Wilkinson, under George Washington's command. And after he entered politics he was reluctant, apparently, to put them down. During the 1804 gubernatorial race in New York, Alexander Hamilton supposedly made derogatory remarks about Burr, which led to their duel and Hamilton's death in Weehawken, New Jersey. In that year Burr cut a grand figure, for as vice president he also presided, with distinction, over the Senate impeachment trial of Justice Samuel Chase. Jefferson had invested much in the jury as the bearer of republican values. Judges like Chase were suspected of being antirepublican aristocratic thinkers who downplayed the importance of the jury. Chase had cut back the role of the jury in a treason trial and thus incurred Jefferson's enmity. Signficantly, the way Burr presided over the Chase impeachment trial provided a model of fairness and rectitude for the way John Marshall would preside over Burr's own treason trial a few years later. Jefferson wanted to see both convicted, but evenhanded judges secured a fair trial for both, and both walked away vindicated.

The behavior that led to Burr's treason trial is still shrouded in mystery. Burr left the East Coast, where because of the killing of

Hamilton in the duel, he was wanted for murder in New York and New Jersey. He started traveling in the western territories from Ohio to New Orleans. His contact in Ohio was Harman Blennerhassett, an Irish expatriate who lived like a feudal lord in his manor on an Ohio River island. In the South his potential ally was his former comrade-in-arms James Wilkinson, who had since been installed as governor of the newly acquired Louisiana territory. Stories or "tall tales" circulated about Burr's plans to raise an expeditionary force to conquer some lands in the Southwest, some belonging to Mexico, and others presumably belonging to the United States. The only thing that came close to an expeditionary force was a motley group of men, no more than a hundred, that gathered on Blennerhassett's island in December 1807 and then, equipped with arms and provisions, headed south. Burr was not with them but he was regarded as their leader. As far as what Burr had in mind, the historian Kent Newmyer puts it this way: He was motivated "by a large set of contingency plans, laced with a large dose of desperation-filled romanticism, all calculated to benefit Aaron Burr."

Not surprisingly, a few men turned on Burr, among them his friend Wilkinson who feared an attack on his own domain. Wilkinson wrote to Jefferson of the nefarious plans, supposedly confirmed by an encrypted letter Burr had sent to Wilkinson. In another incident Blennerhassett disclosed some hostile schemes to an undercover agent sent by Jefferson to investigate plots in the West. On the basis of this evidence and not much more, Jefferson was resolved to see Burr convicted of treason.

Chief Justice John Marshall presided over the jury trial during the summer of 1807 in Richmond, Virginia. The primary charge was treason by "levying war against the United States." The assumption underlying this charge — as in the other branch of treason — was that Burr was a citizen owing allegiance to the United States. (Otherwise every enemy soldier who fought against the United States would be guilty of treason.) In the course of the trial, Marshall made several decisions that have shaped the contours of treason in the United States, most significantly, that treason was a personal crime: It had to be committed by the suspect's own hand. You could not be guilty of treason by conspiring to levy war or by being an accessory to levying war. This makes sense, for if treason is based on personal betrayal, only those who actually commit betrayal can be guilty. This elementary principle is obscured by its technical description, which holds that there is no "constructive" treason. Apparently, the English courts — in one of their represssive uses of the crime — recognized "constructive treason" or treason by conspiracy or complicity. Marshall decided that the English doctrine would not apply in the United States.

If there had been treason by levying war against the United States, then the locus of the crime would have been the events that occurred in organizing and arming the expedition from Blennerhassett's island. Since Burr was not there, it was difficult to link him with the concrete acts of levying war. Burr's acquittal was to be expected as soon as Marshall ruled that the jury had to limit its focus to the events that occurred on the island. Marshall's conduct of the trial and his limiting the role of the jury infuriated the president.

While his restricting the scope of treason was in spirit with the framers' fear of repressive governmental actions, Marshall implicitly made a decision about the nature of war that could have had — and still could have — vast repercussions. Any attempt to overthrow the government of the United States "if carried into execution" constituted levying war against the United States. And further, "the assemblage of a body for the purpose of carrying it into execution" was sufficient. Even more loosely, Marshall quotes a prior case that held that "any force connected with the intention" would constitute the crime of levying war. These loose interpretations of the crime were gratuitous in the context because Marshall's other rulings effectively prevented Burr from being convicted. Implicit in the notion of war, as understood by Marshall and as argued earlier in this book, is the notion of collective action. A single individual acting alone could hardly qualify as levying war. The situation in the Burr case lent itself to the charges of treason because "the assemblage of men" looked like an army.

The implication of the Burr trial is that organized military campaigns — particularly on American soil — are sufficient to constitute the action of levying war. This broad definition of war may come back to shape the course of American jurisprudence. Like the hanging of Major John André — which influenced the perceptions of Roosevelt's military tribunal — the trial of Aaron Burr is one of those searing historical moments with the power to define the course of events centuries later.

Treason after the "Invasion" of 1942

Though there were scattered cases after the Burr trial, there was not much impetus to clarify exactly what treason meant in the United States until the courts had to cope with the fallout from the landing of the eight German saboteurs in the summer of 1942. The same characters whom we encountered in the saga of Roosevelt's military tribunal now return to test the meaning of "betrayal" by those who "owe allegiance to the United States." Three of the four who landed in Florida had friends and relatives of German birth who had become naturalized citizens. Kerling and Thiel went to visit their friend Anthony Cramer in New York. After they met for several hours at the Twin Oaks Inn on Lexington Avenue, Thiel left his money belt with Cramer, and the latter made contact with Thiel's fianceé, Norma Kopp, who was living nearby, and told her that Thiel had come from Germany in a U-boat and that he and the others were receiving instructions from a *Sitz* (hideout) in the Bronx. After the FBI picked up Kerling and Thiel, they arrested Cramer as well. Because he adopted U.S. citizenship in 1936 (an incriminating date for an alleged Nazi sympathizer), they charged him with treason.

While his German friends were tried in summary fashion before a military tribunal, Cramer — the alleged traitor to his adopted country — received a civilian trial with all the protections laid down in the Bill of Rights. The prosecution had to prove guilt beyond reasonable doubt to a jury of citizens. Great hurdles stood between the prosecution and a conviction. The government had to establish that Cramer "adhered to the enemy" and further that the favor he did for Thiel amounted to "aid and comfort to the enemy." The techniques the government used to prove "adherence" illustrated the dangers of making a crime too dependent on internal sentiments about which observers can only speculate. The prosecution introduced evidence that Cramer had studied the Constitution and made marks next to the treason clause, that he had closed the door in the face of someone selling government bonds, and that in 1936 he had gone to Germany to attend the Olympic games in Berlin and met there with Nazi-party officials. All of this evidence is ambiguous, and though Cramer might have sympathized with the Nazis there was no clear proof that he knew of and wished to promote his friends' mission of sabotage.

Establishing that Cramer had given "aid and comfort" to the enemy posed an additional hurdle to conviction. Meeting with saboteurs and taking a money belt into safekeeping hardly looks like much help, but the threshold of treason is admittedly very low. Indeed if the crime is committed in the intention, then all that should matter is the desire to further the enemy mission. In this vague state of the law, the jury convicted but the trial judge, confessing his doubts about whether Cramer knew Thiel and Kerling had explosives with them, declined to impose the death penalty.

In April 1945, with American boys still dying in battle against the Nazis, the Supreme Court reversed Cramer's conviction — one of those courageous actions by the Court that should make us skeptical about dire predictions that civil liberties inevitably suffer in wartime. The main issue for the Court was whether the degree of assistance met the legal threshold of "aid and comfort."

The decision established that whatever the intention and sentiment of the suspected traitor, the government must prove that the defendant actually contributed to the hostile projects of the enemy.

Three Justices dissented, and, ironically, two of them—Justices Hugo Black and William O. Douglas—would prove, two decades later, to be the greatest champions of civil liberties on the Warren court. At the time, however, they were eager to use governmental power to suppress and punish "enemies" of the United States.

Though the libertarian regard for the rights of the criminal suspect prevailed in the case, the government would soon have a chance to put these principles to a more demanding test in a case involving another one of the eight saboteurs of June 1942. At the same time that Kerling and Thiel were meeting with Cramer, Herbert Hans Haupt traveled home to the outskirts of Chicago. His parents, Hans Max and Erna Emma Haupt, received him and got him settled. They "sheltered" him and helped him buy a car and get a job at an optical company. The FBI had Herbert under surveillance and after they arrested him, they went after the parents and four other naturalized German Americans who had contact with the boy. The prosecution portrayed them as a cell eager to help the saboteur. In the end all six were convicted, with the three men sentenced to death and the three women receiving terms of twenty-five years imprisonment. (Chivalry was not dead even in prosecuting traitors!) In June 1943, however, the Court of Appeals reversed the conviction of all six on technical grounds—another fine moment for the rule of law in the heat of war.

Yet the government would not give up. Apparently the prosecutors thought it imperative to establish that some naturalized citizen who aided the saboteurs was guilty of treason. In the second prosecution, they focused all their energies on a single defendant, Hans Max Haupt, the father of the suspected saboteur. It secured another conviction (*Haupt II*), and the trial judge cautiously imposed a sentence of life imprisonment.

On appeal to the Supreme Court, Haupt's lawyers relied on the decision in *Cramer* as well as technical arguments about whether there were really two witnesses to every alleged overt act of trea-son. The FBI saw Herbert going in and out of the Haupts' apart-ment building but it had no witnesses to his parents' actually "sheltering" him. The way the case was framed, one unproven charge — that there were no witnesses of the parents' actually pro-viding their son with room and board — would have been suffi-cient to derail the entire conviction. This time the Court had little doubt about whether to confirm the jury's finding of guilt. Eight votes lined up for the view that this was actually "aid and com-fort." The sole dissenter, Justice Frank Murphy, reasoned that the act of sheltering could not be treasonous because it was compati-ble with parental motives of caring for a son. Murphy was known on the Court for his knowledge of military affairs, but his argu-ment garnered little support. The government scored an impor-tant victory.

Affirming the conviction in *Haupt II* was the last decision by the Supreme Court in the field of treason. There have been other convictions based on World War II incidents, but since that pe-riod, every temptation to prosecute for treason has run aground on a simple problem. Treason requires giving "aid and comfort" to the *enemy*. The matter has never been decided, but many ob-servers think that the term "enemy" refers only to the enemy in a declared war. The well-known American actress Jane Fonda went to Hanoi during the Vietnam War and expressed support for the Vietcong. To her critics this looked like "treason," but absent a declared war, a treason prosecution did not appear to be a prom-ising proposition. I am sure it mattered as well that no one was directly injured by Fonda's lancing words of comfort to the enemy.

The message of the Burr trial might be that the concept of war should be understood more broadly to include undeclared as well as officially declared wars. Admittedly, the concept of war in the context of levying war against the United States does not clarify the concept of the "enemy" because in this context the traitors themselves are the enemy. But the emphasis in Marshall's reasoning is on actual betrayal and the threat to the country. Neither of these considerations requires a formally declared war.

This provides some background for pondering whether John Walker Lindh, the American boy from Marin County, California, committed treason by fighting for the Taliban in armed conflict with American troops as well as with the Northern Alliance in Afghanistan. He was captured while lying in a hospital with other Taliban troops near Mazar-i-Sharif. There is little doubt that Lindh owed allegiance to the United States and that he adhered to the Taliban, giving them aid and comfort. If the Taliban constitute an "enemy" within the meaning of the treason statute, he was clearly guilty.

Many pundits argued that it would be too difficult to provide two witness to the overt act of Lindh's actually fighting for the Taliban. This is probably true, but there are ample witnesses to his recuperating with his fellow troops in the hospital. He learned their language and adopted their manner of dress and grooming. Imagine how much it meant to the embattled Taliban soldiers to know that an American was willing to share their fate. These acts of solidarity are probably enough, under the Haupt standard, to constitute "aid and comfort." But if not, the prosecution could ask the jury to infer participation in combat, precisely as the jury in Haupt inferred "sheltering" of acts of coming and going. Either way, Lindh was guilty.

In the end the Justice Department decided not to press a treason prosecution. Perhaps it thought the classification of the Taliban as the "enemy" was too dicey, a possible ground for reversal on appeal. Or perhaps it was influenced by false concerns about whether there was evidence of adhering and giving aid and comfort. For reasons of their own, they renounced the possibility of the death penalty for treason and charged Lindh primarily with participating in a conspiracy to commit homicide. The press releases described this crime as a conspiracy to kill Americans. But there is no crime of that name. While treason is related to the country of one's allegiance, homicide and conspiracy are universal offenses — not conditioned on the nationality of the victim.

The reason for mentioning the nationality of the victims is that you need some basis for justifying jurisdiction in the American courts. Foreigners engaged in a conspiracy to kill abroad — with no connection to the United States — cannot, under American law, be prosecuted in the United States. That the intended victims were Americans implies that American courts can hear the case. Yet there might be another reason, a psychological ploy, for stressing the Americanness of the victims. This emphasis elicits some of the stigma of treason — of Lindh's turning against his own people to the extent of conspiring to kill them.

If there were some conceptual problems about invoking a treason charge against Lindh, there are even greater problems in thinking about a conspiracy to commit homicide. The Bush administration has now conceded that the Geneva conventions apply to the Taliban detainees at Guantánamo Base on Cuba. But for inexplicable reasons, they have not drawn the inference that these detainees are entitled to be treated as POWs under international law. Of course, it would not make any sense to treat Lindh's cofighters in the Taliban as POWs but to deny this status to Lindh. If they are classified as they should be under international law, neither Lindh nor his co-conspirators can be tried for normal wartime activities. Killing the opponent on the battlefield is about as normal as you can get in fighting a war. Conspiring to kill is implicit in joining the armed forces.

The contradictions begin to pile up. Let's suppose the government ignores the immunity of POWs for battlefield violence. If Lindh is guilty of conspiring to kill, then so are the hundreds of detainees on Guantánamo. Yet while Lindh receives a trial in federal court, the latter face the risk of a conviction and execution by a military tribunal. Lindh's being an American, which is at the foundation of his treason, turns out to be an advantage. He gets a trial in federal court. Others who have committed the same crime face trials in kangaroo courts. Thus the "traitor" gets a fair trial;

the regular soldiers are kept in indefinite detention and face a dubious procedure for determining their guilt. When Lindh goes to trial, the clock should strike thirteen.

The failure intelligently to resolve the Lindh case bespeaks the general moral confusion attendant upon wars in the twenty-first century. We don't know whether we are fighting a war or pursuing justice, or whether the captives are POWs or common criminals. All of this ambivalence comes to the fore in assessing whether it was treason to be fighting with the Taliban. During the investigation of his conduct, high-ranking officials in Washington spoke of Lindh in kindly, avuncular language. President Bush initially described him as a "poor boy, who had been misled." While some — notably New York mayor Rudy Giuliani — wanted to see him executed, the general attitude was a mixture of puzzlement and sympathy for a young man in search of religious meaning. He converts to Islam, goes to the Middle East to study in an authentic manner, and drifts into bad company. To many, he is a victim of circumstance.

The decision not to charge Lindh may portend the general future of treason in the United States. In the age of terrorism there will be no clearer case of betrayal and siding with the enemy. This would have been the proper case in which to push the courts to expand the concept of "enemy" to include de facto enemies in undeclared but congressionally authorized wars. The Burr trial would have been a convincing precedent on the nature of war. But we, the public, do not seem to be so deeply shocked or offended by a religious young man joining the "enemy" that we insist on a prosecution for treason.

There may never be another treason trial in the United States, but we should not conclude from this that loyalty and patriotism are on the decline. It might, paradoxically, be a sign of our strength that we are less prone to use the language of betrayal and treason. This message becomes clear as we turn to the experience of other countries.

The Temptations of Weak Governments

If we glance around the world we notice an extraordinary range of possible treasons.

To paraphrase Tolstoy's opening line in *Anna Karenina*, everyone is patriotic in the same way — paying taxes, serving in the army, playing by the rules. But every traitor is disloyal in his or her own way. There are as many diverse ways of committing treason as there are flags in the United Nations.

The experience of two great powers, Russia and Germany — both with totalitarian backgrounds — illustrates the extremes. If treason has been on the decline for the last half century in the United States, the opposite is true in Russia and the other post-Communist countries. In the fall of 2001 the Russians finally concluded a four-year treason trial and convicted Grigory Pasko for having provided information to a Japanese television station engaged in reporting on the Russian army's dumping nuclear waste at sea. Now, having reviewed all these developments in the Anglo-American world from Edward III to *Haupt II*, one might pose an obvious question: What does talking to reporters have to do with treason?

The Russians have always used very graphic terms to talk about treason. The old Communist term was — "betrayal of the motherland." The new code of democratic Russia relies instead on the concept "betrayal of the government." The current reformers eliminated the death penalty for the offense and dropped some of the more obnoxious variations of treason, such as illegally leaving the country or refusing to return from abroad. Yet the basic structure of the offense is the same as in the days of Stalin and Khrushchev. The Russian analogue to "adhering to the enemy" is an action designed to undermine the international security of the state. Security, as the Russians understand it, seems endangered when foreign journalists write articles that bring the Russian state into disrepute. Whether Pasko did what the prosecutors charge is not as significant as the Russian desire to label this kind of behavior treason.

The Communists pursued Anatoly Shcharansky (Natan Sharansky) — later a minister in the Israeli cabinet — on a similar theory of treason. Shcharansky (Sharansky) had been the contact person in the 1970s for many foreign journalists. He allegedly gave sensitive information to a reporter from Los Angeles, and this was thought to be sufficient to constitute treason under the Soviet code. These charges resulted in a conviction and nine years in prison before he was released in a spy exchange. *Plus ça change, c'est plus la même chose.* The coming of democratic institutions has done little to ameliorate Russian perceptions of betrayal.

In Eastern Europe, in particular in Hungary and the Czech Republic, the concept of treason has played a distinctive role in coming to grips with collaboration by local politicians with the Soviet occupiers. More than thirty years after the event, the Czechs prosecuted two seventy-eight-year-old former Communists — Milos Jakes, last secretary general of the party, and former prime minister Jozef Lenart — for negotiating with the Soviet forces about the formation of a postinvasion government. They were willing to be appointed cabinet ministers under the Soviets. Their trial for treason in 2001 bogged down because at the time of their alleged treason, Lenart enjoyed immunity as a member of Parliament. The current Supreme Court had to decide how they should lift the defendant's immunity when the Parliament that granted it to him no longer existed. This is but one of the problems of using the whip of treason to beat a long-dead regime.

We have an intriguing situation, then, in which treason is on the decline in the Anglo-American world, particularly in the United States, but still of value in the new democracies of Eastern Europe. Why should this be so? We could hazard the general proposition that strong states do not need treason trials to defend themselves. Weaker states do. In the Alien and Sedition Law, enacted in the early stages of the American republic, the government enacted repressive measures to restrict the defamation of governmental officials, measures that the Supreme Court now regards as unconstitutional. The Burr trial reflected not only Jefferson's personal antipathy for Burr but the shared perception that the East Coast states could lose the West either to a foreign power or to an indigenous independence movement. Today the United States has enough confidence in its stability that it need not go to war against internal enemies.

The German Anomaly

Treason in Germany has gone its own way. If you look at the current criminal code, you will be struck by a peculiar feature of its legal definition of the offense. Nowhere does the statute refer to the requirement that the perpetrator of either "high treason" or "state treason" be of German nationality. Anyone who undertakes, by force or by threat of force, to undermine the current constitutional order is guilty. It does not matter whether the threat is articulated by an American in New York or a German in Berlin. The potential penalty is the maximum permitted under German law: life imprisonment.

After unification the Germans tried to apply this provision to the head of the East German secret police, Markus Wolf. During the Cold War he supposedly tried to undermine the stability of the Federal Republic. The West German police did not nab him until he set foot on West German soil, and he was eventually acquitted. The universal nature of the crime is implied in the very fact that a citizen of a different country might be guilty of treason against the Federal Republic.

The original version of the German Criminal Code, enacted in 1871, limits the crime of treason, as do other European codes, to German nationals. At that time Germans distinguished between two forms of treason. The first, called "high treason," focused on threats to the security of the head of state. This provision was reminiscent of a fourteenth-century English statute prohibiting compassing the death of the king. Neither the German nor the English statute explicitly limits the offense to nationals. The second form of treason was called *Landesverrat*, or "state treason." This variation of the offense was based on a *German* national's joining external forces threatening Germany and thus resembles treason as defined today in the U.S. Constitution and the Criminal Code.

Somewhere along the way the Germans changed their code and universalized the offense of treason. They kept the same terminology "high treason" and "treason against the country" but redefined these offenses in a way that eliminated the requirement that the "traitor" belong to the German nation. The "head of state" as the object of protection in "high treason" was replaced by the constitutional order. Seeking to overthrow the German constitutional system might properly be called sedition, but the word "treason" is not apt. The concept of "treason against the country" was redefined in a subtle play on the concept of betrayal. In German as in English, the action of betrayal applies to state secrets as well as to the nation and others to whom we owe loyalty. Today, the "betrayal" of the country refers to the disclosing of state secrets. The "betrayal" of secrets is properly regarded as a universal offense. In the United States we call this "espionage," and we too punish anyone, regardless of nationality, who transmits classified information to those not entitled to receive it.

Espionage is not properly called treason. The best illustration of this point is the prosecution of Ethel and Julius Rosenberg for acquiring and disclosing nuclear secrets to the Soviet Union in the decade after World War II. They were convicted of espionage and sentenced to death on the basis of the testimony of a single witness, David Greenglass. Appealing the case to the Second Circuit, their lawyers ingeniously argued that the essence of their offenses was not simply spying but treason. Because they were guilty of treason, if of anything, they could be convicted only on the basis of "two witnesses to the overt act." Thus they sought refuge in the constitutional rules on prosecuting treason. The appellate court insisted that espionage was essentially different from "giving aid and comfort to the enemy," and the judges were probably right.

Nonetheless, in the peculiar way Germans now speak of treason, the crime still called *Landesverrat* has merged with espionage. The betrayal of secrets has become synonymous with betrayal of the country.

None of this would be so interesting if the historical process of redefining treason were not so surprising. If we look at German legal history as a whole, we would be inclined to think that the change occurred after the end of World War II. The story would go something like this: In revulsion against the nationalist excesses of the Third Reich, the postwar Germans resolved to eliminate the factor of German nationality from the criminal law. Thus they redefined treason to make it like homicide and theft—applicable to everyone, regardless of the country of allegiance. One might even think this renunciation of nationality-based treason reflected a collective consciousness of guilt for the German orgy of nationalist fervor under Hitler. It is a good story but it is false.

The great surprise is that the transformation occurred in 1934, as one of the early reforms introduced by the National Socialists. They made the notion of treason applicable to the entire world. They began the process of transforming the betrayal of country into the betrayal of secrets. The best account I can give of this "reform" is that in a fit of megalomania, Hitler conceived of himself as the *Führer* entitled to respect not just by Germans but by everyone in the world. In effect, he universalized himself as an interest worthy of protection. He was entitled, therefore, to go to war and to use the most repressive measure to defend the existence of his regime. Good evidence for this thesis is found in new statutory language, added in 1934, that made it an offense for anyone to "rob" the *Führer* of his supposedly legitimate regime.

These changes in Nazi law are curious because the drift of German scholarly thinking at the time was to expand the concept of betrayal to encompass the entire criminal law. This was particularly true of the notorious group at the University in Kiel that advocated among other things that Jews should be treated as subhuman beings. One of the proponents of this school was Georg Dahm, who wrote an oft-cited article in 1935 entitled "Betrayal and Felony." The argument was that the essence of crime was not causing harm to others but betraying a personal and intimate relationship with German society and the Fatherland. Thus as the crime of treason was made to look like homicide and theft, Dahm tried to argue that homicide and theft were really like treason.

These conflicting currents might be explained simply as an intersection of a common effort to eliminate the distinctions that prevailed in liberal systems of criminal law. But also it should be noted that Dahm and other Nazi scholars sought status with the regime by developing doctrines that they thought would gain them influence and personal power. This is a common form of self-deception among law professors in general, not only under the Nationalist Socialists. In fact, those in power, then as now, tend to ignore arguments and theories coming from the universities.

After some reflection we can make sense of the National Socialist redefinition of treason. Harder to understand is the way this approach to the crime managed to survive in German-speaking countries after the war. It is found today not only in Germany but in Austria and Switzerland as well. Contemporary lawyers are oblivious to the roots of their current understanding of treason. Or more charitably, one might say that in fact it dovetails with the new mood in the European Union of deemphasizing national identity and rejecting duties to the *Fatherland* and other mystical doctrines tied to the *Volk*. Philosopher Jürgen Habermas has expressed the new mood by coining the phrase *Verfassungs– patriotimus* — patriotism not to the nation but to the constitution of a democratic society.

From the English king to the American republic to the Russian motherland to the German constitution, the object of required loyalty is constantly changing. Perhaps the German model will win out and we will be duty bound to remain steadfast and loyal not to a great leader or a *patria* but to a constitutional order. Yet the German case remains anomalous relative to the general thesis about strong government and weak government. Strong governments like the United States are likely to let treason slip into legal slumber. Germany might follow this pattern as well, even if its statutory formulation makes grandiose claims. Weak governments will continue to invoke charges of treason as a way of shoring up their stability.

Focusing on treason has enabled us to understand what happens when individuals turn against their nations and identify with the enemy. Sometimes they act out of conflicting loyalties; sometimes they simply seek to realize their religious faith and to find what appears to them to be an authentic way of life. The naturalized Americans who identified with the German saboteurs stand for the first category and John Walker Lindh for the second.

Treason is a troubled category of thought. The idea of treason as betrayal of the nation is on the wane in the United States, and the Germans have abandoned the idea altogether. If we reflect further on the influence of Romanticism in the moral thought of the West we will begin to understand why.

CHAPTER SEVEN

Romantic Perversions

Original sin lies like a cancer in the bowels
of an entire civilization.
— *Friedrich Nietzsche*

To understand how and why the Romantic influence over criminal law confounds our thinking about treason, we should take a step back and review the course of our argument. We began with the observation that despite the liberal and individualist influence on the facade of legal discourse, the idea of polycentric collective action runs through contemporary legal thought. I demonstrated this in the context of liability for international aggression, war crimes, crimes against humanity, and genocide. Further, we concluded that — so far as there is collective guilt for these crimes — it is appropriate to treat the nation as the bearer of that guilt. Romantic thinking, leading to the identification of the expansive self with the nation, provides the foundation for this second move. To take this step, we had to reject Jaspers's position recognizing the possibility of collective guilt but denying the nation as an agent capable of wrongdoing.

In sum, we have found plausible the following sequence of moves: Romantics bridge the self and the nation, the nation acts in history, achieving greatness and committing crimes, and for its glory as well as its crimes, the nation must receive a share of both the credit and the blame. Now we must pause to consider the moral premises built into this Romantic approach to legal issues. We cannot simply pick and choose from a cultural movement. Romanticism is burdened with some heavy moral baggage, and we must consider whether we want to accept these negatives along with the positive appeal of Romantic thinking.

To say that the nation is the bearer of collective guilt carries some implications that fly in the face of other premises we hold dear, such as the commitment in the Declaration of Independence that all men, all human beings, are born equal. The concept of the nation — derived etymologically from the Latin noun *natio* meaning "birth — includes all those born and yet to be born. When Lincoln cast his regard back "four score and seven years," he thought not of the American people but of the American nation as the concept embracing generations over time. If the nation is guilty, the conclusion seems to follow that guilt is transmitted to future generations. The passing of guilt from the one generation to the next leads to the conclusion that some children are born guilty and others, of other nations, are not. This is an extreme that I identify as "too much guilt."

Equally disturbing is an implication of Romantic thinking that leads to "too little guilt." Romantics cherish the authenticity of self — the human being fully realized when at home in his or her language and culture. This leads to a deep theoretical problem in criminal responsibility. If terrorists are authentically committed to the premises of their own culture, how can we blame them for committing crimes of violence against those they perceive as their enemies? If we cannot in good conscience blame them for their harmful deeds, we have to think twice about whether we can justifiably punish them. We have the problem either of explaining why they are in fact guilty or why we are prepared to punish in the absence of guilt.

These two issues illustrate some of the excesses of Romanticism. We shall find that as we probe more deeply into the implications of Romantic thinking, we may lose faith in the entire project of building on the Romantic tradition in order to justify any conception of collective guilt. The liberal alternative might, by contrast, begin to look more attractive.

Let us take seriously the possibility that an entire nation is, at a certain moment of time, responsible and guilty for crimes committed in its name. The recurrent example is German guilt for the Holocaust. This is not because we Americans lack other convincing examples of the phenomenon. Many Americans overflow with feelings of guilt — for slavery, for the wartime internment of Japanese Americans, for having subjugated women for so long, for having harbored homophobic sentiments. In some respects we are the showcase example of collective guilt, but the German case has drawn more sustained literary attention and therefore remains at the forefront of the debate about whether collective guilt is morally and conceptually plausible.

The allegation of German guilt recurs in various writings. In his 1996 book *Hitler's Willing Executioners*, Daniel Goldhagen famously charged Germans living in the decades prior to Hitler's rise to power, as well as the Germans living under Hitler, with having nurtured an "eliminationist anti-Semitism," which led directly to genocidal acts. They created the political culture that made the Final Solution thinkable and doable. In an even more recent study of anti-Semitism in the Catholic Church, James Carroll writes: "Hitler's genocidal assault on the Jews became the work of an entire people."

The interesting question is whether these generalizations can be limited in time. Can one speak of German guilt for the years up to 1945, but of no guilt afterward — as though the Russian occupation of Berlin suddenly changed everything? In other words, can one generalize synchronically but not diachronically? Can one sweep up a range of people who lived in a certain decade in a certain geographical area but reject any spatial or temporal extensions?

Suppose we have reliable documentation about the behavior of hundreds of thousands of ordinary Germans in the face of anti-Semitic attacks like those of *Kristallnacht* — the burning down of most of Germany's synagogues coupled with the SS's physical assaults against Jews. What can we infer from this data about the responsibility or guilt of millions of people about whom we have no information at all? Are they complicitous in the German eliminationist culture? If so, why limit the generalization to Germans? Are not Poles, Ukrainians, Slovaks, and Hungarians also implicated? The impulse that leads us to generalize at the level of the nation is the Romantic preoccupation with nations as the bearers of culture. For thoughtful writers like Goldhagen and Carroll, the natural point of reference is the German people organized in a particular political regime, sharing a single history, speaking a single language. On the unspoken assumption that those who perpetrated *Kristallnacht* should be described as Germans, and not more broadly as Europeans or more narrowly as young men of a certain political affiliation who happened to live in Germany, the "German" becomes profiled as an abstract wrongdoer. Here we are reminded of Karl Jaspers's warning that ascribing guilt to the nation replicates the frame of mind that led to anti-Semitism. Behind this particular form of hatred in the Christian West lies the conception of the "Jew" as the eternal deviant; the Jewish nation over time bears the guilt of a few who are said to have killed a man called the Messiah. More will be said later about the roots of anti-Semitism in this perceived "betrayal" on the part of the Jews, but for now we are concerned with a single idea: Is it invariably true that collective guilt leads to the transmission of guilt to the unborn?

The idea that guilt passes from generation to generation expresses, I think, the consequence of attributing guilt to the nation rather than to particular individuals. The nation includes the young and the unborn. Is a child born in the Nazi period exempt? And if the child is born immediately after the collapse of the Third Reich, does it make sense to exempt the child from the culture that has rendered itself guilty? The children, after all, would feel pride about the achievements of their forbears. It follows, it seems, that their identity with the nation should extend to the downside as well as the upside of communal life. The ingredients of mass belief do not suddenly change just because the regime changes. If the nation bears guilt for "eliminationist anti-Semitism," and the nation has a life greater than its constituent members, then the guilt would seem to pass to the next generation — not necessarily to individuals but to the nation as a whole. Thus, by the process of taking the next logical step, we have arrived at the conclusion that if the nation is guilty, the guilt is transmitted from generation to generation.

It is harder than we might think to avoid this particular perversion of collective guilt. The idea dwells deep in the instincts of Western civilization. A primary example is the Christian doctrine of original sin. According to the Book of Genesis, Adam and Eve violated God's command by eating fruit from the tree of knowledge of good and evil. Their disobedience brings to bear God's threat of mortality: If they eat of fruit from the tree of knowledge of good and evil, they will surely die (Gen. 2:17). The Apostle Paul made the grand leap from this tale to the moral stigma affecting all humankind: "[B]y one man sin entered into the world, and death by sin" (Rom. 5:12). Early Christian theologian Augustine coined the label that has remained with us: "The deliberate sin of the First man is the cause of original sin." This doctrine of "the Fall," the idea that human beings are born already affected by sin, has become a theological premise for all Catholics and many Protestants. Baptism became necessary to cleanse the newborn of original sin and to restore the possibility of everlasting life. Thus the doctrine of original sin is tied to the promise of salvation, with the resurrection of Jesus as its demonstration.

There are few ideas more disturbing than the claim that children are born tainted by sin. Not surprisingly, the Enlightenment attitude toward the value of human beings led many to reject the Pauline and Augustinian teaching. According to contemporary Christian theologian Douglas Farrow in the *Oxford Companion to Christian Theology*, many theologians now treat the doctrine of the Fall as a "perversion." The idea that children are born tainted is incompatible with the Jeffersonian creed that all men are created equal — at least if the claim of equality is based on the infinite value of all human beings made in the image of God. A distinctively American version of Christianity — the Church of Jesus Christ of Latter Day Saints — explicitly rejects the doctrine of an everlasting taint originating in the Garden of Eden. According to the second article of founder Joseph Smith's creed: "We believe that men will be punished for their own sins, and not for Adam's transgression." Though Muslims and Jews share with Catholics the same story of creation, they reject the standard Catholic reading of the Fall in Eden.

Though the idea of transmitting guilt by birth is not a common Jewish doctrine, it is recognized in the Hebrew Bible. Under Moses and Joshua, the Jews fought a battle with a tribe called Amalek; according to the version related in Deuteronomy, Amalek attacked from the rear when the Jews were "famished and weary" (Deut. 25:18). In engaging in this maneuver Amalek was "undeterred by fear of God" (ibid.). The description of the Jews' battle with Amalek is very obscure, but it seems to suggest that Amalek was guilty of some war crime, perhaps the first recorded war crime in Western civilization. The Jews are commanded never to forget this crime and to make war against Amalek "throughout the ages" (Exod. 17:16). It is not clear whether this means that the guilt of the tribe passes from generation to generation, but that would at least provide an account of the peculiar Jewish obligation to continue the war against Amalek.

Admittedly there is some ambiguity regarding the obligations imposed on the Jews, for they are simultaneously obligated "to remember what Amalek did to you" (Deut. 25:17) and to "blot out the memory from under Heaven" (ibid., 25:19). This contradiction actually should seem familiar to us for, as we shall see, it is carried forward in Christian attitudes toward the alleged Jewish betrayal of Jesus. The culitivation of memory in the Gospels is coupled with the eliminationist mentality that developed during the Holocaust.

As strong as the religious roots for transmission by birth may be, there is also a counter tradition expressed in the Prophets. Ezekiel preaches, "What do you mean by this repeated proverb concerning the land of Israel, saying, 'The fathers have eaten rotten grapes, and the children's teeth are set on edge.' As I live, says the Lord God, you shall not have occasion to use the proverb in Israel" (Ezek. 18:2). Ezekiel continues in this vein to stress that the father and the son shall each be judged according to his own deeds: "The soul that sins shall die. The son shall not bear the inequity of the father; neither shall the father bear the inequity of the son" (ibid., 18:20). The idea that guilt is transmitted at birth is explicitly rejected. Yet the very fact that it is denounced shows how recurrent and tempting the doctrine is. One finds it not only in the declaration of perpetual war against Amalek but in other doctrines of Jewish law, such as transmission of the taint of bastardy (*mamzerut*) for ten generations. But nothing in Jewish thought comes close to the condemnation of all of humanity in the doctrine of original sin.

The line running from Paul's doctrine of original sin to modern Christian anti-Semitism is easily traced. Both have their origin in the Christian reading of the Fall in Eden. As Elaine Pagels points out in *The Origin of Satan*, anti-Semitism in the Gospels is strongly connected to the Christian invention of the devil as the force of evil. The culminating passage comes in the book of John in which Jesus denounces the Jews as "sons of the devil" (John 8:44). The origins of the devil lie in the Christian reading of the story of Eden, the same reading that generates the myth of the Fall. The devil makes his appearance in the form of the serpent who seduces Eve to eat of the fruit.

Interestingly, the Christian tradition reduced the complex Jewish community, both as it existed at the time of Jesus and as it has evolved through the ages, to a single figure personified in the phrase "son of the devil." As the devil is a timeless figure extending over generations, so too the Jew became a transgenerational enemy of Christianity. The Church's nourishing of anti-Semitism provided a crucible for the stain of collective guilt passing from generation to generation. No wonder that Karl Jaspers warned so strongly against thinking of Germans in the way Christians historically conceptualized the Jews.

The Gospels are rich in arguments linking the collective guilt of the Jews to the ideas of betrayal and treason. But here there is an intriguing reversal. Usually it is the individual who betrays his people. In the story of Jesus as related by Matthew it is first Judas Iscariot and then the Jews who betray Jesus. First Judas betrays Jesus by identifying him and delivering him to the Jewish priests with a kiss. Then the Roman governor allows the Jewish multitude to choose whether to crucify a thief named Barabbas or Jesus, whom Pilate describes as a "just person." The crowd says, "Let him be crucified." Pilate washes his hands and claims that if the Jews confirm the release of Barabbas and the crucifixion of Jesus, he will bear no guilt. Then, in one of the most extraordinary accusations in history, Matthew attributes the following line to the Jews as a collective entity: "His blood be on us and on our children" (Matt. 27:25). It is as though the Jews, by their voluntary choice, brought upon themselves eternal hostility and persecution. Matthew rounds out his accusations by attributing to the Jews a recurrent lie explaining away the resurrection: "His disciples came at night and stole Him away while we slept." The Jews are alleged to have repeated this lie "until this day" (ibid., 28:13). No text could have been better designed to communicate the prejudice that a taint may enter into the soul of people and be passed from parents to children.

Of course, the position of the Church under Popes John XXIII and John Paul II recognizes the legitimacy of the distinctive Jewish relationship to God. But calumny against the Jews dies hard. In May 2001 President Bashar Assad of Syria alleged, in the presence of the pope, that the Jews were guilty not only for killing Jesus but for conspiring to kill the Prophet Mohammad. The willingness of the world to listen to lies of this sort was confirmed at the Durban Convention on Racism in early September 2001, in which anti-Zionist forces from the Muslim world heaped vile epithets on Israel and even directed anti-Semitic remarks to Jewish delegates at the conference. After September 11 the opposite allegations were heard. Everyone in the Muslim world became profiled as a potential terrorist, as we noted in chapter 5, subject to a special brand of justice in the United States. My aim here is not to criticize the Church or any other institutions (or to attribute to them collective guilt) but to search for an understanding of why collective guilt has the propensity to go awry in Western culture.

Karl Jaspers was right in suggesting that adopting the idea that German guilt passes from generation to generation replicates the intellectual indecency of anti-Semitism. From the story of Amalek to the doctrine of original sin, to the birth of anti-Semitism, to the problem of German guilt, we see one baleful and pernicious line of argument. This is surely one of the most regrettable chapters in the history of Western thought. Ezekiel could rail against it, but he could not defeat it.

Let us retrace the steps that have led us, with seeming inevitability, to the doctrine of transmission of guilt by birth. We started with the idea of collective guilt as a way of making sense of the thesis that collective entities must participate in the crimes punished under international law and inferred that this form of guilt attaches to the nation as such. If guilt inheres in the nation itself, and if the nation lives on from generation to generation, so do its achievements, its responsibility, and its guilt. Precisely this idea has generated relentless critique from Ezekiel to Nietzsche to Joseph Smith to Karl Jaspers.

Taking the nation seriously leads, it seems, to the problem of "too much guilt." If Romantic thinking leads invariably to this robust conception of the nation, then we should think twice about succumbing to Romantic sentiment. But that is only half the problem. Romanticism also generates a way of thinking about criminal behavior that results in "too little guilt." This is the problem that must now concern us.

Authenticity without Guilt

The starting point for thinking about this second perversion is the glorification of the inner self at the core of the Romantic movement. The one truth for the Romantic is the coherence of the self. The poet's authenticity ignites the lamp that radiates from the imagination. Existence, reality, and, ultimately, morality come from within. Fichte took Kant's theory of self and converted it into the primary source of reality. For existentialist theologians like Hamann and Schleiermacher, the search for God begins in the fires that burn in the hearth of each personal self.

This preoccupation with internal feelings has moral implications. The important guideline for conduct should not be society's criteria of right and wrong but the internal beat that leads us to express our deepest selves. Isaiah Berlin summarizes the impact of this way of thinking in the German Romantic movement: "By the 1820s you find an outlook in which the state of mind, the motive, is more important than the consequence." The core of morality becomes, in Berlin's words, "[p]urity of heart, integrity, devotion, dedication." As Henry David Thoreau wrote a generation later in *Walden*: "If a man does not keep pace with his companions, perhaps it is because he hears a different drummer. Let him step to the music which he hears."

While the English Romantic poets were celebrating sincerity and imagination in the early nineteenth century, English criminal law also began to look inward. Until this period, the law had always required concrete harm to a person or to property as a condition of criminal liability. The law of treason was the striking exception that made "compassing" or intending the death of the king a crime in itself. Beginning in the early nineteenth century the entire criminal law begins to look like more treason — at least in the respect of stressing intention over the results of action. For the first time it becomes a crime called "attempt" to shoot — and miss — with the intent to kill. There were even some scholars who within a relatively short period began to argue that an attempt to kill was just as bad as actually killing and should be punished accordingly.

Similarly, there was a transformation of larceny from a crime based on the shared image of "thieving" into a crime centered on the *intent* to steal. Embezzlement becomes a crime for the first time even though it is essentially a crime of intention — there is no way to perceive the moment that the clerk decides to keep the money already in his possession. The same transformation is evident in homicide. Though criminal law had long recognized defensive claims based on mistake or accident, we find a progressive reorientation of homicide from a crime based on the centrality of causing death to a crime centered on the intention to kill, with death as a contingent aftermath. We see a critical transformation from a criminal law based on results and the causing of harm to a criminal law anchored in the *mens rea* or "guilty mind" of the offender.

One sees the afterglow of this movement in the contemporary debate about moral luck. One scholar after another has lined up behind the counterintuitive view that consequences are morally irrelevant: All that matters in assessing the blameworthiness of offenders is that over which they have control. Their intentions and bodily movements are within their control, but not the contingent consequences of their actions. According to this view, the aggressors of September 11 are guilty for intending to crash their hijacked airplanes into the World Trade Center and for aiming the planes in that direction, but they are not additionally guilty for the collapse of the towers and the resulting deaths. As bin Laden claimed on a candid videotape released in December 2001, he (and they) did not expect the total destruction of the towers.

It is worth noting how a persistent misreading of Kant's moral philosophy tends to support this metamorphosis of the criminal law. In the *Groundwork of the Metaphysics of Morals*, Kant argues that only a good will could be called moral. The good will is one free of all sensual influence, one that expresses only pure reason and the moral law. Kant's claim about the good will is deep and central to his entire theory of moral autonomy under the law. Yet the theory of the good will has become distorted by subtly shifting the focus from will to intention. The argument becomes that intention is the core of morality, thus dovetailing with Berlin's account of the Romantic emphasis on "purity of heart, integrity, devotion, dedication." This misreading of Kant — the confusion of will with intention — might have been just a confused footnote in the emergence of sincerity as a basis for denying criminal wrongdoing. Yet this particular misreading influenced the entire Romantic movement in the decades after his writing. Kant's emphasis on the self and on autonomy lent itself to interpretation in the minds of thinkers such as Fichte as a basis for glorifying self-expression and the role of the expansive self in history.

We continue to witness this misreading in the way contemporary philosophers glorify "autonomy" as the capacity, supposedly, to do your own thing, when in fact, for Kant, autonomy requires submission to the moral law. Berlin regards Kant as a transitional figure in the Romantic movement not because of what he actually wrote but because of the way his ideas about the will and the importance of freedom lent themselves to misreading by the ensuing generations of Romantics.

The fixation on intentions as the core of criminality leads to the view that only bad intentions are subject to moral censure. Those who sincerely think they are doing the right thing cannot be blamed. They are merely expressing who they are. If we sentence them to prison or even impose the death penalty, as in the cases of Eichmann and McVeigh, it cannot be because they are guilty and deserve punishment; rather, the state has an interest in imposing the sanction. Perhaps the interest of the state lies in making the victims feel vindicated by seeing the offender suffer. Or perhaps the offender is simply a threat to public safety and must be neutralized. We should have more doubts than we do about whether ideological offenders are really guilty and whether the sanctions they suffer are really punishment rather than measures imposed for the sake of social protection.

I refer to this idea as the principle of guiltless sincerity. It is a perversion of Romantic thinking that yields too little guilt. But the doctrine that good intentions are free from blame is, unfortunately, well entrenched in the case law of the courts and in the way scholars and students think about criminal law.

Numerous specific mistakes are attributable to this general belief in the innocence of sincerity. In California, for example, those who kill in the good faith belief that they must kill in self-defense are guilty at most of manslaughter. The reasoning is that murder requires malice and that someone who acts in good-faith self-defense cannot harbor ill will or malice. This doctrine played a key role in the Menendez case in 1995 when two teenage boys who had killed their wealthy parents each convinced some members of their respective juries that they thought their parents were about to kill them, even though at the time of their death the parents were eating strawberries and watching television. Both juries "hung": They could not reach a unanimous verdict that the defendants were guilty or not guilty. At the retrial, the judge instructed the new jury on a narrower definition of self-defense that made their paranoid fantasies of attack (even if they were honestly reported) irrelevant. Shortly thereafter, the lawyer for Ted Kaczynski, the Unabomber, floated an analogous argument based on his client's good faith but eccentric belief that his killings were necessary to combat the evils of technology in society. The argument was correctly rejected but the impulse to excuse on the grounds of sincerity made itself felt.

The most dramatic misapplication of the idea that those who act in good faith cannot be guilty came in 1975 when the House of Lords articulated some doctrines for rape cases that sounded good only because they tapped into the principle of guiltless sincerity. The case itself was one of those bizarre incidents that law students never forget. Four members of the Royal Air Force went drinking together, and after a few too many, one named Morgan told the others that his wife was at home just waiting for intercourse and that she loved to be taken by force. The others believed Morgan, went home with him, and proceeded to force intercourse on his wife despite her screams and fierce resistance. The House of Lords reasoned that this was not really rape. Rape requires an intention to rape, namely to have forced intercourse without consent. If their testimony was credible, they believed in good faith that the victim consented and therefore they could not have had the intention to have intercourse without consent. Nonetheless, the House of Lords confirmed the jury's verdict of guilt: The judges reasoned that the jury could well have believed that the insensitive defendants were lying about their sincere beliefs.

The surprising aftermath is that several leading English scholars wrote that they thought the explanation of the law of rape was right and indeed a great triumph for the principle of *mens rea* — namely that there should be no conviction without a guilty mind. The decision has been applied abroad, most notably in Israel and in Canada. The principle of the Morgan case — that a sincere belief in consent will excuse a rape — is still considered sound in the United Kingdom, even though Parliament has made efforts to overthrow the doctrine by legislation.

Women around the world (whether feminists or not) were in a state of shock. That the House of Lords could so casually have dismissed the interests of female victims was beyond belief. The Lords seemed to be indifferent to the plight of rape victims. Perhaps. But it is also possible that they were simply seduced by the principle of guiltless sincerity.

As I had written as early as 1978, the fundamental mistake of the decision was failing to grasp a more sensible standard for rape, namely that someone who forces himself on another should be guilty of rape if the victim has not consented and if the offender negligently believes that she has. Someone who acts negligently still tenders sincere beliefs that he is doing the right thing. The negligence consists precisely in failing to attend to all the signals that should alert a reasonable person to the conclusion that the conduct is wrong and illegal. For example, in the Morgan case, there were ample cues that would have led normal, reasonable people to think twice about whether their sexual partner had actually consented. The fact that Mrs. Morgan was screaming and resisting should have prompted the offenders to be more skeptical about the statements of a soused husband in a pub. They were obviously negligent about whether the victim had consented to intercourse, and that should have been enough to support their conviction.

We have encountered this idea before in discussing the problem of unlawful orders in the military. The soldier who follows orders also acts in good faith. He or she thinks that because the order has been given this must be the right thing to do. In the case of unlawful orders, say, to kill civilians, the Nuremberg rule was that the soldier had to know that the order was unlawful and decide nonetheless to go ahead and commit the atrocity. This standard conforms to the principle of guiltless sincerity. Without knowledge that the order is unlawful, the soldier has a clean mind and a clean conscience. How can we blame him for committing inhuman deeds?

The Rome Statute prescribing the law of the International Criminal Court has reformed the standard to include the equivalent of negligent misperceptions. If the order given by a military commander is "manifestly unlawful," then the subordinate has no excuse for following it. "Manifestly unlawful" means that the order would appear unlawful to a reasonable person. If the soldier does not realize that such an order is unlawful, it is his own fault.

This is a useful standard. As applied in the Morgan case, it is fair to say that Mrs. Morgan "manifestly" did not consent to intercourse. If the perpetrators did not realize that she did not consent, it was their own fault, their own negligence.

The only problem with this standard of negligence is that many misguided legal thinkers believe that negligence cannot be a proper basis for guilt because the inadvertently negligent actor does not choose to do wrong. The principle of guiltless sincerity rears its perverted mien. To be guilty, supposedly, one must be aware that one is deviating from right conduct. If one simply is deceived, misguided, and oblivious to the moral cues of one's situation, one cannot be guilty.

The most difficult cases are those of ideological offenders acting within the confines of total cultures — the terrorists of September 11, the Palestinian suicide bombers who deceive themselves into thinking that they are martyrs for their country and their faith, the followers of David Koresh holed up in their compound in Waco, Texas, even Timothy McVeigh who lived and acted in a culture that supported his extreme version of the Constitution. They might engage in conduct that is manifestly unlawful but within the confines of their particular culture it is difficult if not impossible for them to see it.

Ideological offenders are becoming a common feature of the landscape of criminal law. From Adolf Hitler, to Yigal Amir, to Ted Kaczynski, to Timothy McVeigh, to Osama bin Laden, we are cursed by a growing army of offenders who are authentic in their hatreds and in their commitment to violence. There is probably no more serious challenge to the theory of criminal law than to figure out what we are doing when we purport to punish these people.

Refuting the doctrine of "guiltless sincerity" is not so easy. Legal systems do in fact sanction ideological offenders, but if we pause to reflect on the meaning of guilt and punishment in these cases, we run into difficulty. What is the sense of blaming and punishing if the defendants see themselves as martyrs? What are we doing to them when they have no sense whatsoever of personal guilt?

To avoid this distortion of Romantic sincerity, we must make some rather strong moral claims. First, we have to assert that there is an objective moral crime called harming and killing innocent people. For anyone who takes moral reality seriously, this is not too daunting a thought. Moral reality implies that propositions about right and wrong have a truth value—that is, they actually say something about the world. But, second, we have to make an argument about the blameworthiness and guilt of those who commit this wrong in good faith, in the sincere belief that under certain circumstances it is right to kill innocent people. They are guilty for failing to grasp and to act in conformity with moral truth. This might be right, but I cannot escape the feeling that this attribution of guilt for ignorance of universal truths carries the ring of moral dogmatism.

One problem with formulating and applying a universal proposition about killing innocent people is that virtually all the ideological offenders I have mentioned believed in one way or another that their victims belonged to a class of people who were aggressing against them. Their ideology was never simply to kill innocents but rather to eliminate what they perceived, correctly or incorrectly, to be some kind of threat. Hitler and his followers thought that Jews were strangling the nation. Amir, the assassin of Yitzhak Rabin, believed that Rabin was a *rodef*, an aggressor, threatening the life of Israel. Kaczynski thought that technology was ruining civilization. The aggressors of September 11 allegedly felt invaded by the existence of Israel and the presence of American troops in Saudi Arabia. The litany of paranoid perceptions goes on and on. But, irrational fears or not, these offenders would not have described their actions as the killing of totally innocent people. Their factual errors add to the difficulty of blaming them for ignorance of universal moral truth. Perhaps they knew the moral truth but just disagreed about its application in practice.

The distortion of guiltless sincerity is an ever-recurring threat to clear thinking about guilt in the criminal law. Like the distortion of transmission by birth, this implication of Romantic thinking calls into question not only the project of attributing collective guilt but the project of understanding the very concept of guilt. We are, as it were, at a crisis of faith in our original thesis. Our attempt to understand international criminal law has led to the thesis that nations engage in collective actions and participate in aggression, war crimes, crimes against humanity, and genocide. To account for this firm belief in nations as collective agents, we turned to the Romantic tradition in search of an answer. But now we see that the entire enterprise suffers from serious risks of distorted thinking. We are prone to accepting too much guilt in the theory of transmission by birth and too little in the doctrine of guiltless sincerity.

To begin the contrary case in favor of collective guilt we have to pause and reflect on the possible advantages and disadvantages of supporting a conception of guilt that takes collective entities, and particularly the nation, seriously.

Distributing Guilt

I meant by my remark about Kant that
the principle of my will must always be
such that it can become the principle of
general laws.
— *Adoph Eichmann, during his trial
in Jerusalem*

Enlightened liberal thinkers have good reason to be disturbed by the implications of Romanticism for punishing guilty actions. The two moral perversions of Romantic thinking—transmission by birth and guiltless sincerity—should be enough to make one dubious about Romantic thinking in the law. If that were not enough, the critic of Romanticism can point to the potentially chauvinistic tendencies of Herder, Fichte, Wordsworth, and Byron. Even if communal self-love does not erupt in xenophobic and bellicose policies, taking the nation seriously as a collective entity has its own problems. It generates a receptivity to collective guilt that in turn leads to the practice of collective punishment. These ideas shock the liberal conscience because wholesale punishment implies the arbitrary punishment of some people not for what they have done but simply because they are members of the same group. The paradigm for these fears is German military retaliation against entire villages simply because one resident of the village attacked a German soldier.

Yet there is another way of thinking about collective guilt, one that is compatible and indeed enhances the principle of individual responsibility. This alternative is suggested by the principle of distributing responsibility and guilt among all parties — and only those parties — that actively participate in the occurrence of evil. This practice is familiar to us from the way the law of accidents distributes liability on the basis of relative fault. This body of law, called torts, used to be an all-or-nothing affair. Either the defendant was liable for all the damage he caused or for none of it. Now the defendant can be liable for a portion of the damage, depending on the degree of his responsibility. If two cars collide and cause damage to each other and their respective passengers, the two drivers (or their insurance companies) will pay for the damage in proportion to the negligence of each. If one is thought be 60 percent at fault, he will pay for 60 percent of the damage caused. If another is thought be 40 percent liable, she will pay 40 percent of the total. It is hard to deny that this more nuanced approach is fairer and more accurately reflects the actual responsibility of those involved in the incident.

A similar idea underlies the defense of provocation in the common law of homicide, at least as this concept was historically understood. A killing could be reduced from murder to manslaughter if the victim "provoked" the incident; the victim was thought to have contributed to his or her own demise. If the victim was practically accountable for the homicidal incident, then it only seemed fair to punish the defendant less. The less harm you cause, the less you must pay — either in the private law of accident or the criminal law of homicide.

My plea is that we begin to think, in general, about criminal guilt in line with this principle of distribution according to relative fault. If a nation bears guilt for the homicidal tendencies of its people, then individual perpetrators should arguably be less guilty and their punishment should be mitigated. As the provoked killer is guilty only of manslaughter, the killers who act in the name of the nation should — if the analogy holds — be liable for a mitigated offense.

This is an appealing, humanistic way to think about collective guilt, and it would have the virtue of broadening the inquiry in a criminal trial to include some of the tasks now filled by the truth commissions that have sprung up in transitional societies from South Africa to El Salvador. If this humanistic way of thinking about guilt could carry the day, we might see some grounds for vindicating a Romantic attitude toward nations as actors in history.

The criminal trial focuses our attention on the person in the dock. And in recent years these have been prominent figures of government — Goering, Eichmann, Pinochet, Milosevic, the military junta in Argentina. These are the "dictators" to whom all blame is directed. But no dictator rules in a vacuum. To muster power he must enjoy the support of the military, the implicit emotional consent of business leaders and professionals, and the tolerance of the public as a whole. In the face of a dissenting public incessantly banging on pots (as in the 2002 protests in Buenos Aires) or marching in the streets (as in Dresden in the dying days of Soviet Communism), no dictator can maintain power. The failure to protest generates a basis for holding the public at least partially responsibile for the ongoing dictatorship. This is one way to understand Karl Jaspers's penetrating comment: We are politically guilty for the way we are governed.

The great temptation of criminal trials is to convict and move on. We blame the primary figures and ignore the guilt of collectives for generating the crime, thereby deceiving ourselves that we have solved the problem. The glaring example of this self-deception is the trial and conviction of Ramzi Yousef and others for the 1993 bombing of the World Trade Center. It was obvious that this crime was the outgrowth of an entire culture of hatred cultivated in the mosques and the streets of the Islamic world. At some level we must have known that the defendants were representative of a much greater conspiracy of hate. We underestimated the cultural depth of responsibility for the paroxysm of violence and eventually paid the price of our self-deception.

The twin seductions of blaming and forgetting are almost irresistible. We are politically hardwired to look for ways to believe that justice has been done and to forget the collective guilt behind the crime. We enjoy the illusion that the problem goes away simply because some individuals are punished. This process of forgetting is what some people call "closure."

For the sake of broader inquiry in criminal trials, we should welcome the relevance of collective guilt. Communist courts once claimed that in every criminal trial they investigated the social causes of the crime as well as the guilt of the individual perpetrator. Whether they actually did this or not, at least their ideology tried to orient the criminal process toward broader questions that touched the entire society. This is my aspiration as well, but I am troubled by the philosophical problems posed by the project. It is not entirely clear how the guilt of the nation — even if we assume that it exists — becomes relevant in judging the degree of responsibility and punishment that should properly fall on the actual perpetrator.

The Model of Complicity

It was not easy for legal cultures to accept the idea that some people can be complicitous in actions executed by others. If one person provides assistance, advice, or the means of execution to another and the latter carries out the deed, the actual perpetrator is the one traditionally thought to be stained by the deed. The person who executes the deed has blood on his or her hands. Traditional Jewish law went so far as to hold that only the actual perpetrator could be guilty. *Ain schlichut b-avirah* is the Talmudic saying: No one can be the agent of another in committing crime. The same principle is found in the moral philosophy of Immanuel Kant, who claimed that lying to a would-be murderer was impermissible. If I were hiding Jews from the Nazis, and the Gestapo knocked at my door, I supposedly could not lie to them, even if my purpose was to protect the people in hiding. This bizarre moral teaching could make sense only if it is assumed that by telling the truth and thereby assisting murder by the Gestapo,

I did not render myself an accomplice in the killing. If I were responsible either for lying on the one hand, or complicity in murder on the other, the correct moral choice would obviously be to lie and avoid the murder. In the end, then, Kant subscribes to the principle found in Jewish law that no one can be accomplice in someone else's crime.

In the course of history, however, all legal systems have come to recognize the principle of becoming implicated in crimes carried out by other people. The person who provides the advice, the assistance, the means, or the weapons becomes "an accomplice" in the crime, also called an "aider-and-abettor" or an "accessory." A good example is the *Morgan* case discussed in the previous chapter. Morgan deceived his friends in the bar into believing that his wife desired to be subjected to forcible intercourse. They went ahead and committed the deed. If they were guilty, Morgan would also be guilty by extension. His guilt would derive from the guilt of those who actually laid hands on Mrs. Morgan. (If they were found not guilty, there would be a difficult problem in determining whether the accomplice Morgan could be nonetheless held liable.)

A famous case in Germany, decided before the new criminal code was enacted in 1975, illustrates the principle of complicity as it functions in practice. The KGB ordered an agent named Stashchinsky to commit assassinations in Germany. At his trial for murder, Stashchinsky claimed that he was merely the servant of the KGB, that it was the dominant party in the relationship. Therefore, even though the KGB was not before the court, it should be regarded as the principal perpetrator, and he, Stashchinsky, should be treated as an accessory, receiving a lesser punishment. It was an ingenious argument drawing on precedents in German law. In one of these prior cases, a nurse killed a suffering infant on orders from the mother. The Supreme Court of Germany agreed that Stashchinsky was but the servant of the KGB and therefore bore reduced liability for the assassinations.

This is quite a remarkable idea: The person who pulls the trigger can be treated as an aider-and-abetter, an accessory to the crime. In 1975 the German legislature rejected this in favor of the principle that as between the accomplice and the perpetrator, the actual perpetrator is always fully responsible for the deed. American and English courts avoid this dispute by holding to the common law doctrine that all participants in the crime are punished at the same level. But this view oversimplifies the problem by suppressing important distinctions. Our moral intuitions certainly suggest that the accessory is less guilty than the actual perpetrator. A good example is the reduced guilt of Ariel Sharon for the massacres in the Palestinian camps of Sabra and Shatila during the 1982 war in Lebanon. Israel's defense minister of the time, Sharon opened the gates and allowed the Lebanese Phalangist soldiers to carry out the killings on their own enthusiastic initiative. The Israeli committee of inquiry was right in concluding that Sharon bore indirect responsibility for the atrocity, but in their view his guilt was less egregious than that of the soldiers who actually shed blood.

Whatever the official teaching of the common law, it would be hard to believe that the courts do not show leniency in sentencing accomplices who merely wait outside in the car while the perpetrator commits the robbery. The principle of leniency in these cases resembles the idea in comparative negligence cases of imposing liability according to the degree of the actor's contribution to the harm that occurs. Unlike the approach in accident law, however, there is no fixed sum of guilt that must be divided among the parties. In these cases, the distribution of negligence between plaintiff and defendant starts from the premise that their relative shares must add up to 100 percent. The distribution is a zero-sum game: If one side is allocated more fault, the other side get less. In cases of complicity, however, the total punishment will be greater than 100 percent of what one person acting alone would receive. Distribution in complicity, therefore, is not a zero-sum inquiry. The perpetrator can be treated as 100 percent guilty and the accomplice as 80 percent guilty.

The basis for distribution in cases of complicity is not the malicious attitude of the participants, for all of them typically have the same desire and intention of promoting the final result — be it the death of victim, the destruction of property, or sexual aggression. The difference in degrees of guilt is based on the relative dominance of the parties in the interaction leading to the collective commission of the crime. The Stashchinsky decision was based on the idea that the KGB directors were the dominant or hegemonic force in the carrying out of the crime. The mitigation of Sharon's guilt was based on the perception that the Phalangists were active and autonomous actors who bore a full share of guilt, thereby implicitly reducing Sharon's guilt.

An inquiry into relative dominance requires subtle judgments about power and influence. Needless to say, these questions elude objective determination; the court conducting the inquiry could well be influenced by its own political agenda. The danger of political manipulation tempts us to give up the inquiry and to treat all perpetrators as guilty in the same way, precisely as the common law holds. Yet this temptation obscures important moral intuitions about relative degrees of participation. We are caught, then, between the dangers of politics on the one hand and moral oversimplification on the other.

The argument that collective guilt should mitigate the guilt of individual offenders became acute in the 1961 prosecution of Adolf Eichmann in Jerusalem. It is appealing to think that the guilt of the German nation as a whole should have partially excused Eichmann and perhaps saved him from the death penalty. He was guilty to be sure, but guilty like so many others of a collective crime. The Stashchinsky principle could provide a way of recognizing that in cases of genocide and other collective offenses, there are in fact two perpetrators — the individual and the nation.

If we assume that the German nation is guilty for the Holocaust, the question is whether this guilt stands in the same relationship to Eichmann's guilt as does the responsibility of the KGB commanders to Stashchinsky. One would like to think so, but unfortunately the analogy founders on a critical difference. The German nation acted through Eichmann as well as through other agents of the "Final Solution." But the relationship was not causal. While the KGB commanders were complicitous, indeed the dominant party in Stashchinsky's killings, the German nation is not complicitous in Eichmann's crimes in quite the same way.

This point requires some explanation. A relationship of complicity requires interaction between two completely independent parties. We have to be able to think of the organization called the KGB, as represented by its commanders, as distinct and separate from Stashchinsky as an individual. If this is the case, then the KGB can become the dominant party in the relationship, and Stashchinsky can become the dependent accessory. The relationship between the German nation and Eichmann does not fall into the categories of domination and subordination. The relationship is more like that between an orchestra and its first violinist. The orchestra expresses itself through the first violinist as well as through other individual musicians, but the collective orchestral entity does not cause the drummer or the violinist to play. It would not be correct to say that the orchestra dominates its members or is complicitous in their playing. The model for understanding the orchestra and its musicians, therefore, is not causal. Rather, it is expressive.

There are, admittedly, some disanologies between an orchestra and a nation that acts through its members. An orchestra plays according to a musical score and responds to the direction of a conductor. But the orchestra's execution of the score is still a collective phenomenon. The musicians constitute the orchestra but the latter entity has a collective existence of its own and it would be incorrect to say that this collective entity causes or dominates the playing of its members.

Because the orchestra has an independent collective existence, we can speak of the pride of the orchestra for a good performance and its responsibility for a bad one — "bad" as evidenced perhaps by weak coordination, lack of spirit, and imbalance in timbre and tone. The same kind of participatory sharing of positive responsibility occurs in all artistic performance, even as between the artists and the audience. It is not an accident that successful, well-recognized players will turn to the audience and express their appreciation by applauding for the audience. Good taste may inhibit the blaming of audiences that show little emotional support for the performance, but the sharing of responsibility for both good and bad performances is hard to deny.

Everyone who teaches large participatory classes — or even small seminars — knows that success in teaching depends, in part, on the collective mood generated by the students as well as the professor. Classes as a whole can be positively responsible for a high level of tolerant, challenging discourse and they can be negatively responsible for a mood of grade-grubbing and intellectual hostility. For reasons I explore later, I resist using the word "guilt" to talk about the negative responsibility of an orchestra or a class. I have less difficulty in speaking about the guilt of nations.

The critical point, for present purposes, is that the relationship between the nation and the individual is best understood by analogy to that between the orchestra and the violinist. In both cases the collective expresses itself though the actions of the individual. The challenging question is how, under this model of expression, the responsibility (or guilt) of the collective can mitigate the responsibility of its constituent members. To make sense of this mitigating effect, we would have to assume that the responsibility inheres in the collective as such — not in the collective as the sum total of its individual members. To express this point precisely we need to recall Rousseau's distinction, discussed earlier, between the "associative" and the "aggregative" conception of society. The difference, it will be recalled, is that associative guilt attaches to the nation as abstracted from its individual members. The aggregative guilt of the nation, by contrast, is nothing more than the sum of its parts — the total guilt of all the individuals in the society.

In order for the nation to bear a portion of the guilt and thus to relieve Eichmann of part of his, we must think of this guilt not as an aggregative but as an associative attribute of the nation. The guilt must adhere to the nation as such and not to the individual members. If the nation's guilt were simply an aggregation of the guilt of its citizens, then for the purposes of sentencing a particular offender like Eichmann, the guilt of the nation would either be tautological or irrelevant. It would be tautological to claim that Eichmann should be punished less because his own guilt, projected onto the nation, provided a basis for mitigating his crime. It would be irrelevant to invoke the guilt of other SS agents who also engaged in the systematic killing of Jews, for though their guilt might be part of an aggregated German guilt, their role would have nothing to do with blaming and punishing Eichmann. In order to make the claim, then, that German guilt should mitigate Eichmann's guilt, we have to think of the nation and its guilt in a fully robust Romantic sense. We must regard the nation as an independent agent capable of its own wrongdoing and its own irreducible guilt.

The troubling question is how and why the associative guilt of the nation could function to reduce the individual guilt of criminal actors. For these purposes we must put the analogy of the orchestra behind us. The analogy helped us understand the sense in which a collective can act and express itself through its constituent members, but it is strained to speak of the guilt of the orchestra in the same way we are inclined to think about the guilt of the nation for crimes committed in its name.

We should turn our attention now to the contexts in which we are inclined to take collective guilt seriously — namely, when evil becomes routine, and popular sentiment supports acts of discrimination and violence. Hannah Arendt coined the phrase "banality of evil" to describe the degenerate climate of the Third Reich, but the sad truth is that these climates of moral degeneracy are all around us — in every school in Palestine that teaches hatred of the Jews; in every *madrasa* in Pakistan that teaches contempt for infidels; in every yeshiva that preaches the permissibility of assassinating political leaders; in every society that stigmatizes difference, legitimates hatred, or inculcates a disposition toward acceptable violence.

We can recognize the collective guilt for these pernicious attitudes and yet question whether this guilt has any bearing on the culpability and punishment of individual offenders. Hannah Arendt failed to address this question. Though others have noted the problem, the theoretical assessment of mitigation remains underdeveloped. The burden is on us to explore the banality of evil — and collective guilt for its survival — as a mitigating factor in sentencing offenders like Eichmann.

The problem is that evil opinions of the masses do not *cause* individuals like Eichmann to believe what they believe or do what they do. The relationship might be one of influence but not of causation. The widespread antipathy for Muslims in Serbia did not cause Milosevic to undertake a program of ethnic cleansing. Nor did the widespread belief in the second-class humanity of blacks induce Americans to promote and defend the practice of slavery. Therefore, the theory of mitigation in this context cannot be based on a model of causation and cannot be as straightforward as the doctrine of complicity. Indeed, one should be skeptical about whether mass attitudes and collective guilt are relevant at all.

But I wish to argue that they are. In order to make the case for an alternative view of mitigation on the basis of collective guilt, we have to turn our attention to the general problems of free will and criminal culpability.

The Possibility of Self-Correction

To give a proper account of collective guilt as a mitigating factor, I must engage the reader in a detour about the general nature of culpability and freedom of the will. The entire structure of criminal liability is based on the idea that people are free to abstain from committing crimes and that they therefore are guilty for submitting to their desires when they should not.

From this elementary model lawyers infer a number of grounds for excusing people who lack voluntary control over their actions. The examples are duress (acting with a gun to one's head), personal necessity (cannibalizing a human being when there is no other way to stay alive), and insanity (being governed by "irresistible impulses" generated by mental illness). All of these excuses are based on variations of a causal model of responsibility. If some external factor causes me to act, I cannot be held accountable for commiting a crime against an innocent person. The common metaphor in legal discussions is that the "will is overborne" by the overwhelming pressure of the situation.

From this elementary causal model, jurists and scholars have thought for centuries that if all of our behavior were caused by natural forces, then we could not be guilty of anything. This view about general causation is called determinism. If nature determines our conduct, it is said, there is no room left for personal responsibility and guilt. Guilt presupposes, therefore, freedom of the will, and freedom in this sense stands in logical opposition to the idea that the external forces determine our conduct. Among the religiously faithful there has always been a tendency to think of humans acting freely as God supposedly acts freely—without a prior cause. Thus it is commonly said that original sin entered the world because Adam and Eve freely chose to disobey God. Auschwitz was possible because human beings chose—of their uncaused free will—to do evil.

Among philosophers this idea of free will has been disputed for centuries. Kant denied that there could be any uncaused action in the physical world, but he tried to save the doctrine of free will by imagining two distinct realms of causation. He posited that in the world of sensual impulse, physical factors determine the actions of both animals and humans; in the realm of freedom beyond the five senses, actions are caused not by sensual impulses but by the dictates of reason. For actions freely chosen, these two worlds coincide in some mysterious way.

Among contemporary philosophers very few defend the idea, still accepted by theologians, of a will uncaused by antecedent causes. They argue, plausibly, that if a will of this sort did exist, it would float without an anchor in the physical world and therefore it would bob around in a random manner — hardly a proper basis for moral responsibility. Instead of seeing a contradiction between freedom and determinism, the modern tendency is to see the two as compatible. When philosopher Roderick Chisholm sought to defend the traditional view by analogy to the way God acts, his philosophical opponent Harry Frankfurt labeled the argument as "quaint."

Frankfurt himself develops a conception of free will that provides a useful model for gauging how conventional attitudes might be applied to the assessment of individual guilt. The key move in Frankfurt's system is elaborating the distinction between first-order and second-order desires. First-order desires are the typical temptations that beset all of us who contemplate criminal acts — stealing a book, killing an enemy, or cheating on our income tax. Second-order desires or volitions are our decisions about whether to identify with or reject the first-order desires. Frankfurt's conception of a person derives from this structure. A "person" is an agent who has second-order volitions and chooses either to go with or to go against his first-order desires. A human being without second-order volitions is a "wanton": someone who gives in to every first-order desire.

Suppose that someone has a first-order desire to discriminate against people who look different and are treated as outsiders in the society. He has a "will" to exclude "the other" and perhaps even to inflict violence on the group so defined, thus taking the first step toward genocide. At the second level of volition, a person can decide whether to submit to this desire or to resist it. "A person exercises freedom of the will," Frankfurt writes, "in securing conformity of his will to his second-order volitions." Admittedly, there is some ambiguity as to whether the person who acts freely must be able to succeed in every effort to control his first-order desires. Frankfurt admits: "When a person acts, the desire by which he is moved is either the will he wants or a will he wants to be without." In other words, it is possible that at the second level of volition, a morally sensitive person might sincerely want not to discriminate against "others" in his professional relationships, but finds, upon reflection, that he only reads and talks to colleagues who closely resemble him in race, gender, and religion. When he realizes this, he might appropriately feel guilt for not being able to conform his will to his second-order volition not to discriminate. This is "the will he wants to be without."

Frankfurt probably means, however, that in a case of an unsuccessful second-order volition, the will is not free at all, but it strikes me as a useful emendation of the theory to treat this case as unsuccessfully executed free will. The advantage of this extension of the theory is that it provides an account of feeling guilty as well as of free will. As Frankfurt notes, "A person who does not have freedom feels its lack" when he becomes aware of the "discrepancy between his will and his second-order volitions." Kant has a similar line about when individuals become aware of the possibility of freedom, namely when they are acting one way and realize that morality requires them to do the opposite. These are precisely the occasions when people feel guilty. They realize that they should act otherwise but nonetheless submit to first-order desires that are inconsistent with their principles.

These feelings of guilt would be inappropriate and "neurotic" if the actor consistently violated his internal principles and then flagellated himself for having done so. To say that his will is free requires that at least sometimes he succeed in controlling his first-order desires. He must have a disposition to effectuate his second-order volitions, and if he consistently fails to conform his will to these principles, it would difficult to say that he is at all disposed to do so.

One of Frankfurt's intriguing premises is that the category of persons — agents who act on second-order volitions — need not coincide with human beings. There are some human beings who are not persons and some persons who are not human beings. The former category are the wantons. They submit to their first-order desires, whatever they may happen to be. They have no second-order volitions to control their desires. Small children are in this category, as are others who simply act on their desires without reflection. Significantly, as we realize by exploring the amendment to Frankfurt's theory, these beings without second-order volitions are incapable of feeling guilt. They never sense the discrepancy between a second-order volition and what they are actually doing.

Frankfurt's definition of persons as agents capable of conforming their will to their second-order volitions could serve us well in generating a new foundation for our intuitions of collective guilt. After exploring the way Frankfurt's theory works itself out with regard to individual guilt, we must consider the possibility that collectives also have second-order volitions and that they are guilty when they fail to conform their first-order desires to them.

The conventional views about free will and culpability in the criminal law are far less sophisticated than Frankfurt's elaborate two-tiered structure. The prevailing view in Europe as well as the United States is that individual offenders are culpable when they engage in unlawful action with the *mens rea* required by the definition of the offense. That is, as the particular statute requires, they purposely, knowingly, recklessly, or negligently engage in conduct that satisfies the elements of the offense. There are some differences among theorists about the relevance of personal excuses in assessing culpability but this in-house debate does not bear on our efforts to understand free will as a foundation for judgments of culpability.

In the criminal law, free will is simply taken for granted. Perhaps this is because we assume that people formulate their criminal intentions in societies in which the particular criminal action is routinely criticized and condemned. But let us suppose we live in a world in which it is conventionally acceptable to hate Jews as "Christ-killers" or to regard blacks as subhuman or to think of gays as perverse and unworthy members of the species; not so long ago these were the dominant opinions in the United States. Suppose, further, that in this world of hate it is perfectly acceptable to commit physical assault against these people who are nominally protected under the law but nonetheless routinely despised and demeaned. This behavior might be formally against the law, but nonetheless commonplace. If the dominant system of beliefs encourages actions like *Kristallnacht*, lynchings, gay bashing, or domestic violence, those who succumb to the social norm are certainly still to blame, but one has to wonder whether they *alone* are to blame and whether they alone must bear the guilt.

This problems bears some resemblance to the perversion of Romantic thinking that we labeled "guiltless sincerity." The criminal who is faithful to the malicious attitudes of his own society is a sincere representative of his or her culture. With their respect for the exotic and the authentic, Romantics find it hard — or should find it hard — to blame ideological terrorists like Palestinian suicide bombers and the perpetrators of the September 11 attacks. The corrective for this view is to recognize that some actions are intrinsically wrong regardless of local enmities. The universal principle of wrongful conduct lies at the foundation of the liberal theory of human rights. Without something like a general theory of wrongful conduct, we would find it hard to make sense of the idea of punishing these ideological offenders who, in their own minds, are doing the right thing. In the context of this chapter, my claim is slightly different: egregious human rights offenders might find some ground for mitigation in the banality of their wrongheaded views of the world around them.

Guilt does not consist simply in surrendering to first-order desires to inflict harm on innocent persons. The assessment of guilt requires a second-order decision — namely, reflecting upon the intended action and deciding to go ahead with the criminal deed despite a second-order volition to do the right thing. Generally, we can rely upon popular views of right and wrong as guides to the realization of this volition, to avoid giving way to the temptation to do wrong. That is, the potential criminal in a normally diverse society has an opportunity for self-correction, to revise his criminal impulse in light of the prevailing moral norms of the society. What happens in a society in which all the external signals point in favor of going through with a criminal action? This moral condition generates the banality of evil. When this happens, when the prevailing sentiments in society support rather than contradict first-order malicious attitudes to violate the rights of others, then we confront a problem in blaming the offender fully for the deed.

Many of the issues we are discussing came to the fore in the late 1990s trials of the border guards in East Germany who tried to kill their fellow citizens making a run for the wall separating the two Germanies. After unification, the government of the enlarged Federal Republic prosecuted several guards for having violated the East German law prohibiting attempted murder. Their defense was that a local statute legitimated their shooting to kill under the circumstances. The German Supreme Court would not recognize the statute as a ground for justifying the conduct because it constituted, in the language of philosopher Gustav Radbruch, "legislated wrongdoing." It was a violation of the universal principles of humanity, including a hypothesized international right to leave one's country.

Many observers objected to this ruling as disrespectful of the law of the German Democratic Republic. More interesting for our purposes is the question whether the border guards were fully to blame for having violated the law of attempted murder. Their argument could well have been that the general climate of opinion surrounding their actions should mitigate their guilt. They did the wrong thing but under the circumstances of their position and the culture in which they operated, they were at least partially excused for not having been able to apply a second-order volition to respect human life.

The guards could have picked up many clues that their shootings were not entirely free of social stigma. Their actions were not publicized in the local newspapers. After a shooting incident they were transferred to other positions. There was a general sense that this was a dirty job—perhaps necessary in the minds of the state's political leaders but nonetheless unsavory. These clues of moral wrongdoing might justify the conclusion that the border guards were fully to blame for their conduct. It strikes me as more humane, however, to recognize that the culture in which they lived—including the Communist regime—bore part of the guilt for making their actions seem almost acceptable. There is some evidence that the courts were motivated by this theory of mitigated guilt, for they sentenced the convicted guards to suspended terms of less than two years in prison.

German law recognizes a formal basis for mitigating guilt on the grounds of cultural influence. If suspects are mistaken about the wrongful nature of their conduct, as the border guards arguably were, they can be excused if their mistake is "unavoidable." This is equivalent to the Catholic doctrine of invincible error. The avoidability of an error is not simply a matter of moral right and wrong in the abstract sense. To assess the degree to which an error is to be excused as invincible, one has to probe the general attitudes that prevail in the community. It might be an excusable error in the United States, for example, to think that sexual relations with a stepdaughter are legally permissible, though in fact the local law prohibits the relationship as incest. Those who engage in errors of this type might act criminally—in violation of the law—but they are not to blame. The German border guards plausibly claimed their error about the legality of the shooting was unavoidable and therefore free from blame. The German courts disagreed.

Significantly, the excuse of unavoidable ignorance is not based — even metaphorically — on a causal argument. There is no suggestion that the will is "overborne" by ignorance. The excuse is grounded in the difficulty of self-correction, of conforming the will to second-order desires in the face of widespread beliefs in the correctness of the conduct.

Making the case for mitigation in this way arguably puts the cart before the horse. The guilt of the offenders might be mitigated in a case like the German border-guard case but it does not follow that the nation or some other collective in East Germany is guilty for having created the moral environment that makes the decision for the guards more difficult.

When a social attitude favoring aberrant behavior takes hold, it is difficult to pin down its sources and therefore it is difficult to make the inference from the banality of evil to the nation's guilt. We may safely assume, however, that these immoral climates of opinion do not come about by accident. They require teachers, religious leaders, politicians, policies of the state, and a network of supportive laws. And they come to express a collective sentiment — whether we call the collective society, the state, the nation, or by the name of a political party. However this collective is identified, it seems plausible to say that it is represented by the government when the state brings a criminal prosecution. The people bring the indictment against the offender, and in these cases where evil has become banal, the people constituting the society bear some of the guilt.

One might think of this guilt as a kind of treason committed by the nation or the government against its loyal citizens. The state and the nation it represents have a duty to contribute to the flourishing, both physical and moral, of individual members of society. To do this they must create — or at least not suppress — a climate of opinion in which potential offenders can exercise their second-order power of self-correction. By enforcing orthodoxy, by restricting the range of morally appealing options, the state deprives its citizens of the essential condition for a moral life —

namely, the possibility of critical moral self-assessment. When the state or the society denies people the possibility of self-correction, it commits a wrong. It betrays its duty to create circumstances of moral action, and it bears part of the guilt for the crimes that result.

We have before us a humanistic theory of collective guilt, a theory that provides a plausible basis for mitigating the penalties of those who commit horrendous crimes. The theory is not simply an argument of state forfeiture — namely that the state has misbehaved and therefore cannot punish the crime fully. The argument is based rather on the distribution of guilt between offender and society, between the offender and the nation in which his life is expressed. My conclusion is that this conception of distributed guilt should have had a bearing on the sentencing of Eichmann; it should have influenced our perception of the crime committed by Timothy McVeigh; it should have come into play when the East German border guards were put on trial for doing what the ideology of their society preached. The crimes these men committed expressed not only their personal guilt but also the collective guilt of those who deprived the offenders of their second-order critical sensibilities.

In a way he probably did not anticipate, Frankfurt's theory of the person might lead us to support this conception of the nation as a bearer of collective guilt. Does the nation constitute a "person" as an agent with second-order volitions? It is a possibility worth exploring. The nation or a society as a whole may have desires — sometimes conflicting desires — just as individual citizens do. For example, at the time of the founding, from 1787 to 1791, the American people had the desire to unite in a single union, to guarantee individual rights, yet to retain slavery within its existing borders. They wanted to abolish the slave trade after 1808 and yet protect slave owners against the loss of their "property" when slaves escaped to free territory. These desires obviously could not fit together in a single consistent constitution. Our collective second-order volition at the time was *not* to choose among these conflicting wills but to anchor all of them in the Constitution supplemented by the Bill of Rights.

Among those not deciding among conflicting objectives, however, were some groups whose second-order volition was to respect the equality of all human beings made in God's image. But, as Lincoln noted with pain in his Second Inaugural Address, others "read the same Bible and pray[ed] to the same God" but still believed that one human being could claim ownership over another. For the abolitionists, the critical second-order principle was expressed in the Declaration of Independence: "We hold these principles to be self-evident, that all men are created equal." We failed to conform the Constitution to this higher order principle and that failure itself was the occasion of deep feelings of anger and guilt on the part of articulate Americans like William Lloyd Garrison, who denounced the Constitution as a "pact with the devil."

Reading Lincoln's speeches, particularly the Gettysburg Address and the Second Inaugural Address, one gets the impression that the nation as a whole bears the guilt for slavery. At Gettysburg Lincoln spoke only of the nation, never of North and South. The nation would experience "a new birth of freedom." It would overcome its guilt for the mistakes of the Constitution by reviving the unity that was present "four score and seven years ago" when the delegates from thirteen states unanimously pledged their "lives," their "fortunes," and their "sacred honor" for the sake of independence. After reelection to a second term, as the war was approaching its end, Lincoln reflected on the collective suffering of the nation:

> The Almighty has His own purposes. "Woe unto the world because of offenses; for it must needs be that offenses come, but woe to that man by whom the offense cometh." If we shall suppose that American slavery is one of those offenses which, in the providence of God, must needs come, but which, having continued through His appointed time, He now wills to remove, and that He gives to both

North and South this terrible war as the woe due to those by whom the offense came . . .

The North and South had to suffer together for their collective offense of maintaining and tolerating slavery. His recognition of this collective guilt enabled Lincoln to be generous toward the vanquished foe and to commit himself to a policy of "malice toward none, with charity for all." This was collective guilt in the service of compassion for those who led the rebellion against the United States.

Let us review the intellectual journey that has led us to this point. The aim has been to devise a theory of collective guilt that could mitigate the guilt of criminals like Eichmann. The first attempt was to reason by analogy to causal theories of complicity represented by the Stashchinsky case. This inquiry led us into a cul de sac because the relationship between collective action by the nation and individual action by the citizen is not causal. Because complicity presupposes a causal relationship, we cannot say that the nation is complicitous in the crime. As a result, we turned to the possibility of a noncausal theory based on the collective guilt of society for at least partially depriving the offender of the possibility of self-correction. Those who participate in creating the banality of evil bear a portion of the guilt for the accidental offender whose actions bespeak the mentality of the crowd.

Romantic attitudes toward the nation are at least partially vindicated. The theory of distributing guilt provides a humanistic defense of collective guilt—a doctrine that is generally regarded as repressive and violative of individual interests. This implication of taking the nation seriously stands in ongoing tension with the Romantic perversions of original sin and guiltless sincerity. In order to defend the humanistic uses of collective guilt, we should consider non-Romantic sources for taking the nation and its guilt seriously. The quest for these sources leads us to a historical inquiry into the origin of guilt in Western culture.

CHAPTER NINE

Shadows of the Past

I advised her to keep away from the tree.
She said she wouldn't. I foresee trouble.
Will emigrate.
  — *Mark Twain, The Diaries of*
  Adam and Eve

Our attraction to collective guilt, despite its vices, suggests a residual memory of a time when nations made a deeper mark on our consciousness than did individuals. Imagine a world in which only the nation could enter into a covenant with God. Think of a time when warfare meant the obliteration of entire peoples. Nations were not merely part of the chorus of history. They were the only players on the stage.

This is the world of the Bible. By immersing ourselves in its stories we can gain another perspective on current quandaries about crime and guilt. We can learn to see the problem transposed, where the primary issue is not collective guilt but a world in which the primary puzzle is whether individuals can stand alone, separated from their nations, and be found guilty for their personal crimes.

The first eleven chapters of Genesis address the history of all humanity. Beginning in Genesis 12, we read the national saga of a people called the Hebrews — *Ivriim* — literally, the ones who had "crossed over" from someplace else. (Only much later are they called Jews.) God tells Abraham to go forth from his native land and to begin a journey that will make him the founder of a great

179

nation. The rest of Genesis details the stories of the four generations from Abraham to Joseph, the forebears of the Hebrew people, in all of their human follies and intrigues. The book is designed to entertain, and it highlights the adventures, loves, and crimes of individuals whose names have carried mythical significance for the thousands of generations of readers steeped in the culture of the Bible.

When Christians, Jews, and Muslims think about collective guilt, their minds invariably run in grooves that were etched in this ancient culture in which individuals act, but the issues at stake are the fate of humanity and of specific nations. As we have seen, the entire doctrine of original sin turns on an interpretation of the actions of Adam and Eve in Eden, but this is not the only story invested with mythical significance. When Abraham banishes his firstborn son Ishmael to the desert, Muslims read this separation as the beginning of the great divide between two warring families of cousins—the Jews and the Arabs. When some highly charged event occurs—such as Lot's daughters committing incest with their father—the incident is understood as the origin of specific nations, in this case, the Ammonites and the Moabites. Their conception in incest explains their expulsion from the congregation of Israel. Genesis recounts the mythical beginnings not only of humanity but of the nations that have existed in the ancient world.

No other book has imprinted itself so deeply on the cultural instincts of at least half the world's population, and it is a book that resonates with collective guilt. Yet when entering the text of Genesis with a view to the question of guilt, we encounter an immediate problem. In cases where one expects to find individuals described as guilty for their sins or as having feelings of guilt for what they have done, there is no mention of the word. Adam and Eve feel no guilt after their disobedience of God. Cain feels no guilt after engaging in apparent incest by "knowing his wife," a woman generally assumed to be his sister. Noah's son Ham feels no guilt after "uncovering his father's nakedness" and thereby bringing a curse upon his children. The best translation for "guilt" into Hebrew is *asham*, but this word does not appear until Chapter 26, more than half way through the narrative.

The biblical concept that comes closet to "guilt" prior to chapter 26 is *avon*, which is the word used in the Hebrew text to explain what Cain feels when he petitions God, after killing Abel, that his *avon* is too much to bear. The usual translation of this term is "punishment," thus yielding Cain's complaint that his being exiled as "a fugitive and wanderer on the earth" is an excessive punishment. God places a mark on Cain to ensure that others will not kill him. However, *avon* can also be translated as "sin" or "crime," which would transform Cain's complaint into a confession of guilt. His being a "fugitive and a wanderer on the earth" is converted into part of the crime of fratricide. He realizes what he has done and cannot bear the thought of becoming disconnected from all those who are meaningful to him. His response to his isolation is to marry; father a son, Enoch; and found the first city recorded in this mythical history.

The correct translation of *avon* is controversial because, in the world of the Bible, the crime and the punishment are understood as conceptually interchangeable. As pollution and the purification are two sides of the same phenomenon, a crime and its condemnation are a single deed viewed from different perspectives. This is important to keep in mind as we explore the emergence of "guilt" and "punishment" in the biblical narrative.

A Recurrent Tale of Pollution and Guilt

The idea of guilt—if not the precise word—presents itself in the very beginning of Abraham's story. There is a famine in the land, which leads Abraham (still called Abram) and Sarah (Sarai) to leave Canaan and take up residence in Egypt under the kingship of Pharaoh (Gen. 12:10). Thus begins a story that recurs three times in the narrative of Genesis. The pattern is always the same:

One of the fathers of the Jewish people is about to enter a foreign land where he suspects that the barbarians will kill him and take his wife. This leads to adultery or a state of near adultery. The sin of adultery — even if committed by mistake — inflicts a pollution upon the land. This pollution is eventually called "guilt."

The first incident of guilt occurs when Abram, fearful for his life, tells Pharaoh that Sarai is his sister. Technically, she *is* his sister because she is the daughter of his father, Terah, by another mother, but this excuse hardly spares Pharaoh the torment of committing the great sin of sleeping with another man's wife. Pharaoh takes Sarai into his harem. A plague then descends upon "Pharaoh and his household" as a sign that a sexual sin has occurred or is about to occur (Gen. 12:17). Pharaoh understands the plague as a sign that something is askew in the natural order and infers that Abram must have been lying to him. He confronts Sarai's husband: "Why did you say, she is my sister so that I might have taken her as my wife?" (ibid., 12:19). He tells Abraham and his entourage to leave.

In a later retelling of the same story, after the renaming of the couple, Abraham tells the same lie to King Abimelech in the land of Gerar (Gen. 20:3). This time the truth is revealed not by a plague but by God's coming to the king in a dream and saying "'You are to die because of the woman that you have taken, for she is a married woman'" (ibid., 22:3). Abimelech interprets the "you" to refer to his entire people. He thinks collectively, in a way parallel to the sign of adultery that came to Pharaoh in a plague on his entire household. As we learn later, a curse has come upon all of Gerar: The women are not able to give birth. The dream and the curse inform the potentate that some sin has occurred or is about to occur in his land.

Still within the framework of the dream, Abimelech enters into a disputation with God about whether in light of "the integrity of his heart," he and his "righteous nation" deserve to die (Gen. 20:4). He makes the kind of argument that a modern criminal lawyer would make on behalf of a client who made an unavoidable mistake: "He himself said to me, 'She is my sister'! and she also said, 'He is my brother'" (ibid., 20:5). The aim here is not to blame Abraham and Sarah but to generate an excuse for Abimelech based on his "integrity" and "purity of hands" (ibid.). In the first telling of the story, guilt appears as a form of pollution that infects the land. The plagues come whether Pharaoh is totally innocent in his heart or not. The deed is enough. The scene is reminiscent of the opening of *Oedipus Rex* in which plagues descend upon Thebes in recognition of the unnatural facts — yet to be discovered — that Oedipus has slain his father and married his mother. Both Oedipus and Pharaoh are guilty merely for having crossed a forbidden line. Whether they are personally blameworthy is irrelevant.

In the story of Abraham and Abimelech we encounter guilt in the sense of personal blameworthiness. God concedes that purity of heart does matter: "And God said to him in a dream, 'Yes, I know that you did this in the integrity of your heart. For I also kept you from sinning against me. Therefore I did not let you touch her'" (Gen. 20:6). This is a curious form of divine intervention, suggesting that as long as Abimelech's heart remains pure he could not commit adultery with Sarah, even by mistake.

Yet some wrong does occur merely in the act described in Gen. 20:2 as Abimelech's "taking" Sarah into his household. He does not touch her but he must still make amends for this act of "taking" though it, too, is committed by mistake. He must restore Sarah to Abraham and hope that Abraham, now described for the first time as a "prophet," will pray for him. Abimelech complies, and though he needs Abraham's prayers, he lances an accusation against Abraham that will echo later in the Book of Genesis: "What have you done to us? In what have I offended you that you have brought on me and my kingdom a great sin." The stain upon the kingdom is now described as a "sin" (*chata-ah*). The word is used earlier in Genesis to describe the condition of corruption that had fallen on Sodom and Gomorrah, a corruption so great that destruction of the city was the only suitable divine remedy. Understandably, Abimelech is concerned that the mere act of taking Sarah into his household might bring a penalty of this gravity upon his kingdom.

Abimelech's concerns shift the burden of explanation to Abraham. Why did he engage in this action that could visit serious harm on another land? Abraham offers two arguments on his behalf. The first, that he thought that Gerar was a land "without reverence for God" (Gen. 20:11) and that the inhabitants would slay him and take his wife. As a wanderer still looking for the land promised to him, he cannot grasp that other lands where he sojourns are civilized and have a proper moral code respecting human life and the sanctity of marriage. Though the Egyptian pharaoh had treated him properly the first time he passed Sarah off as his sister, he still thinks that foreigners lack basic principles of decency and morality.

His second argument is that Sarah was, in fact, his sister — daughter of the same father, though by a different mother. (Though prohibited later in Leviticus, this was not considered incest in Abraham's culture because, I surmise, the daughter of a different mother is likely to have grown up in a different household.) Still, Abraham seeks to hide in what seems to us today a legalism. He undoubtedly sought to deceive both Pharaoh and Abimelech but now claims that it was all a misunderstanding. He meant one thing by "sister," but they understood something else.

The structure of Abraham's and Abimelech's arguments differs. Abimelech addresses himself to God and makes claims about the inner state of his heart. His soul is clean, and therefore, he claims, he should not be guilty in the eyes of God. Abraham directs his argument not to God but to secular considerations. He argues not about his inner being but rather about cultural difference. As a foreigner, he cannot, he says, be blamed for bearing suspicion toward a different culture or for using the word "sister" in a way that produces misunderstanding.

It is not clear whether Abimelech is persuaded by these arguments or whether he recalls God's instruction to respect Abraham as a prophet. Both factors seem to move him to "restore" Sarah to Abraham and to give him gifts of sheep, oxen, and servants. He adapts to Abraham's argument that it was all a misunderstanding by describing his gift to Sarah as giving silver to her "brother" — thus accepting Abraham's description of the relationship. Abraham meets his side of the bargain by praying to God, with the result that the women of Gerar could once more conceive and give birth.

Multiple conceptions of guilt emerge from this short, rich tale. Initially, guilt is conceptualized as a collective phenomenon. Abimelech accuses Abraham of bringing a sin upon the land. It besets the entire country. A curse falls on the women of Gerar: They cannot conceive. Yet this collective guilt comes in several refined variations. As compared to the single state of sin in the tale of Abram and Pharaoh, the guilt of Abimelech might be greater or lesser. The greater sin would have been to commit adultery by having sexual relationships with Sarah, a married woman; the lesser, "taking" her into the household and thus creating the risk of adultery. Further, there is a difference in both of these cases between acting with or without personal guilt. Both Abimelech and Abraham seek to deny their personal blameworthiness for having created an objective condition at odds with the moral order. Abimelech appeals to the innocence of his heart, Abraham to cultural misunderstanding. Finally, there is a difference between guilt in relationship to God (Abimelech) and guilt in relationship to other human beings (Abraham). No less than eight variations in the types of guilt emerge from the combination of these factors.

Missing from the list, however, is the subjective experience of *feeling* guilty. There is no indication that any of the characters in the drama feel anything but mistreated and misunderstood. We have yet to comprehend how the distinctively modern phenomenon of feeling guilty emerges from the historical background of biblical guilt. Significantly, the Hebrew word most commonly translated as "guilt" — *asham* — does not appear in this tale of Abraham and Abimelech. However, the substance of guilt may be there without the use of the word itself. In the third telling of the same basic story, we finally encounter the technical term for guilt.

The third version begins with another famine that drives Abraham and Sarah's son, Isaac, and his wife Rebecca to return to "sojourn" in Gerar. There they encounter another (or possibly the same) king named Abimelech. The men of the community admire Rebecca's beauty, which leads Isaac to repeat the classic lie that she is his sister. (For Isaac to have uttered this falsehood in good faith, he must have had a very strained conception of sisterhood. Rebecca was the daughter of Bethuel, who was Abraham's nephew — thus Rebecca was a first cousin once removed.) The distinguishing feature of this third story is the way Abimelech discovers the lie. The truth comes neither with a plague nor in a dream. Abimelech looks out the window one day and sees Isaac and Rebecca engaged in some activity that is described by the mysterious verb *l-tsachek*. Having observed this phenomenon he realizes that they are not brother and sister and immediately confronts Isaac with the lie. His accusation against Isaac repeats the syntax of Abimelech's denunciation of Abraham, but this time the word "guilt" takes the place of "sin": "What is this you have done to us? One of the people might easily have lain with your wife and you would have brought guilt upon us" (Gen. 26:10).

What could the couple have been doing such that Abimelech could realize immediately that they were not brother and sister? The only thing we can imagine is that they were being sexually affectionate — fondling and petting — and that the incest taboo informs Abimelech's perception. He knows that they are not brother and sister because, if they were, they would not be engaged in incestuous foreplay in public.

That the incest taboo is known in Gerar is itself significant. The Hebrew patriarchs Abraham and Isaac seem constantly to be underestimating the moral sophistication of their neighbors. They fail to recognize the power of their God to influence the moral judgment of those who pray to different gods. In modern terms, we would say that they were provincial and xenophobic. They do not yet understand the universality of the moral prohibitions against adultery and incest.

The Hebrew text supports our interpretation of the activity of Isaac and Rebecca as sexual foreplay. Though scholars still debate the precise meaning of the verb *l-tzachek*, the root clearly implies laughter and sport. In fact, this is the root of Isaac's name in Hebrew, *Yitzhak*, which he received because Sarah laughed when she was told that she would conceive at her advanced age (Gen. 18:13). The same verb appears in other key passages in which some sexually tinged activities in public generate deep social conflict. It is used to describe what Ishmael does to Isaac (ibid., 21:9), an activity so offensive that Sarah resolves to send him away. The usual translation of the verb in this context as "mocking" misses the sexual overtones of the act. The other revealing use of the verb is in the description of the way the Hebrews danced and "rose to play"when they were worshiping the Golden Calf (Exod. 32:6). The unspecified activity of Isaac and Rebecca is of a piece with these other erotic activities that are presented as the source of corruption and conflict.

The remedy for guilt, in the sense the term is used in the Hebrew Bible, is to bring a sacrifice to the Temple. The sacrifice cleanses the guilt. Remarkably, the word used in chapter 5 of Leviticus to describe a whole range of sacrifices is also guilt — *asham*. A guilt sacrifice is prescribed to atone for specific sins, burnt offerings for others. The crossover in meaning between the deed and the remedy recalls the controversy about translating *avon*, the word that Cain uses in his complaint that his sin/punishment is too difficult to bear. With regard to guilt (*asham*) as well as Cain's sin/punishment (*avon*), this easy interchange of the negative and the positive, the contamination and the decontamination, reveals the tight conceptual connection between the two.

Walter Burkert, a prominent historian of Greek religion and culture, has a different take on this easy association of guilt and punishment in the ancient world. He suggests that those who committed the offense requiring a sacrificial response actually tendered personal feelings of guilt and projected these subjective feelings onto the sacrifice. This account does not seem to square with the language of the Bible, but perhaps both are correct.

Shame in Place of Guilt

A striking characteristic of the awakening in Eden (or the Fall in Christian thought) is that — despite the great sin of disobedience — there is no discussion of guilt or feelings of unworthiness on the part of Adam and Eve. Instead the story is framed as a disquisition on the birth of shame. When Adam and Eve are separated into distinct beings, "[t]he two of them were naked, the man and his wife, yet they felt no shame" (Gen. 2:25). After they ate of the fruit from the tree of the knowledge of good and evil, "the eyes of both of them were opened and they perceived that they were naked; and they sewed together fig leaves" (ibid., 3:7). Many different things were supposed to happen upon tasting the fruit, but none of them indicates a reason to be ashamed. According to a literal reading of God's threat ("you shall surely die"), they should have expired upon taking the first bite. According to the serpent's promise, they should have become like gods. (Gen. 3:5, "God knows that in the day you eat of it you shall become as gods knowing good and evil.") At the very minimum, they should have acquired some knowledge of moral values. But none of this is captured in the text, which describes a reaction of shame, expressed in their seeking to cover themselves.

This is a serious puzzle. How do we account for the dissonance between the threats and promises tied to eating the forbidden fruit, on the one hand, and the onset of shame, on the other? One standard interpretation is that suddenly Adam and Eve become aware of the procreative capacities in their genitals. Thus they become aware of being like God in their capacity to generate new life. This explains their attention being drawn to their sexual parts, but why should they feel shame as a result? And what knowledge have they acquired? Is it of good or of evil?

Perhaps the story is written against the background of the common human experience of feeling shame about the exposure of the genitals and therefore as soon as Adam and Eve become aware of their procreative power they feel shame about being naked. People ordinarily are indeed embarrassed or ashamed about having their genitals exposed. It is not clear why. Perhaps the thought is that our sexual appetites reveal how much like animals we really are and that this is the root consciousness of shame. But we actually share four basic functions with animals: sex, excretion, eating, and sleeping. We feel shame about the first two (the second being so taboo that it is not even discussed in the Bible), but the latter two animal impulses are the mainstay of all long-distance airplane flights. Doing things that animals also do will sometimes trigger a sense of shame, sometimes not. It is not these four actions themselves that matter but whether we have control over time, place, and manner. As anyone who has spent time in a nudist colony knows, the shame felt in being naked in front of strangers is easily overcome. It is hardly a necessary feature of being human — of being like gods or of having knowledge of good and evil.

The most telling line in this story is that upon eating the fruit "the eyes of both of them were opened" (Gen. 3:7). The core experience of shame is feeling exposed, being subject to the gaze of another. There is no suggestion in the text that either Adam or Eve judge each other harshly, blame each other, or feel anything in particular — only that they are aware of each other's eyes. And their first reaction is to sense the nakedness of that part of the body that makes them different from each other. For the first time, they become aware that they are distinct beings. When they were first created they were naked but felt no shame because they were not aware of their difference.

Becoming like God or, as the serpent promises, like "gods" is to learn to appreciate distinctions. The Biblical creation itself is founded on building distinctions into the world. The world is organized into the sharply defined categories of night and day, earth and sky, land and sea, plants and animals, animals and humans, life and death, good and evil — and finally, man and woman. The knowledge of good and evil is not substantive knowledge of the sort later recorded in the Ten Commandments but rather the elementary knowledge that the world is organized by distinctions. The categorical separation of good and evil typifies the full range of distinctions that lie at the foundation of God's creation.

The thesis, then, is that "nakedness" is a metaphor for separation, for being different, a feature of men and women that is most obvious when their genitals are exposed. We find validation of this interpretation a few sentences later when God comes into the Garden and purports not to know where Adam is (Gen. 3:9). (This is, of course, an amusing state of affairs for a supposedly omniscient God.) The divine search for Adam enables the man, now with eyes open, to say that he was hiding (ibid., 3:10). He heard the voice of God in the Garden and felt something that made him sense his nakedness and compelled him to hide. That feeling is rendered in Hebrew as *irah* and the word is typically translated as "fear." The better translation in a religious context is "awe" or "reverence." Adam says, "I heard the sound of You in the Garden, and I was afraid because I was naked" (ibid.). If nakedness is essentially connected to shame, then the passage becomes incoherent. But if we focus on the phenomenon of separation and the possibility of revering God as an independent force, the passage conveys a clear theological message. Adam felt naked because he was in awe of God. He could not feel awe unless he also felt independent and able to see God as a power separate from himself. Adam and Eve feel shame toward each other, but their sentiment toward God is not shame but awe and respect. The common theme is separation. They can feel shame when their eyes tell them that they are separate beings, and they can feel awe toward God only after they become like gods themselves, understanding the distinction between the human and the divine.

Shame in individuals, we can conclude, has a sound grounding both in our experience and in our mythology. The feature that makes it different from responsibility and guilt, however, is its nonrational quality. There is nothing logical about feeling shame about the exposure of one's genitals. Nor is there anything well reasoned about minorities feeling ashamed of the way they are, with the resulting desire to conceal their origins and stay "in the closet." On the whole, it seems that the practice of coming out liberates people from the strictures of shame. Yet at the same time, feeling ashamed, for say cheating or committing adultery, is a healthy reaction that strengthens our ties with others.

A rather simple distinction holds between shame and guilt. People feel shame for *who and what they are*, and guilt for *what they have done*. This connection between shame and the objective facts of our identity explains why shame can connect with parts of the body and stand totally outside the criteria of responsibility. Guilt about what you have done can make you feel shame for who you are to have done such a thing. But the inverse relationship does not hold. That is, someone might feel shame about a physical deformity and attempt to conceal it. But there would be no reason to feel guilt about an accidental feature of one's body.

Though we now nourish a sharp distinction between guilt and shame and speak of some cultures as shame-cultures and others as guilt-cultures, it seems safe to assume that the ancient world understood these concepts in a way different from our own. In contemplating whether Oedipus feels guilt or shame for his fated patricide and incest, it is often said that the Greeks at the time of Sophocles did not distinguish between guilt and shame. There are signs of both in the play. When Oedipus discovers his crime, he craves punishment as though he were guilty in the modern sense, but the method of his self-inflicted punishment — putting out his eyes and going into exile — resonates with shame. He literally cannot bear to see others looking at him. He cannot have his children look upon him with the knowledge that they are the offspring of an incestuous marriage. Wanting to suffer — to be in the position of the sacrificial animal — is a characteristic response of those who feel guilt. Wanting to avoid the gaze of others is central to the experience of shame.

The Evolution of Subjective Guilt

In the last 2,500 years in the West, we have undergone a major transformation in our thinking about guilt. The evolution toward our current approach has required the transition from the objective phenomenon of pollution to the subjective condition of blameworthiness. Though we retain a memory of the ancient idea of guilt as a stain upon the community, the focus has shifted to the modern idea that individuals feel guilty. Recall the argument in Roth's *The Human Stain* about why the entire college should feel guilty for its hounding of Coleman Silk. The logic begins with personal feelings of guilt and reasons outward toward the probable feelings of others.

Along with this change, there has been a shift from guilt as a fixed quantity, the same for everyone, to the concept of guilt as a matter of degree. There is some suggestion of greater and lesser guilt in the story of Abraham and Abimelech. Yet the greater or lesser guilt still tainted everyone. The striking assumption of modernity is that some individuals are more guilty than others. Their relative degrees of guilt depend on two factors: first, how much they contribute or how close they come to causing physical harm, and second, their internal knowledge of the action and its risks. The principal who controls the actions leading to harm is more guilty than the accessory who merely aids in the execution of the plan. Those who take risks intentionally are worse than those who do so inadvertently. These assumptions about relative guilt are built into the way we now think about crime and punishment. The modern conception of guilt is not categorical but rather a matter of degree.

These shifts from the external to the internal, and from the absolute to the relative, signal another conceptual transformation. The notion of guilt in the biblical culture was connected with a particular kind of response — the sacrifice of animals in a religious ritual. In the modern secular understanding of guilt, the linkage is not with sacrifice in the Temple but with punishment prescribed in court. As Herbert Morris writes, "To be guilty is, among other things, both to owe something to another and to be the justified object of their hostility." Morris emphasizes the element of indebtedness in guilt, a factor that provides a bridge between the duty to bring a sacrifice and the duty to suffer punishment. This connection is suggested by the close association in German between *Schuld* (guilt) and *Verschulden* (debt). It is supported as well by the way in which the Hebrew terms migrate back and forth between the problem and the remedy, between the pollution and the purification, the guilt and the punishment.

The secularization of guilt should not, however, lead us to forget one very important aspect of guilt in the modern understanding. As Paul Ricouer points out in *The Symbolism of Evil*, the guilty person suffers from a particular sense of unworthiness, a loss of self-esteem that leads to a craving for punishment as the fitting externalization of his inner self-depreciation. One might add that in our current post-apartheid and post-Communist political situation, the need for punishment can be satisfied as well by a public confession of guilt.

Our modern condition now allows for the possibility of guilt in the absence of harm. It now seems plausible to say that someone who aims to kill, then shoots and misses, is just as guilty as someone who shoot and kills. There are many who say that the two categories of offenders should be punished the same way. Of course, this would have seemed absurd to the ancients. It would be equivalent to suggesting today that the intention to pollute is equivalent to actual pollution.

This transformation of guilt is much too deep and too radical to be attributed to any single historical process. It is difficult even to date it precisely. It would seem to be older than the rebellion of the German Romantics against the French Enlightenment in the beginning of the nineteenth century, but it is not clear when the shift occurred. Did it take place with the preaching of the Hebrew prophets? With the emergence of Christianity and its conception of individual salvation? Or with the sixteenth-century Protestant doctrine of salvation by faith alone? These religious movements in themselves cannot explain either the secularization of guilt or the grading of guilt as a matter of degree. Nor can the history of religion account for the modern phenomenon of free-floating guilt and its detachment from all external anchors. The modern condition is best expressed in the plight of Kafka's Josef K, who knows that he is regarded as guilty for something but does not know what. He must wander the maze of the law in search of the trial that will resolve his anxiety about his internal state of unworthiness. It is as though he is Oedipus, but with the plagues on Thebes internalized and without a truth that he can discover.

Among all these transformations, the critical shift for purposes of this study lies in the presumed point of departure in assessing guilt as collective or individual. Our entire investigation has taken for granted that the burden of proof is on the advocate of collective guilt. But for the ancients, particularly the ancient Hebrews, collective guilt was the norm. Though we must accept the conventional assumption that individual guilt is well understood and collective guilt problematic, it is hard for me to believe that we can entirely escape the influence of the past.

Many of the Romantics were themselves deeply engaged by the biblical stories we have surveyed here. For Johann Georg Hamann, reading the history of the Hebrews was a transformative experience; he found in this history of a particular people a general message about the evolution of each human spirit. Johann Gottfried Herder became a scholar of biblical poetry. Taking the Bible seriously nurtured the Romantic fascination with cultural particularity. The universalist pretension of the Enlightenment yielded in the face of a revered text celebrating the story of a single nation in its struggle for survival.

Though the Bible may have less of a grip on our imagination today, we cannot easily escape its influence. Our moral sentiments are still informed by the Ten Commandments, and our sentiments about guilt and punishment stand in constant dialogue with ancient understandings. The biblical assumptions about collective agency and guilt as pollution seep though our liberal defenses and open us to the plausibility of attaching guilt to nations as well as to individuals.

Living with Guilt

The King, subject to violent mood swings, asked his chief craftsman to engrave a ring with a single slogan that would get him through his depressions and temper his ecstasies. The craftsman returned with a ring bearing the line: "This too shall pass."
— *Jewish Folktale*

The result of war is sometimes glory, but more often guilt. Losers feel guilty for letting down their comrades in arms, and they may tender similar feelings toward the home front and their political leaders. Winners may make things worse by subjecting them to trials for alleged war crimes. The victors, for their part, cannot easily escape guilt for the actions that seemed necessary to win the war. Their morally sensitive countrymen never allow them to forget, for example, that they engaged in actions like nuking Hiroshima or confining Japanese Americans in security camps. Even survivors feel guilty. In *We Were Soldiers,* a 2002 film designed to glorify bravery in Vietnam, the commander of the costly American victory in Ia Dang Valley, Lt. Col. Hal Moore, says, "I can never forgive myself that my men died and I did not."

Coping with Guilt: Denial

If a nation is guilty for crimes against innocent peoples and individuals, the guilt is multiplied. The burden is so great that we invariably seek refuge in denial. We refuse to recognize the actions done by us and in our name until something happens — something like the death of Coleman Silk in *The Human Stain*—to awaken our human capacity for empathy and shared suffering. For Germans living after the war, the critical experience was apparently a television series — named *Holocaust*—that told the story of one Jewish family in the Third Reich exposed to systematic persecution and mass murder. About half the adult population, twenty million people, watched some portion of the television series when it was first broadcast in January 1979. Suddenly, hundreds of thousands of people understood for the first time the depth of the crime that their fellow countrymen had committed. The experience had the effect of adding the term *"der Holocaust"* to the German language.

Discovering guilt has become a standard theme in psychological drama. We see the beginnings of this genre in *Oedipus Rex*, an entire play devoted to the investigation of something the protagonist Oedipus could conceivably have known at the outset: He has killed his father and married his mother. Both he and his mother, Jocasta, claim not to be aware of their involvement in an incestuous relationship (it is possible, I suppose, that she would not recognize her own son). They must wait until they are overwhelmed with clues that bring home to them both their need to be punished and their need literally to avoid seeing and being seen by their children.

In Genesis, the three parallel narratives of deception and adultery address the same process of discovery. In the beginning Pharaoh reads the plagues to learn of guilt in the land; then Abimelech finds clues in a dream; and finally the later Abimelech sees it with his own eyes, trained in a culture in which brother and sister do not commit incest. All of these stories illustrate the process of inferring guilt from some way of perceiving the truth behind the pretenses of language and lies (plagues, dreams, visual evidence). As soon as the king learns that the woman alleged to be a man's sister is married to him, the guilt is obvious.

The temptation today is to cope with guilt by denial. Often, we know precisely what we have done, but we do not feel guilty. Raskolnikov in Dostoyevsky's *Crime and Punishment* has become the exemplar of the modern man who knows intellectually that he has killed but fails to grasp the moral aspects of his actions. He must go through a tortured process of self-realization before he grasps the moral depth of what he's done. This is the condition of all ideological killers, all those caught in a culture of authenticity and insulated from blame and guilt because their societies tell them they are doing the right thing. This was the condition of Timothy McVeigh, who thought he was a war hero in the spirit of Alexander Hamilton and Thomas Jefferson. This is Yigal Amir, who felt no remorse for killing a prime minister who sought to bring peace between Arabs and Jews. And this is Slobodan Milosevic, who has chosen the supreme vehicle of denial—namely, defending his actions in an international court against accusations of genocide.

The process of discovery culminates in a sudden explosion of conscience. Repression yields and the truth overwhelms. The reaction can often be violent, as in the case of Oedipus; or, as in the case of Athena College, it can be therapeutic and generate posthumous efforts toward reconciliation. Importantly, this process of exploration and discovery applies to groups as well as to individuals. An entire culture can support slavery, but the mass of people will be able to ignore the suffering of their fellow human beings only for so long. Sooner or later the truth will break through, and the abolitionist spirit will be born. They will find it bizarre, as Lincoln does in his Second Inaugural Address, "that any men should dare to ask a just God's assistance in wringing their bread from the sweat of other men's faces." Once the political insight takes hold, the converts cannot but feel guilt for having been on the side of oppression and injustice.

Coping with Guilt: Displacement

Understandably, the prospect of collective guilt generates denial and resistance. We deny our guilt in particular cases, and to buttress our positions, many deny even the possibility of collective guilt. Any move to recall our roots in the biblical culture of collective guilt is labeled "barbarous." And yet even those who advocate the exclusivity of individual guilt must cope with intuitions that move them in the opposite direction. A good solution might be to displace the notion of guilt into neighboring conceptual territory—in particular, the domains of shame and responsibility. Of course, not all assertions about shame and responsibility would be displacements of sentiments of guilt, for there may be many cases in which one of these alternative concepts does indeed fit the facts better than does the notion of collective guilt. The most we can do is to look at some writers and, with respect for their arguments, consider whether the claims of shame and responsibility are doing the work that the notion of collective guilt should be doing.

Let me begin with an essay by a German philosopher named Anton Leist about his and his compatriots' reactions upon visiting Auschwitz. He notes that he and some other Germans experience shame when they visit the death camp while others of his compatriots do not. The problem arises, then, whether there are grounds for these two groups to subject each other's reactions to criticism. He cannot say to his emotionally neutral compatriots, "You are in fact ashamed" the way he could say, "You and I, we are guilty for what happened here." Nor can he say, the way he might to a child who just ate the frosting off his friend's birthday cake, "You ought to feel ashamed of yourself." This admonition, appropriate for the peccadilloes of children, hardly fits the gravity of crimes against humanity. At the same time, they cannot appropriately say to him, "Don't be ridiculous. There is nothing here for *us* to be ashamed about." German tourists might plausibly regard "shame" as an excessive reaction when they visit Machu Picchu and first learn of the Inca practice of human sacrifice. But Germans in Auschwitz, Americans in Hiroshima, Japanese in Nanjing, and nationals everywhere at the sites of mass criminality committed in the names of their own nations might appropriately feel shame for what their fellow countrymen have done.

The curious thing about shame is that it can arise for good as well as bad reasons. One sound reason to be ashamed is that one has — or one's countrymen have — in fact committed a horrendous crime, a realization that might make it difficult to endure the gaze of the victims or their families. An irrational reason for shame is that one might have some physical deformity like a hunchback or six fingers. Equally irrational is the shame felt by rape victims or by those belonging to a discriminated-against minority. Concentration camp survivors, for example, feel shame for several reasons — as victims, as members of despised minorities, and as those physically deformed by the numbers burned into their forearms.

The shame that Leist feels seems to be rational. He should be highly conscious of the great crime committed at the death camps but for reasons that we have yet to lay bare, he gravitates more toward the sentiment of shame than to the possibility of shared guilt for the crimes of his forebears.

The relationship of Jews to Christians reveals a different interplay of guilt and shame. Christian anti-Semitism begins with accusations of Jewish guilt for having "killed Christ." The tradition of stigmatizing Jews in Western cultures generates in modern Jews a sense of shame for being the marginalized bearers of a vilified religion. ("If so many people have hated us, they must have had a reason!") Part of that shame arises simply from their fate as victims. In the same way that rape victims often feel ashamed and wish to conceal their identity, Auschwitz survivors and those who identify with them might share in this irrational shame. As result they might conceal their origins, convert to Christianity, or seek to adopt the manners of the Christian majority — there are many mechanisms for coping with disdain in the eyes of others.

But let us not forget that Matthew charges the Jews not with shame but with guilt for the crucifixion. In the words of Matthew, the Jewish crowd says to Pilate: "His blood be on us and on our children" (Matt. 27:25). Though until very recently many Christians sincerely believed in the accusations recorded in the Gospels, Jews could not have been rationally expected to take these charges of guilt seriously. (Think, by analogy, of blacks listening to the arguments of racists and concluding that, yes, they were indeed inferior beings.) Even though guilt could not plausibly fit their situation in Western culture, Jews might well have felt shame simply as members of, as Justice Frankfurter put it, with some exaggeration, "the most vilified and persecuted minority in history."

The appeal of shame to people like Leist is that it is purely subjective and limited to the psychology of the person who feels it. Every person is entitled to feel shame or not to feel it, in a purely personal way. One gay man might feel shame and prefer to remain in the closet; another might march in gay pride parades; a third might be indifferent to his sexual orientation. Their shame (or pride) tell us nothing about whether they *deserve* to feel any of these sentiments. Nor need they fault others or suggest that others ought to share these purely personal reactions. The discourse of shame is well suited to a culture preoccupied with psychological causes and relativist values (e.g., "What is true for me need not be true for you").

The only problem is that the *same* sentiment may be experienced by both aggressors and victims. Both Leist and the survivors of the camps feel shame. We are tempted to say that the former is *rational* and the latter is not. But qualifying shame this way would defeat the relativist purpose of seeking refuge in shame rather than guilt. What could make shame rational except its being backed up by a real crime that provides a basis for feeling guilt? If the shame is rational, therefore, the best account of the feeling is that it reflects a sense of shared guilt that one would rather not admit. The discourse of shame has the advantage of tact. To assert collective guilt for the Holocaust bears the aggressive implication that others, too, are guilty and therefore should feel guilty. This is a charge that those living in the midst of the allegedly guilty may be reluctant to make.

A good example of this reluctance appears in a thoughtful essay by András Sajó about living as a Jew in post-Holocaust Hungary. Sajó argues that Hungarian Christians should feel collective shame for their participation in the mass murder of Jews after the German invasion in March 1944. As recognition of this shame, he writes, they should be willing to make reparations to the victims and their families. Sajó is committed to the liberal principles that individuals are the only agents who can render themselves guilty, and therefore he relies upon the notion of collective shame to make his charges against Hungarians as a group. It might have been more accurate (though perhaps less tactful) for Sajó to use the idiom of guilt to make his case. Upon more careful examination of his arguments, we find that he is, in fact, talking about guilt in the vocabulary of shame.

At the outset we should recognize the dissonance between shame and Sajó's proposal of compensation. A charge of collective shame hardly provides a basis for imposing a duty to make compensation. Even if I feel shame for what I personally have done, I am not sure why I would want to compensate someone who has suffered as a result of my action. That would not make me feel less ashamed. But if it is guilt that I am feeling, then compensation might restore my relationship with the victim and reduce the hostility directed toward me. *Wiedergutmachung* — or making things whole again — is a response not to shame but to guilt. If the Hungarian Christians felt shame about their own, their parents', or their grandparents' role in the murder of Hungarian Jews, the appropriate response would be to try to hide, to cover themselves in order to avoid the gaze of those they injured. This response would not satisfy Sajó. He wants them to come out, to stand up and be counted. Ideally, they should confess. These are our usual expectations of people whom we regard as guilty for what they have done.

In a seminar about his article, Sajó conceded that he had a personal motive for wanting to attribute collective shame (in fact, collective guilt) to the Hungarian nation in which he lived. He is both Hungarian and an assimilated secular Jew. He would like to see his offspring merge into the Hungarian majority. Yet if the dominant society rejects its responsibility and its guilt, his total assimilation into the Hungarian nation could easily seem to him like a betrayal of his Jewish roots. To understand Sajó's situation, we need only ask what it would be like to live as African Americans in the United States if the dominant white political class felt no guilt — no unease whatever — about having used guns and chains to bring their ancestors to American soil. Suppose the whites expressed the attitude: "You are free now, the past is irrelevant." I should think that this mass amnesia of the dominant culture toward the crimes of the past would be unbearable, both to blacks and whites. The recognition of guilt provides a bridge for the victims and those who identify with the victims to enter into normal social relations.

Thus it becomes clear that collective guilt, when expressed to the victims and their descendants, fulfills an important social function. Confession — or at least the absence of systematic denial — facilitates reconciliation. I am not sure that an admission of shame could accomplish the same end. After all, the confessed shame may have irrational roots; it may reflect the labeling effect of others and say nothing about the legitimacy of the victims' grievance.

If there is some displacement from the conception of guilt to an acceptable discourse about shame, there may be a similar process implied by the widespread desire to use the idiom of responsibility in place of the idea of guilt. Responsibility appeals to us because it makes so few demands. It means simply that one person must respond, give an account, to another. The duty to give an answer might arise without any personal fault; for example, it might be based solely on having caused harm or being the person in charge when the harm occurred. In an early essay, legal philosopher H.L.A. Hart denoted various senses of responsibility, including causal responsibility and criminal responsibility. The term "responsibility" has analogues based on verbs for "responding" or "answering" in almost all languages and provides a bridge connecting criminal law with private law and administrative law.

The ubiquitous concept of responsibility is the lawyer's friend. It does the job of justifying both punishment and civil sanctions, and it carries few metaphysical pretensions.

The notion of responsibility has several attributes that are absent in the concept of guilt. First, the idea of responsibility extends to future behavior. Students are responsible for certain cases prescribed by the class syllabus. They must literally answer in class when questioned about the material. A responsible person is one who can be counted on, not only to give an accounting of past actions, but to do what he or she is supposed to do. Second, the concept of responsibility entails more subtle negations than does the concept of guilt.

The opposite of being guilty is simply being "not guilty" or innocent. But there are two variations in the negation of responsibility, and they represent drastically different ideas. A *nonresponsible* person is someone who cannot be expected to give any account at all. By contrast, an *irresponsible* person is someone who if he is honest will give a self-incriminating account, that is, he will admit that he is likely not to fulfill his "responsibilities." Neither the nonresponsible nor the irresponsible person can be relied upon in the future. The former might do the right thing but without planning to do it; the latter is likely to make plans that will preclude doing the right thing. This fine distinction appears to be an unusual feature of the English language.

Third, by describing someone as responsible, nonresponsible, or irresponsible, we are saying something about their character, how they will behave over time. By contrast, guilt is always connected to a particular deed in the past. People do not have "guilty" characters; they engage in actions for which they are guilty. But the statement "She is responsible" is ambiguous, implying either that she might be responsible in general or responsible only for a particular deed, and in the latter case, the deed might be past, present, or future. And fourth, responsibility carries no necessary consequences, while guilt is closely connected to punishment — either an expectation of punishment by the criminal law or a craving for punishment in the case of one who feels guilty.

Admittedly, there are many situations in which the concept of responsibility rather than guilt seems to be appropriate. We noted this in discussing the participation of an orchestra in a bad performance. The individual members of the orchestra might be responsible for a desultory performance but it would be odd to describe them as guilty. The reason the term "guilt" is inappropriate in this and other contexts, I believe, is that guilt is historically associated with a remedy of purification — for instance, the guilt offering in Leviticus. Guilt is associated in Christianity with acts of penance, and in modern secular states with symbolic penance, such as community service. In the case of "responsibility," there is nothing to purify, nothing to cleanse. This is, to be sure, part of the appeal of the idiom: It carries fewer overtones of the ancient beliefs that we think we have shed.

Finally, the great appeal of "responsibility" is that it is not associated with doctrines that transmit guilt from generation to generation. The stripped-down concept of responsibility is free of all the Romantic overtones of a living nation and the virtues of authenticity. A young German who goes to Israel to work on a kibbutz may feel a need to make amends for the past, and he may participate in a shared sense of guilt, but he cannot be charged with "responsibility" for the crimes of his grandfathers.

Responsibility functions like promising. The one who has promised is liable for breaches of the promise, those that have occurred and those that have not occurred. The same is true of responsibility. If a single person can be responsible for a child in his care, then a team of baby-sitters can commit themselves and take responsibility as well. If something happens to the child, they — all together and as individuals — must provide an accounting, and they may have to stand responsible in the sense of accepting civil liability.

In the end, then, the concepts of shame and responsibility cannot do the work that we require of guilt and collective guilt. Collective shame cannot account for the desire to impose a duty of reparation on wrongdoers, nor can it account for the difference between rational and irrational shame. It cannot distinguish between the sentiments of shame felt by those whose compatriots have committed a "shameful" act of brutality as compared to the shame felt by the victims themselves for having been branded as inferior and humiliated.

The principle of collective guilt is honored as much in denial and displacement as in explicit advocacy. The words themselves — "collective guilt" — repel many because of their association with an ancient world of organically perceived nations. The concept of the collective seems to leave no room for the liberal ideal of the fully autonomous person who acts in independence of his society and his culture. The biblical associations make the idea seem too primitive for modern thinkers. And yet the idea of collective guilt, camouflaged in the language of shame and responsibility, still percolates through our political judgment and our social practices. If we focus less on the language of guilt and more on the underlying sentiments, we might be surprised at how the pervasive tradition of collectivist thinking continues to shape the modern mind.

The Social Meaning of Collective Guilt

Recall the story of András Sajó. Some response by the dominant society to the crimes against his people was necessary for him to resolve his problem of conflicting loyalties. He could not think seriously about assimilation unless he knew that the culture he was leaving behind was adequately respected. He called the desired response "collective shame for the Holocaust." In fact he was thinking about guilt, but the important point for him was that silence by the dominant group about the sins of the past was simply unbearable.

Even if the guilty are not punished, their confession of guilt puts them in a morally subordinate position that enables the former victims to regain lost dignity. This perspective on collective guilt enables us to understand the European and Israeli practice of punishing Holocaust denial, the crime the Germans call "the lie about Auschwitz." At first blush, it is hard to understand why anyone should object to writers denying that Jews were systematically murdered. Why is it insulting and demeaning for Jews to be told, in an extreme version of denial, "You are just like everybody else. No one wants to hurt you now, and nobody wanted to kill you then?" Presumably it would not be a crime for someone to deny that the Exodus from Egypt ever occurred or that the Patriarch Abraham ever lived. These facts are more central to Jewish identity than the death camps of the Third Reich. And yet Holocaust denial — but not the denial of the Exodus — is punished as a crime in many jurisdictions.

The only way to make sense of the criminal prohibitions in force in most European countries is to think of Holocaust denial as a way of saying that no one could possibly be guilty, or personally touched, by these crimes of the past. If it never happened, no one could possibly feel guilty about it. Denial of the Holocaust, then, is much worse than silence, for in the latter case one might suppose that even though silent, many people feel a personal debt arising from the crimes of the past. If denial of the event becomes the official orthodoxy, however, there is hardly a basis for finding solace in beliefs that lie below the surface of official silence. Would it be enough to have a truth commission that articulates a public truth about the crimes of the past? I am not sure. It is important that the dominant group recognize its moral burden. It must not only speak the truth but make a symbolic bow, an act of self-deprecation, in order to acknowledge the relative dignity of those who have suffered.

And would a sense of collective responsibility accomplish the same end? Curiously, if young Americans said today "We feel responsible for slavery," the statement would not ring true. Why should they be responsible for actions taken over a century and a half ago? But their guilt, arising by virtue of identification with the history of their nation, would make sense. Remarkably, even children of twentieth-century immigrants can and do feel guilt for a nineteenth-century collective crime. American history has an extraordinary pull on the children of immigrants. It confers on them a new identity and gives them a stake in a psychological past that is not even part of their or their family's lived experience. By saying that they feel guilt for slavery, they would be saying that they see the effects of the nineteenth-century crime in the problems of race relations all around them, and that they feel personally touched and unworthy that these circumstances of discrimination should constitute part of their psychological history. Their authenticity as whole beings requires them not only to feel pride in the American experiment, but also to recognize the crimes of the American nation and to accept the guilt that follows from wrongdoing.

Americans, in fact, seem to have an inclination to recognize social guilt. We are constantly discovering the evils of our past ways. In our robust egalitarian culture, we witness a newly discovered and shared sense of guilt for the sins of Columbus, the elimination of Native American culture, the oppression of women, and the persecution of homosexuals. Most significantly, our politically correct speech serves as a constant reminder of our collective guilt. The words by which subordination was expressed in the past have become taboo. As we ritualistically avoid the "N" word and all its analogues, we remind ourselves and each other that our language provides an etymological transcript of our evil ways.

The proof of collective guilt in politically correct speech is evident not just in the avoidance of certain words, but in the anxiety about using words that border on forbidden territory. To use a word like "niggardly" or "spooks" generates self-consciousness, a sense of possibly having crossed the line. The speaker says to himself: "Perhaps like Coleman Silk in *The Human Stain* I will be taken to be one of those bigots who still exist among us." The same anxiety is felt by any professor who forthrightly addresses issues of race and racism in class or takes on the dangers of falsely accusing men of rape in criminal law. Some of the fear may stem from being falsely branded by the others as belonging "to the wrong side." But part of it also stems from participating in a collective experience of stigmatizing attitudes of the past as oppressive and seeking to signal that covenant with justice in our daily use of language.

It is not surprising that every society has its characteristic way of expressing its guilt for the sins of the past. For Americans, the reforming of language is our ongoing project. For Continental Europeans, it is the preservation of public truths about genocide. For South Africans, it is enough to hear the stories and confessions of past oppression. For the Japanese, the constitutional renunciation of war serves as a constant reminder. The common element is a recognition that cultural continuity and the flourishing of the nation require the use of memory to institutionalize our guilt as well as our cultural triumphs.

This kind of collective guilt inheres in the nation, but it tells us nothing about the guilt of any particular person alive today. We remember and recognize our continuity with those in the past who, for one reason or another, routinely said and did things that we would today regard as unthinkable. In a peculiar way we feel even more aware of these past crimes and more guilty for their occurrence than we would expect of people at the time they occurred. After all, they were insulated from the truth by their historical circumstances. I cannot blame Thomas Jefferson for keeping slaves, and yet today it would be an unspeakable crime. Those who act enmeshed in a particular culture are less able to exercise their second-order powers of self-correction, but with the benefit of hindsight we all reach refined judgments about the wrongs of prior generations. Our only problem is that we do not yet have hindsight about our potential excesses in condemning others who adhere to now stigmatized attitudes like racism, sexism, homophobia, or anti-Semitism. Nor do we fully know whether our fighting wars abroad or neglecting poverty at home will be judged by future generations to be a basis for *their* collective guilt.

Collective guilt is, in fact, on the rise. We tend to feel increasingly touched and connected to the misfortunes that befall others. We feel guilty about polluting the environment if we throw a bottle on the street. We feel contaminated by wearing tennis shoes made by child labor on the other side of the world. We feel metaphysical guilt, as Jaspers would say, that people are starving or dying of AIDS somewhere in the world. In harboring all these feelings, we fall prey to the illusion of omnipotence. We want to matter so much to the events of the world that we assume guilt where, in fact, the events may be far beyond our control.

No Shame in Glory or Guilt

In early 2002 the United States found itself basking in success. Having achieved a technologically impressive victory in Afghanistan, the Bush administration could cherish the glory of winning a war on the ground and vindicating America's honor as the world's sole superpower. The moment of satisfaction was well deserved, but it would surely be transient. The glory would give way to unexpected disappointments. There would inevitably come military setbacks, mistakes, failures in the field.

And as the Bush administration was to be admired on many fronts — supporting reform in Afghanistan and standing faithfully behind the unpopular democratic states of Israel and Taiwan — it was also laying the groundwork for later regrets. The president's first stab at defining the procedures for military tribunals met with criticism from civil libertarians and constitutionalists like myself. As a result the Justice Department reformed the procedures in March 2002 but still failed to guarantee some of the protections found in court-martial trials — not to mention jury trials under the Sixth Amendment. The most notable shortcoming was the failure to guarantee review by an independent civilian court. But the executive branch cannot unilaterally close the courts and rule out the use of the writ of habeas corpus to test the legality of their proposed procedures. The Supreme Court has the final word. This is why Roosevelt failed to lock out the courts in 1942 and why the Bush administration was destined to fail in the same maneuver sixty years later.

In the age of terrorism the Bush administration has yet to work out the contours of the basic concepts surrounding its military campaigns. It has flirted with vague definitions of the enemy — all Muslim fundamentalists, all international terrorists, the "axis of evil," all unreliable possessors of nuclear and biological weapons. It has toyed with invading Iraq, with or without the backup of other Western nations, and considered intervening in several arenas of international conflict at the same time. Sooner or later, the vagueness of the campaign will produce occasions of regret. And as is always possible when our technical abilities outdistance our understanding of what we are doing, we risk an incident that will cost the lives of many innocent people. If a blunder of great proportion occurs, we will look back on our own time as a period of indifference to the values and concepts that define our willingness to seek honor and glory (and of course security) in going to war. There will be ample reason for collective responsibility and even guilt.

In the immediate wake of September 11 we were unsure whether a horrendous crime had occurred — like Timothy McVeigh's blowing up of the federal building in Oklahoma City — or whether this was a sneak military attack, an act of war analogous to Pearl Harbor. Time has not resolved our confusions. Long after their capture, President Bush continued to refer to the detainees in Guantánamo Base as "killers" but failed to acknowledge that in warfare both sides engage in legitimate killing. "Killing" could be relevant only if we treated the entire campaign against Al Qaeda and the Taliban as a criminal prosecution or, if this was a case of warfare, as the war crime of killing civilians. The penalty for our ambiguity is paid by the detainees who have the benefit of being treated neither as criminal suspects granted constitutional protections nor as prisoners of war with the attendant right not to respond to interrogations.

With regard to military tribunals and detentions without trial, supporters of the Bush administration love to quote the cant that the Constitution is not a suicide pact, thereby justifying incursions into civil liberties. Instead they should think about the Constitution as an invitation to courage. Had they respect for our tradition, they would insist on full constitutional protections for all suspects and all prisoners — even if granting these rights creates the risk that a few terrorists might get away.

The most puzzling paradox of all is the failure of will in the prosecution of John Walker Lindh. In an age of born-again patriots, the government was afraid to invoke the stigma of treason against someone who openly fought for the enemy. The Walker Lindh prosecution, more than any other, reveals the Administration's lack of legal integrity. By charging Lindh with a conspiracy to kill Americans they brought to bear a set of categories that prevents us from distinguishing coherently between Lindh and his cofighters in the Taliban. If one is guilty of a conspiracy to kill, they all are. But one gets a trial in federal court; the others are exposed to trial in military tribunals.

As the public sharing the glory of military victory, we bear responsibility for failing to insist more clearly on clarity at the top — clarity about objectives, about the concepts used to describe our opponents, and about the international legal and constitutional limits of power. We should not forget that, as Jaspers argued, we are accountable and indeed guilty for the way we are governed.

In the end, the Romantic quest for honor and glory — for the realization of the self in national assertion — brings us back to the universality of the human condition. The commitment to honor and the urge for glory spring from who we are — not as Americans or Germans or Taliban, but as human beings. We all share the capacity to flourish in our victories and to suffer in our defeats. We experience the pain of being victims and the collective sharing of both guilt and shame for our transgressions.

Our capacity for feeling guilt underscores our humanity more than its affirms our allegiance to a particular nation. All human beings—and only human beings—feel guilt. Animals may fear punishment and may experience shame, but they do not conceptualize their fears and anxieties as a failing of the self. Our capacity for guilt, then, distinguishes us as a species and reminds us that beyond our Romantic attachments, we are still children of the Enlightenment. The very fact of guilt, as we now understand it, serves the liberal view of the world, a vision of individuals standing apart from their nations, each responsible solely for his or her own crimes.

The thesis that frames this entire essay, then, is that the experience of guilt and of collective guilt carries a humanistic message. Not only does our capacity for experiencing guilt remind us of our humanity, but collective guilt offers an opportunity for a more humane and sensitive approach to establishing degrees of guilt and determining just sentences in criminal cases. Collective guilt attaches to the nation or to the subculture of which the defendant is part—so far as the prevailing opinion in these groups shapes the thinking on those who contemplate criminal acts. The "banality of evil" compromises the ability of individuals to engage in the self-correction of their criminal impulses. Individual criminals are surely guilty for their crimes. But they are not guilty alone.

Learning to think about these issues in more subtle ways spares us from the temptation to use criminal trials as the vehicle for transferring our guilt to the suspects in the dock. The trial of "evil," of those who are repugnant to us, should also be an occasion to examine our own role in the occurrence of the crime and to invoke our own collective guilt as a factor mitigating the sentence of those whom we want to blame and punish.

Thinking about collective guilt, however, leads to two excesses of Romantic thinking about the self as an aspect of collective experience. The first is transmission of guilt by birth (too much guilt) and the second, insulation of authentic actors from blame (too little guilt). The primary examples of the former are the theological doctrine of original sin, anti-Semitism, and any other doctrine that transmits sin from generation to generation. We can guard against this corruption of guilt by holding firm to the teaching of Ezekiel that the sins of the fathers not be visited on the sons.

Of perhaps greater difficulty is the latter problem of ideological criminals, a phenomenon that, with religious fanaticism on the rise, seems to be all too common. There is no doubt that those who kill because they believe it is their religious duty to do so are nevertheless murderers and deserve to be punished. But it remains difficult to explain their punishment to ourselves when the offenders are impervious to our reasons. We do not communicate condemnation to suspects when they are convinced that they did the right thing. The challenge is to find the proper middle way that mitigates punishment on the basis of society's compromising its citizens' capacity for self-correction, and yet stops short of excusing offenders because they are sincere in their actions.

We would do well to recognize the place of guilt and collective guilt in our cultural lives. But there remains a question about what we can appropriately feel guilty for. It is natural for us, as authentic and rooted human beings, to feel pride for the achievements and guilt for those wrongs brought about by the groups that define our biographies and inform who we are. The problem, in the end, lies not in the nature of guilt but in the scope of agency. Who acts in the world? Individuals act. As the Romantics have taught us, groups and nations also act. And we act through them. The questions of agency and guilt will remain contested. May the debate begin anew — with firm recognition that ours is not a simple world of individuals but a more complicated world in which we seek agency in solidarity with others.

The nations of the world will act. May they do so not with guilt but with glory.

Preface

x) . . . *of the arguments in this book*. The two relevant articles are George P. Fletcher, "Fairness and Utility in Tort Theory," 85 *Harvard Law Review* 537 (1972), and George P. Fletcher, "The Metamorphosis of Larceny," 89 *Harvard Law Review* 269 (1976).

x) . . . *about the leading Palsgraf case . . . Palsgraf v. Long Island Railroad Company*, 248 N.Y. 339; 162 N.E. 99 (1928).

x) . . . *from a hundred sources.*" 162 N.E. at 103.

x) . . . *as equivalent to "the duty to be obeyed" . . .* 162 N.E. at 100.

xi) . . . *to scientific policy-making.* See Bruce Ackerman, *Private Property and the Constitution* (Yale 1977). The problem of contradictions or "antinomies" in the law was discussed also in the influential book, Roberto Mangabeira Unger, *Knowledge and Politics* (Free Press 1975).

xii) . . . Roots of Romanticism *a few years ago . . .* Berlin's work is widely discussed in the text of this book.

xiii) . . . *on the equal treatment of all*. The books mentioned in this paragraph are George P. Fletcher, *Loyalty: An Essay on the Morality of Relationships* (OUP 1992) and Charles Taylor, *Sources of the Self: The Making of Modern Identity* (Harvard 1989).

xiii) . . . *in book form in April 2001.* See George P. Fletcher, *Our Secret Constitution: How Lincoln Redefined American Democracy* (Oxford 2001).

xv) . . . *of the* Yale Law Journal. See George P. Fletcher, "Liberals and Romantics at War: The Problem of Collective Guilt," 111 *Yale Law Journal* (2002) 1499.

Chapter One

2) . . . *concept eludes easy definition.* Domestic terrorism is defined in 18 United States Code § 2331, as amended slightly by the 2001 U.S.A. Patriot Act, as follows:

> The term "domestic terrorism" means activities that —
> (A) involve acts dangerous to human life that are a violation of the criminal laws of the United States or of any State;
> (B) appear to be intended —
> (i) to intimidate or coerce a civilian population;
> (ii) to influence the policy of a government by intimidation or coercion; or
> (iii) to affect the conduct of a government by mass destruction, assassination, or kidnaping; and
> (C) occur primarily within the territorial jurisdiction of the United States.
> Terrorism becomes international if, as the statute provides, there is a significant international component in the location of the crime, the intended victims, or the place of asylum.

4) . . . *corruption of governments that fail to prosecute.* The evil of *impunidad* is recognized in the Preamble to the 1998 Rome Statute, which prescribes the law applicable in the proposed International Criminal Court: "Determined to put an end to impunity for the perpetrators of these crimes . . ."

4) . . . *the number of offenders to be punished.* The full version of the *lex talionis* is found in Exod. 21:21–24: "But if other damage ensues, then the penalty shall be life for life, eye for eye, tooth for tooth, hand for hand, foot for foot, burn for burn, wound for wound, bruise for bruise."

6) . . . *protections of the Geneva conventions.* The status of prisoners of war is regulated in the Geneva Convention relative to the Treatment of Prisoners of War, August 12, 1949, in particular, Article 4, defining the requirements of POW status.

6) . . . *are entitled to representation by counsel.* Whether the Fifth and Sixth Amendments apply abroad is a matter of some controversy. The leading case in the Supreme Court is *United States v. Verdugo-Urquidez*, 494 U.S. 259 (1990), which holds that the Fourth Amendment prohibiting unreasonable searches and seizures does not apply abroad. But that case does not resolve the problem whether other constitutional rights like the Miranda rule and the right to a jury trial restrict the actions of the U.S. government abroad.

8) . . . *a single "nation under God" that must "long endure."* Gettysburg Address, November 19, 1863. For an analysis of the address, see George P. Fletcher, *Our Secret Constitution: How Lincoln Redefined American Democracy* (Oxford University Press, 2001).

10) . . . *the oft-repeated lyrics of Pete Seeger.* The Pete Seeger lyrics come from "The Ballad of October 16th," on *Songs for John Doe* (Almanac Records, 1941).

10) . . . *Send the Marines!"* From "Send the Marines," on *That Was the Year That Was* (Warner Brothers, 1965).

11) . . . *eerie (if vague) predictive quality?"* Stephen Holden, "Critics Notebook: Film Portrayals to Stir the Soul," *New York Times*, January 4, 2002, page E1.

12) . . . *make the world safe for democracy."* Woodrow Wilson's famous declaration appears in his War Message of April 2, 1917, and can be found at James D. Richardson's *Compilation of the Messages and Papers of the Presidents*, Vol. 17 (Bureau of National Literature, 1917), 8231.

14) . . . izzat *in Arabic and Persian culture* . . . See David Mandel-

baum, *Women's Seclusion and Men's Honor: Sex Roles in North India* (University of Arizona Press, 1988) 20.

15) . . . *excusing a homicide committed in a duel.* Kant (1724–1804) discusses dueling in "The Doctrine of Right," which is the first part of Immanuel Kant, *The Metaphysics of Morals* (Cambridge, Mary Gregor trans., 1991) (1797).

15) . . . *according to its inherent impulses.* Fichte's (1762–1814) best-known nationalist tract is Johann Gottlieb Fichte, *Addresses to the German Nation* (Open Court, R. Jones and G. Turnbull trans., 1922).

16) . . . *Romantic indulgence in sentiment . . .* Schleiermacher (1768–1834) developed his theological views in Friedrich Schleiermacher, *On Religion: Speeches to Its Cultured Despisers* (1799).

16) . . . *its own path in the development of legal institutions.* Friedrich Carl von Savigny developed his case against legislation in Frederick Charles von Savigny, *Of the Vocation of Our Age for Legislation and Jurisprudence* (Littlewood & Co., Abraham Hayard trans., 1986) (1831).

16) . . . *Romantic sacrifice for the nation.* Henry David Thoreau (1817–1862) defended John Brown in, "The Last Days of John Brown," reprinted in Henry David Thoreau, *Reform Papers* (Princeton University Press, 1973). Ralph Waldo Emerson (1803–1882) described him as a "hero of romance." See Robert Ferguson, "Story and Narrative in the Trial of John Brown," 6 *Yale Journal of Law and the Humanities* (1994) 37.

16) . . . *fought in the uprising of 1848.* For a discussion of Francis Lieber's views, see *Our Secret Constitution* (Oxford University Press, 2001) at pp. 70–74.

16) . . . *far more uplifting and worthy.*" Barbara Ehrenreich, *Blood Rites: Origins and History of the Passions of War* (Holt, 1997), 13.

17) . . . *spontaneous overflow of powerful feelings.*" This quote from Wordsworth (1770–1850) appears in the "Preface" to William Wordsworth, *Lyrical Ballads* (2nd ed., 1800).

18) . . . *not been logic but experience . . .* The line from Holmes (1841–1935) is found in Oliver Wendell Holmes Jr., *The Common Law* (Little, Brown, 1881) 1.

18) . . . *echoed great Romantic themes.* Anne Dailey, "Holmes and the Romantic Mind," 48 *Duke Law Journal* (1988) 429.

19) . . . *the world of sensual impulse.* Kant's views on humanity and morality are found in Immanuel Kant, *Groundwork of the Metaphysics of Morals* (Cambridge, Mary Gregor trans., 1998) (1785).

23) . . . *reaches out to the mysteries of the universe.* William Blake (1757–1827) made this expansionist observation in his "Auguries of Innocence," *Songs and Ballads* (1808).

23) . . . *than are dreamt of in your philosophy."* Hamlet's admonition to Horatio appears in *Hamlet*, Act I, Scene 5.

Chapter Two

26) . . . *personal autonomy and other liberal values."* Nancy Rosenblum, *Another Liberalism: Romanticism and the Reconstruction of Liberal Thought* (Harvard University Press, 1987).

26) . . . *the principles of justice.* The classic statement of Rawls's derivation of his two principles of justice is John Rawls, *A Theory of Justice* (Harvard, 1971). For an adaptation of Rawls's views to include community attachments, see William Kymlicka, *Multicultural Citizenship* (Oxford University Press, 1996).

27) . . . *spirit of the Enlightenment:* . . . For a statement of the three propositions defining the attitudes of the Enlightenment, see Isaiah Berlin, *The Roots of Romanticism* (Princeton University Press, 1999) 21–22.

28) . . . *passions of the self.* On the theology of Johann Georg Hamann (1730–1788), see Isaiah Berlin, *Three Critics of the Enlightenment* (Princeton University Press, 2000) 317.

28) . . . *higher spirits beyond.* See William Wordsworth, *Lyrical Ballads* (2nd ed., 1800).

29) . . . *phenomenon of imprecise generalization.* Wittgenstein (1889–1951) developed his theory of family resemblance in Ludwig Wittgenstein, *Philosophical Investigations* (MacMillan, 1953).

31) . . . *Rawls, Dworkin, Ackerman* . . . The leading books written

by American liberals are John Rawls, op. cit.; Bruce Ackerman, *Social Justice in the Liberal State* (Yale, 1981); Ronald Dworkin, *Taking Rights Seriously* (Harvard University Press, 1978); Joseph Raz, *The Morality of Freedom* (Oxford University Press, 1988).

31) . . . *presumably the same in all human beings.* Pinker's theory of Mentalese is developed in Steven Pinker, *The Language Instinct: How the Mind Creates Language* (Harper, 2000) 44–74.

32) . . . *roots in a particular language.* Herder (1744–1803) set forth his views on language in Johann Gottfried Herder, *On the Origin of Language* (Ungar, John Moran ed. and trans., 1967).

32) . . . *Earth's first blood, have titles manifold.*" Wordsworth wrote "We Must Be Free or Die" in 1802.

33) . . . *through the discourse of lawyers* . . . For my previous reflections on the nature of reasonableness in the law, see "The Right and Reasonable," 98 *Harvard Law Review* (1985) 949.

34) . . . *"fairness" and "reasonableness" dozens of times.* In the Rome Statute on the International Criminal Court, some of the expressions based on "reasonableness" are "reasonable basis" (Article 15(3)), "reasonable measures" (Article 28(a)(ii)), "reasonable grounds"(Article 58 (1)(a)), "unreasonable period" (Article 60(4)), and "reasonable time" (Article 60(1)). The term "fairness" appears in Rome Statute in the expressions "fair and regular trial" (Article 2(a)(vi)), "fair representation of male and female judges" (Article 8(a)(iii)), and a "fair and expeditious" trial (Article 64(2)).

35) . . . *single formula of moral equality.* My liberal universalist side took precedence in an article exploring the religious roots of the concept of equality: "In God's Image: The Religious Imperative of Equality under Law," 99 *Columbia Law Review* (1999) 1608.

36) . . . *Rousseau's* volunté generale, *or general will.* The classic exposition of *volunté generale* is Jean-Jacques Rousseau, *The Social Contract* (Penguin, Maurice Cranston trans., 1987).

37) . . . *acting in an aggregative sense.* Ackerman has developed his views on constitutional theory in Bruce A. Ackerman, *We the People: Foundations* (Harvard University Press, 1991), and *We the People: Transformations (Vol. 2)* (Harvard University Press, 1998).

38) . . . *conceptions of "collective responsibility" as "barbarous."* H. D.

Lewis made these comments in "Collective Responsibility," originally published in 1948, reprinted in *Collective Responsibility: Applied Ethics 17* (Rowman & Littlefield, Larry May and Stacey Hoffman eds., 1991).

40) . . . *Glendon wrote an influential book complaining* . . . See Mary Ann Glendon, *Rights Talk: The Impoverishment of Political Discourse* (Free Press, 1991).

40) . . . *identical in most European countries."* The Schwarzenberger quote found in George Schwarzenberger and E. D. Brown, *A Manual of International Law 43* (Professional Books, Ltd. 6th ed., 1976).

Chapter Three

44) . . . *subjects constituting the state—did not count.* It is surprisingly difficult to find an explicit discussion in the literature of the transition toward individual criminal liability. It is worth consulting the following: Telford Taylor (Chief American prosecutor in Nuremberg), *The Anatomy of the Nuremberg Trials: A Personal Memoir* (Little, Brown, 1992); Nina Jørgensen, *The Responsibility of States for International Crimes* (Oxford University Press, 2000) 73–76 (discussing individual versus collective responsibility under the heading of "individualism versus holism"); George Schwarzenberger, "The Problem of an International Criminal Law," *3 Current Legal Problems* (1950) 263, 275–76; Cf. David J. Cohen, "Bureaucracy, Justice, and Collective Responsibility in the World War II War Crimes Trials," *18 Rechtshistorisches Journal* (1999) 313, 323: "[A]ny attempt to deal with . . . criminality of the Nazi kind without focusing on problems of collective action is likely to prove inadequate."

44) . . . *jurisdiction over natural [as opposed to legal] persons* . . ." The official citation to the Rome Statute of the International Criminal Court of July 17, 1998, is U.N. Doc. A.CONF/183/9.

45) . . . *gentlemen in Rome did "protest too much."* In the quote from Hamlet, Queen Gertrude herself says with regard to the play within the play, "The lady protests too much, methinks." *Hamlet*, Act III, Scene 2.

47) . . . jus-in-bello, *or law-in-war.* On *jus ad bellum* and *jus in bello*, see Michael Walzer, *Just and Unjust Wars* (3d ed. Basic Books,

2000) 21 (referring to the "logical independence and the "dualism" of the two categories); see also Yoram Dinstein, *War, Aggression, and Self-Defense* (Grotius, 1988) 12 (noting that *jus in bello* applies as soon as the state of war arises).

47) . . . *Vietnam, Iraq, and finally Afghanistan.* The joint congressional resolution to initiate the war in Afghanistan, September 18, 2001, is cited as 107 Public Law 40; 115 Statutes 224, and provides:

> That the President is authorized to use all necessary and appropriate force against those nations, organizations, or persons he determines planned, authorized, committed, or aided the terrorist attacks that occurred on September 11, 2001, or harbored such organizations or persons, in order to prevent any future acts of international terrorism against the United States by such nations, organizations or persons.

50) . . . *a state for purposes of international law.* For the decision treating the Bosnian Serbian regime as equivalent to a state, see *Kadic v. Karadic,* 70 F.3d 232 (2ⁿᵈ Cir. 1995).

50) . . . *Constitution and the Bill of Rights five times* . . . The term "war" appears in the following provisions of the Constitution: Article I, Sec. 8, Cl. 11 (congressional power to declare war); Article I, Sec. 10, Cl. 3 (states may not engage in war unless attacked); Article III, Sec. 3, Cl. 1 (treason defined as waging war against the United States); Third Amendment (on quartering soldiers in wartime); Fifth Amendment (exception for cases in the militia in wartime). The term "armed conflict" appears in the definition of war crimes in the Rome Statute, Article 8(2)(b). According to Article 5(1) of the Statute, the jurisdiction of the Court should be "limited to the most serious crimes of concern to the international community as a whole."

51) . . . *constitute a crime under international law.* According to the Rome Statute Article 5(1)(d), "the crime of aggression" will be included within the Court's jurisdiction, but so far the United Nations has not been able to formulate a definition of the crime.

52) . . . *of any other State" would be sufficient.* See United Nations General Assembly Resolution 3314 (XXIX), December 14, 1974, Articles 1 and 3(c).

54) *War crimes exist* . . . The first prosecution of a war crime recognized in the American courts was *In re Yamashita*, 327 U.S. 1 (1946) (upholding a military tribunal for the trial of a Japanese general, invoked by an American commander in the Philippines on his own initiative). After the war Congress made it a federal offense to commit a grave breach of the Geneva Convention. 18 United States Code § 2443. The name of this offense was changed to "war crimes" in 1997. The war crime is punishable only if committed by a U.S. soldier or against a U.S. citizen.

55) . . . *a mere servant of the state.* Rousseau's discussion of soldiers in warfare is found in *The Social Contract* (Penguin, Maurice Cranston trans., 1987) at 56.

56) . . . *safe surrender is no longer possible.* The crime of "no quarter" is defined in the Hague Convention (IV) Respecting the Laws and Customs of War on Land, October 18, 1907, art. 23(d), 36 Stat. 2277, 2302, 205 Consol. T.S. 277, 293, and the Rome Statute, Art. 8(2)(b)(xii).

56) . . . *a method of warfare."* "Pillaging a town" is prohibited in the Hague Convention Article 23; Rome Statute Article 8(2)(b)(xvi). The use of "starvation" as a weapon is prohibited in the 1977 Geneva Protocol II Additional to the Geneva Convention of August 12, 1949, Article 14; Rome Statute Article 8(2)(b)(xxv).

58) . . . *not entitled to their protection."* For the quoted provision from Lieber's code, see *Instructions for the Government of Armies of the United States in the Field*, prepared by Francis Lieber, promulgated as General Order No. 100 by President Lincoln, 24 April 1863, Article 52.

58) . . . *no imminent attack against him.* On the imminence requirement in the law of self-defense, see George P. Fletcher, *A Crime of Self-Defense: Bernhard Goetz and the Law on Trial* (Free Press, 1988).

60) . . . *regarded as state action."* For an example of conduct by a state official see *D.T. ex rel. M.T. v. Indep. Sch. Dist. No. 16*, 894 F.2d 1176, 1186 (10th Cir. 1990) (a teacher, a state employee, was charged with sexual harassment for purely private conduct during the summer vacation).

63) . . . *victim is an American citizen.* On the federal law of war crimes, see note on page 54.

63) . . . *apparent on the face of the statute.* On the definition of crimes against humanity, see Rome Statute Article 7.

64) . . . *whenever and wherever they occur.* In early June 2001, a Belgian court convicted four Rwandans, including two Catholic Hutu nuns, of complicity in the murder of seven thousand Tutsis seeking refuge in their monastery. The *Economist* noted that "this was the first time that a jury of citizens from one country had judged defendants for war crimes committed in another." "Judging Genocide," *Economist*, June 16, 2001. The jurisdiction of the Belgian court was based on Art. 7 of the Law of June 16, 1993, granting Belgian courts jurisdiction over genocide as defined in the Genocide Convention regardless of where the offense occurred or by whom or against whom the offense was committed. The statute was amended on February 10, 1999. See "*Loi relative à la repression des violations graves de droit international humanitaire* [Law concerning the prosecution of grave breaches of international humanitarian law]"(Feb. 10 1999), published in the *Moniteur Belge* (Mar. 23 1999) § 7.

64) . . . *the killings committed by others.* The Kahan Commission in Israel determined that as minister of defense in 1982 Ariel Sharon bore "indirect responsibility" for the killings executed by the Phalangists. See Anthony Lewis, "Politics in Court," *New York Times*, November 16, 1984, page 23A.

66) . . . *outside of organizational influences and structures.* On the definition of genocide, see Rome Statute Article 6, originally defined in the Convention on the Prevention and Punishment of the Crime of Genocide, adopted Dec. 9, 1948, S. Exec. Doc. O, 81-1 (1949), 78 U.N.T.S. 277.

66) . . . *two victims, the individual and the group.* On hate crimes, see James Jacobs and Kimberly Potter, *Hate Crimes: Criminal Law and Identity Politics* (Oxford University Press, 1998) 29–44 (discussing the variety of hate-crime legislation in the United States). The Model Statute drafted by the Anti-Defamation League defines an offense of "intimidation" based on committing a specified form of physical violence "by reason of the actual or perceived race, color, religion, national origin or sexual orientation of another individual." Ibid. at 33. For a thoughtful

critique of hate-crime legislation, see Anthony M. Dillof, "Punishing Bias: An Examination of the Theoretical Foundations of Bias Crime Statutes," 91 *Northwestern University Law Review* (1997) 1015.

67) . . . *proposal to protect politically defined groups*." On the U.N. decision, see Leo Kuper, *Prevention of Genocide* (Yale University Press, 1985) 126–47.

69) *The Hutus were originally peasant farmers*. See Alison des Forges, *Leave None to Tell the Story: Genocide in Rwanda* (Human Rights Watch, 1999).

Chapter Four

71) . . . *with Bernard Williams* . . . The conversation took place, as I recall, on a bus from Oxford to Heathrow airport in December 2000.

72) . . . *detailed in the Book of Leviticus* . . . The provisions on the scapegoat are found in Leviticus 16. This passage is read in synagogues on the Jewish Day of Atonement. One commentator refers to the institution of sending the scapegoat to Azazel as "the most embarassing feature of the ancient ritual." See *The Torah: A Modern Commentary* (Union of American Hebrew Congregations, W. Gunter Plaut ed., 1981) 859.

72) . . . *entitled to inflict that punishment*. Legal scholars have thought surprisingly little about the psychological complexities of the criminal process. For an exception, see Albert A. Ehrenzweig, *Psychoanalytic Jurisprudence; On Ethics, Aesthetics, and Law — On Crime, Tort, and Procedure* (Oceana, 1971).

73) . . . *notably Margaret Gilbert and John Searle* . . . See generally Margaret Gilbert, *Sociality and Responsibility: New Essays in Plural Subject Theory* (Rowman and Littlefield, 2000); John R. Searle, *The Construction of Social Reality* (Free Press, 1995) 23–26.

74) . . . *San Fernando Valley parking lot*. The Rodney King incident occurred shortly after midnight on March 3, 1991. For a detailed study of the state and federal cases, see George P. Fletcher, *With Justice for Some: Victims' Rights in Criminal Trials* (Addison-Wesley, 1995).

75) . . . *commit atrocities on the civilian population*. For the Su-

preme Court's decision in the case, see *In re Yamashita*, 327 U.S. 1 (1946).

77) *The philosopher Karl Jaspers* . . . The German version of Jaspers's monograph is found in Karl Jaspers, *Was is der Mensch* (Piper, 2000) 329–51. The English translation has been republished as Karl Jaspers, *The Question of German Guilt* (Fordham, E. B. Ashton ed., 2002).

78) . . . *the Crown commuted the sentence to six months in prison.* See *Regina v. Dudley and Stephens*, 14 Queens Bench Division 273 (1884).

79) . . . *it is part of my own being.*" See Sigmund Freud, "Some Additional Notes on Dream Interpretation As a Whole," in *19 The Complete Psychological Works of Sigmund Freud* (Hogarth Press and the Institute of Psycho-Analysis, 1961) 133.

80) . . . *a Talmudic analysis of sacrificing one to save many.* See *Talmud Yerushalmi*, Terumot 8:41. According to the analysis in this passage, if the aggressor names a particular suspect and threatens to destroy the town if he is not turned over, it is permissible to surrender him to save the town. The assumption is that if the authorities name a suspect, they have reasonable grounds to believe that he is guilty of some wrongdoing. Also, if the suspect is named, the guilt of choosing the victim does not fall upon the town. See generally, David Daube, *Collaboration with Tyranny in Rabbinic Law: The Riddell Memorial Lectures* (Oxford University Press, 1965).

81) *In his recent novel* . . . See Philip Roth, *The Human Stain* (Houghton Mifflin, 2000).

84) . . . *Eichmann in Jerusalem.* See Hannah Arendt, *Eichmann in Jerusalem: A Report on the Banality of Evil* (Penguin, 1994).

86) . . . *November 19, 1863.* For an analysis of the Gettysburg Address, see Fletcher, *Our Secret Constitution* 35–56.

87) . . . *liberty of the world).* De Gaulle made the statement in London on March 1, 1941. Charles De Gaulle, *Discours et messages: 1940–1946* (Plon, 1946) at 73.

89) . . . *abandoned lands owned by no one.* The leading case in this area is *Mabo v. Queensland* (1992) 107 Australian Law Reports 1.

Chapter Five

92) . . . *"it is politics by other means."* The full thought from Carl von Clausewitz, *On War* (1832) is "The ultimate object of war is political. To attain this object fully, the enemy must be disarmed. Disarming the enemy becomes therefore the immediate object of hostilities."

93) . . . *he or she is acting contrary to the law.* The Model Penal Code (American Law Institute 1962) provides in § 2.10: "It is an affirmative defense that the actor, in engaging in the conduct charged to constitute an offense, does no more than execute an order of his superior in the armed services that he does not know to be unlawful." In other words, if he knows that the order is unlawful he forfeits the right to rely on superior's order as a defense.

93) *The Rome Statute has expanded even this emphasis* . . . The Rome Statute turns the presumption of the MPC on its head and provides in Article 33 that relying on superior orders should not provide a defense unless:

(a) The person was under a legal obligation to obey orders of the Government or the superior in question;

(b) The person did not know that the order was unlawful; and

(c) The order was not manifestly unlawful.

For the purposes of this book, orders to commit genocide or crimes against humanity are manifestly unlawful.

95) . . . *a complacent "good German" during the Third Reich.* See Hannah Arendt, *Eichmann in Jerusalem: A Report on the Banality of Evil* (Penguin, 1994) 90.

95) . . . *Erik Erickson struck closer to the mark.* See Erik H. Erickson, *Childhood and Society* (W. W. Norton, 1950).

96) . . . *eight German spies in the summer of 1942.* The factual account offered here draws heavily on the following sources: Francis Biddle, *In Brief Authority* (Doubleday, 1962) 323–45; Gary Cohen, "The Keystone Kommandos," *The Atlantic* (February 2002) 46–59; David J. Danielski, "The Saboteurs' Case," *1 Journal of Supreme Court History* 61 (1996); Boris I. Bittker, "The World War II German Sabo-

teur Case and Writs of Certiorari before Judgment by the Court of Appeals: A Tale of *Nunc pro Tunc* Jurisdiction," *14 Const. Commentary* 431 (1997); Ex parte *Quirin*, 317 U.S. 1 (1942).

97) *Haupt went home to his parents.* See *Haupt v. United States*, 330 U.S. 631 (1947).

97) . . . *the FBI was watching.* See *Cramer v. United States*, 325 U.S. I (1945).

98) . . . *documents stuffed into his boots.* The case is discussed in *Quirin*, 317 U.S. at 13, note 9.

99) . . . *still on the books.* At the time of the Quirin trial, the provision was numbered 10 United States Code § 1554. It is now number 18 U.S.C. § 904.

101) . . . *directly to anarchy or despotism.*" The quote is found in Ex parte *Milligan*, 71 U.S. 2, 120 (1866).

101) *Are all the laws but one . . .*" This famous line in Lincoln's speech has become the title of a book on the problem of circumventing the Constitution in time of emergencies. William Rehnquist, *All the Laws but One: Civil Liberties in Wartime* (Knopf, 1998).

102) . . . *suicide pact.*" Justice Arthur Goldberg made this incidental comment in *Kennedy v. Mendoza-Martinez*, 372 U.S. 144, 160 (1963), favoring the rights of citizens not to be divested of citizenship for draft evasion.

102) . . . *for being a public enemy.*" See Francis Lieber, *General Order No. 100: Instructions for the Government of Armies of the United States in the Field* Article 56 (1863).

106) . . . *are treated as spies, and suffer death.*" See Lieber, *General Order 100: Instructions for the Government of Armies of the United States in the Field*, Article 83.

106) . . . *trial and punishment by military tribunals.*" The quote from Justice Stone's opinion is found in *Quirin* at p. 31.

107) . . . *acts which render their belligerency unlawful.*" This is also found at *Quirin*, ibid.

109) . . . *their belligerency unlawful.*" See *Quirin*, ibid.

109) *Today, owing to the jurisprudential strides . . .*" Primary rules define offenses; secondary rules prescribe the formulas for making con-

tracts, acquiring licenses, and so on. The rules for acquiring combatancy status are secondary rules. See H.L.A. Hart, *The Concept of Law*
(Oxford University Press 2nd ed., 1994) 80–81.

110) *Never mind that.* The closest provisions to spying that are to be
found in the international treaties on warfare are the restrictions in the
1907 Hague Convention defining the limits of the power of state to
punishing spying. See e.g., Article 30 ("A spy taken in the act shall not
be punished without previous trial").

110) . . . *procedures designed for courts-martial.* The key provisions
were known as Articles 46½ and Article 50 of the Articles of War, Title
10 of the United States Code then in force. Both required certification of
the decision to a military appeal panel before submitting the case to the
president. This procedure was not observed prior to the execution of six
defendants in *Quirin.*

111) . . . *the exemption of petty offenses* . . . See *Schick v. United
States*, 195 U.S. 65 (1904). There was a time when the prosecution for
contempt of court was exempt from the requirement of a jury for the
same historical reasons, but the Supreme Court reversed this policy in
Bloom v. Illinois, 391 U.S. 194 (1968).

113) . . . *two-thirds vote to impose the death penalty.* The President's
Executive Order of November 13, 2001, was published at 66 Federal
Register 57831–57836 (November 16, 2001), referred to hereafter as
the Bush Order.

113) . . . *if he, Bush, so decides.* Bush Order § 4(c)(8): ". . . submission of the record of the trial, including any conviction or sentence, for
review and final decision by me or by the Secretary of Defense if so
designated by me for that purpose."

113) . . . *and proceed with one of these tribunals.* Bush Order § 2(a):

The term "individual subject to this order" shall mean any individual who is not a United States citizen with respect to whom I determine from time to time in writing that:
(1) there is reason to believe that such individual, at the relevant
    times, (i) is or was a member of the organization known as al
    Qaeda; (ii) has engaged in, aided or abetted, or conspired to

commit, acts of international terrorism, or acts in preparation therefor, that have caused, threaten to cause, or have as their aim to cause, injury to or adverse effects on the United States, its citizens, national security, foreign policy, or economy; or (iii) has knowingly harbored one or more individuals described in subparagraphs (i) or (ii) of subsection 2(a)(1) of this order; and

(2) it is in the interest of the United States that such individual be subject to this order.

115) ... *namely the foreigners, the "terrorists."* For the views of Carl Schmitt on these issues, see Carl Schmitt, *The Concept of the Political* (University of Chicago Press, George Schwab trans., 1996).

115) ... *the laws of war, without a jury."* Laurence Tribe, "Trial by Fury," *The New Republic*, December 10, 2001.

115) ... *does not violate the Constitution."* See testimony of Cass Sunstein, Senate Judiciary Committee, December 4, 2001.

115) ... *a jury trial in every criminal prosecution.* U.S. Constitution, Article III, §2, clause 3 provides, in part: "The Trial of all Crimes, except in Cases of Impeachment, shall be by Jury." The Sixth Amendment provides, in part: "In all criminal prosecutions, the accused shall enjoy the right to a speedy and public trial, by an impartial jury of the State and district wherein the crime shall have been committed."

Chapter Six

118) ... *to constitute treason against the king.* The treason statute is cited as 25 Edw. III, stat. 5, c.2.

119) *"If I come upon the King I will kill him."* See "Crohagan's Case," *172 English Reporter* 891 (Kings Bench 1634).

120) ... *to constitute this "open deed."* For a review of the views expressed by common law scholars on this issue, see George P. Fletcher, *Rethinking Criminal Law* (Oxford University Press, 2000) 207–215.

121) ... *giving them Aid and Comfort."* U.S. Constitution, Article III, sec. 3, clause 1 provides in its entirety:

Treason against the United States, shall consist only in levying War against them, or in adhering to their Enemies, giving them Aid and Comfort. No Person shall be convicted of Treason unless on the Testimony of two Witnesses to the same overt Act, or on Confession in open Court.

122) . . . *against Aaron Burr in 1807.* My description of the Aaron Burr case relies heavily on the excellent analysis provided by R. Kent Newmyer, *John Marshall and the Heroic Age of the Supreme Court* (Louisiana State, 2001) 175–202.

122) . . . *and thus incurred Jefferson's enmity.* Chase was accused of improper behavior in *United States v. Fries*, 9 F.Cas. 924, 934 (D. Penn. 1800).

123) . . . *all calculated to benefit Aaron Burr."* Newmyer at 181.

124) . . . *constituted levying war against the United States* . . . Ibid., at 187.

124) . . . *into execution" was sufficient.* Ibid.

124) . . . *"any force connected with the intention."* . . . This is the language of Justice Samuel Chase in the Fries treason trial. See ibid.

125) . . . *they arrested Cramer as well.* The statement of facts is drawn from *Cramer v. United States*, 325 U.S. I (1945).

127) . . . *Warren court.* The additional dissenter was Justice Stanley Reed.

127) . . . *twenty-five years imprisonment.* See *United States v. Haupt*, 136 F.2d 661 (7th Cir. 1943).

127) . . . *a sentence of life imprisonment.* See *Haupt v. United States*, 330 U.S. 631 (1947).

129) . . . *no crime of that name.* Murder is defined in language of the common law in 18 USC § 1111, and manslaughter is defined in § 1112. The reference to American nationals appears in a sentencing provision, 18 USC § 2332, which specifies that anyone who commits murder or manslaughter, as defined in § 1111 or § 1112, against a U.S. national abroad, shall be punished for specific terms. A conspiracy to commit homicide against a U.S. national is punished according to § 2332(b).

The indictment against Lindh incorrectly identifies § 2332(b) as the basis of the prosecution; in fact it is only about the sentence in case the victim or intended victim is a U.S. national abroad.

132) *"betrayal of the government."* The relevant provision under the old RSFSR Criminal Code was § 64. My own experiences intervening in Soviet antidissident trials is recorded in Telford Taylor, *Courts of Terror* (Vintage, 1976). The corresponding provision of the new Russian Criminal Code of 1996 is § 275. The Soviet crime was the first to be mentioned among specific offenses; the new provision comes near the end of the Code.

133) *. . . on a similar theory of treason.* For thoughts based on my own experience as one of Shcharansky's lawyers, see my op-ed piece "Shcharansky: Remembering to Remember," *Los Angeles Times*, March 14, 1980, part II, page 7.

135) *. . . and thus resembles treason as defined today.* See *Strafgesetzbuch für das Deutsche Reich* § 80 (Hans Rüdorff ed., J. Guttentag 1890) (high treason); ibid., § 87 (state treason by sympathizing with the enemy); ibid., § 88 (state treason by taking up arms against Germany).

135) *Espionage is not properly called treason.* The current French Criminal Code distinguishes between treason, which only French nationals can commit, and espionage, which anybody can commit. See Code Pénal 411-1 (1994) (requiring for *trahison* that one of a specified list of acts be commited by a "French" person or someone in the French military service).

136) *. . . the judges were probably right.* See *United States v. Rosenberg*, 195 F.2d 583 (2nd Cir. 1952). Nonetheless it is quite common, even for lawyers and judges, to refer to the crime of the Rosenbergs as treason. See *Glass v. Louisiana*, 471 U.S. 1080, 1091 note 32 (1985) (Brennan, J., dissenting) (referring to mishaps when "Ethel Rosenberg was electrocuted for treason").

136) *The great surprise is that the transformation occurred in 1934 . . .* The relevant changes occurred in the Gesetz zur Änderung von Vorschriften des Strafrechts und des Strafverfahrens, v. 2.5.1934 (RGBl. I S. 341), reprinted in *Die Strafgesetzgebung der Jahre* 1931 *bis* 1935 (Legislation for the Years 1931–35) (Ernst Schäfer and Hans V. Dohanyi

eds., J.C.B. Mohr, 1936). Section 81 of the 1934 statute, Rüdorff, *Straf-gesetzbuch für das Deutsche Reich*, describes the act of treason as rob-bing the President or Chancellor, the Reich or another member of the government of the Reich of his constitutional power (*"Wer es unternim-mit, den Reichspräsidenten oder den Reichskanzler oder en anderes Mitglied der Reichsregierung seiner verfaffungsmässigen Gewalt zu berauben"*).

Chapter Seven

141) . . . *Hitler's genocidal assault on the Jews became the work of an entire people."* Carroll concludes this declaration, in his book *Constantine's Sword: The Church and the Jews* (Houghton Mifflin, 2001), ". . . and an entire civilization was prepared to let it happen." See page 28 of his text.

143) . . . *many theologians now treat the doctrine of the Fall as a "perversion."* See Farrow's entry on the Fall on page 233 of *The Oxford Companion to Christian Thought* (Oxford University Press, Adrian Hastings et al., eds., 2000).

144) . . . *for their own sins, and not for Adam's transgression."* I am quoting Article 2 of the *Mormon Articles of Faith*. The text can be found online at <*http://www.sacred-texts.com/mor/morartf.txt*>.

145) . . . *the Christian invention of the devil as the force of evil.* Pagels's insight is articulated on pages 102–105 of her book *The Origin of Satan* (Random House, 1995).

147) . . . *and even directed anti-Semitic remarks to Jewish delegates at the conference.* See Jeff Jacoby, "Durban, Racism, and Islamism," *Boston Globe*, September 3, 2001, page A15 (commenting on a vote by nongovernmental organizations to brand Israel "a racist Apartheid state" and to urge the U.N. to reinstate its notorious resolution equating Zionism with racism).

148) . . . *the state of mind, the motive, is more important than the consequence."* See Isaiah Berlin's *The Roots of Romanticism* (Princeton University Press, 1999) 10.

148) . . . *"purity of heart, integrity, dedication, devotion."* Ibid.

148) . . . *Let him step to the music which he hears."* This appears in the conclusion of Thoreau's *Walden*, written in 1854.

149) . . . *that only a good will could be called moral.* Immanuel Kant, *Groundwork of the Metaphysics of Morals* 7 (Cambridge, Mary Gregor trans., 1998).

151) . . . *law students never forget.* The House of Lords' decision is *Regina v. Morgan*, 1976 A.C. 182 (H.L. 1976).

153) . . . *the subordinate has no excuse for following it.* This rule appears in Article 33 of the Rome Statute of the International Criminal Court, paragraph 1(c).

Chapter Eight

158) . . . *actual responsibility of those involved in the incident.* German law has recognized comparative negligence since 1900. See German Civil Code § 254 (establishing that liability for negligence depends "on the extent to which one party or the other caused the damage"). Until the last few days Anglo-American courts applied the rule of contributory negligence, which implied that if negligent, the plaintiff could not recover anything. The leading case changing the law is *Li v. Yellow Cab Co.*, 532 P.2d 1226, 1243 (Cal. 1975).

158) . . . *the criminal law of homicide.* For cases illustrating the principle of provocation, see *Rex v. Simpson*, 84 L.J.K.B. 1893 (Crim. App. 1915); *White v. State*, 72 S.W. 173 (1902). For analysis of these old cases, see George P. Fletcher, *Rethinking Criminal Law* (Little, Brown, 1978) 245–46.

160) *No one can be the agent of another in committing crime.* See 2 *Encyclopedia Talmudica* (Philipp Feldheim, 1974) 154–64.

161) *No one can be accomplice in someone else's crime.* See Immanuel Kant, "On a Supposed Right to Tell Lies," from *Benevolent Motives in Critique of Practical Reason and Other Works on the Theory of Ethics* (Longmans, Green, T. K. Abbott ed., 1909).

161) *A famous case in Germany* . . . See Judgment of October 19, 1962, 18 BGHSt, 87.

162) . . . *fully responsible for the deed.* German Criminal Code § 25(1)

defining *Täterschaft* or "Perpetration" provides: "Someone will be punished as a perpetrator if he commits the act himself or through another person." This effectively overrules the Staschinsky ruling because if he commits the act himself he must at least be punished as a full perpetrator (even if he theoretically is just an accessory).

162) . . . *soldiers who actually shed blood*. See note page 64.

164) . . . *two completely independent parties*. For further notes on the comparative law of complicity, see George P. Fletcher, *Basic Concepts of Criminal Law* (Oxford University Press, 1996), 188–203.

166) . . . *the degenerate climate of the Third Reich* . . . Hannah Arendt, *Eichmann in Jerusalem: A Report on the Banality of Evil* (Penguin, 1994). David J. Cohen anticipates the argument made here that the banality of evil should have had a mitigating effect on Eichmann's punishment. He criticizes Arendt for failing to see this point. David J. Cohen, "Bureaucracy, Justice, and Collective Responsibility in the World War II War Crimes Trials," 18 *Rechtshistorisches Journal* (1999) 316 ("On the one hand, having made the best case, the case the defense did not make, for Eichmann's innocence by locating his crimes within the larger bureaucratic, moral, political, legal, and social context of Nazi occupied Europe, she completely denies the relevance of that context for an assessment of his guilt.")

168) . . . *generated by mental illness)*. These excuses are surveyed in George P. Fletcher. *Rethinking Criminal Law* (Oxford University Press, 2000) 774–855.

169) . . . *coincide in some mysterious way*. See Kant's own analysis of the third antinomy between freedom and determinism in Immanuel Kant, *The Critique of Pure Reason* (Dutton, J.M.D. Meiklejohn trans., 1978).

169) . . . *Harry Frankfurt labeled the theological view as "quaint."* Frankfurt's essay is "Freedom of the Will and the Concept of a Person" in Harry Frankfurt, *The Importance of What We Care About: Philosophical Essays* (Cambridge, 1988) 11. Chisholm's views appear in "Freedom and Action" in *Freedom and Determinism* (Random House, 1966).

173) . . . *East German law prohibiting attempted murder*. For an il-

luminating discussion of the borderguards case, see Manfred Gabriel, "Coming to Grips with the East German Border Guards Case," 38 *Columbia Journal of Transnational Law* (1999) 275.

174) . . . *excused if their mistake is "unavoidable."* German Criminal Code § 17 provides: "If at the time of the deed the actor lacks the insight to understand the wrongful nature of his action, he acts without culpability, provided he could not have avoided making the mistake. If he could have avoided the mistake, the penalty may be mitigated according to the rules of § 49 (1). (The latter provisions permit reduction of the penalty to no more than 75 percent of the maximum allowed.)

176) . . . *of the crime committed by Timothy McVeigh.* For an earlier account particularly sympathetic to the influences on McVeigh, see George P. Fletcher, "Unsound Constitution," *The New Republic*, June 23, 1997, page14.

177) . . . *Constitution as a "pact with the devil."* Garrison (1805–1879) carried out his abolitionist campaign in the pages of his newspaper the *Liberator*, which was first published in 1831. He directed the phrases "pact with the devil" specifically against the Compromise of 1850 and the newly enacted Fugitive Slave Law.

177) . . . *experience "a new birth of freedom."* The late Charles Black wrote a stirring book drawing on these words in the Gettysburg Address. See Charles L. Black, *A New Birth of Freedom: Human Rights, Named and Unnamed* (Grosset/Putnam, 1997). I analyze the quoted phrase in the context of the entire address in *Our Secret Constitution*, at 53.

178) . . . *by whom the offense came."* Second Inaugural Address, delivered March 4, 1864. For the historical context of the address, see Ronald C. White, Jr., *Lincoln's Greatest Speech* (Simon & Schuster, 2002).

Chapter Nine

179) . . . *are they called Jews.*) The term "Jew" comes from *yehudi*, which refers to a resident of the province of Judah. See 2 Kings 18:28 (referring to *yehudit* as the Hebrew language). See generally *The Ency-*

clopedia of the Jewish Religion (Holt, Rinehart, Z. Werblowsky and G. Wigoder eds., 1965) 211.

181) . . . *as conceptually interchangeable.* The linguistic phenomenon is well summarized in *Etz Hayim: Torah and Commentary* (Rabbinical Assembly, David L. Lieber, sr. ed., 2001) 27 n.13, in a comment on the editor's choice of "punishment" as the proper translation.

182) . . . *for she is a married woman."* I take responsibility for the translations of the Hebrew Bible that appear in the text. I have relied upon various sources and checked each for its accuracy.

184) . . . *prohibited later in Leviticus.* See Calum Carmichael, *Law, Legend, and Incest in the Bible: Leviticus 18–20.* (Cornell, 1997).

187) . . . *guilt and punishment in the ancient world.* Walter Burkert, "Greek Tragedy and Sacrificial Ritual," 7 *Greek, Roman and Byzantine Studies* (1966) 87, 112 (noting that "the community is knit together in the common experience of shock and guilt" at the time of sacrifices).

191) . . . *distinction holds between shame and guilt.* Discussing "shame" has become fashionable in the psychoanalytic literature, see, e.g., Donald L. Nathanson, *Shame and Pride: Affect, Sex, and the Birth of Self* (W. W. Norton, 1992). For a philosophical analysis, it is hard to improve on Max Scheler, "Shame and Feelings of Modesty," in *Person and Self-Value* 1 (M. S. Frings trans., 1987).

191) . . . *did not distinguish between guilt and shame.* Bernard Williams, *Shame and Necessity* (University of California Press, 1993) 88–89.

193) . . . *justified object of their hostility."* Herbert Morris, *On Guilt and Innocence: Essays in Legal Philosophy and Moral Psychology* (University of California Press, 1976) 120.

193) *As Paul Ricouer points out . . .* Paul Ricoeur, *The Symbolism of Evil* (Harper and Row, Emerson Buchanan trans., 1969) 144–46.

194) . . . *Kafka's Josef K . . .* Franz Kafka, *The Trial* (Schocken, Willa and Edwin Muir trans., 1995).

Chapter Ten

196) . . . *my men died and I did not."* The film is based on the personal account of Hal Moore in Harold G. Moore, Joseph L. Galloway,

We Were Soldiers Once . . . and Young: Ia Drang—The Battle That Changed the War in Vietnam (Random House, 1992) 197.

197) *. . . systematic persecution and mass murder.* William Drozdiak, "Hitler Legacy Haunts Germany Still; Fifty Years after Rise, Nation Sifts Lessons," *Washington Post,* January 30, 1983, at page A1.

197) *We see the beginnings of this genre . . .* Sophocles, *Oedipus Rex* (Dover Thrift Editions, F. Storr trans., 1912). The text is not clear as to whether the pollution derives primarily from the patricide or the incest. The following lines of the chorus suggest that the incest is at least a major factor: "Time found thee out—Time who sees everything—Unwittingly guilty; and arraigns thee now consort ill-sorted, unto whom are bred sons of thy getting, in thine own birthbed."

198) *. . . Alexander Hamilton and Thomas Jefferson.* See George P. Fletcher, "Unsound Constitution," *The New Republic,* June 23, 1997, at p. 14.

198) *. . . the sweat of other men's faces."* Second Inaugural Address, delivered March 4, 1864.

199) *. . . is labeled "barbarous."* See note above page 38.

199) *. . . reactions upon visiting Auschwitz.* Anton Leist, "Scham und deutsches Nationalbewußtsein [Shame and German National Consciousness]," *in Aktuelle Fragen politischer Philosophie [Current Issues in Political Philosophy]* 369 (Peter Koller and Klaus Puhl eds., 1997).

200) *. . . they must have had a reason!"* As the Jewish cop Robert Gold says in David Mamet's film *Homicide* (1991), "There has been so much anti-Semitisim in the last four thousand years, the Jews must have been doing something wrong."

201) *". . . the most vilified and persecuted minority in history."* West *Virginia State Board of Education v. Barnette,* 319 U.S. 624, 646 (Frankfurter, J., dissenting).

201–02) *. . . as a Jew in post-Holocaust Hungary.* András Sajó, "Affordable Shame," in *The Paradoxes of Unintended Consequences* (Lord Dahrendorf et al. eds., 2000) 163.

202) *In a seminar about his article, Sajó . . .* The seminar took place at the Cardozo Law School in New York City in February 2001.

203) . . . *H.L.A. Hart denoted various senses* . . . H.L.A. Hart, "Varieties of Responsibility," 83 *Law Quarterly Review* (1967) 346.

207) . . . *the lie about Auschwitz."* § 130 StGB (providing, in part, that the following acts are criminal and punishable by up to three years in prison: acting in a way likely to disturb the public order by cursing, heaping contempt, or defaming a segment of the population, and thus attacking the dignity of these persons). This provision is interpreted to penalize Holocaust denial. T. Lenckner in Schoenke-Schroeder, Strafgesetzbuch: Kommentar § 30 at 1214–15 n.1 (26th ed. 2001). Holocaust denial is also subject to prosecution as a criminal insult according to StGB § 185. For a review of the German case law, see Eric Stein, "History Against Free Speech: The New German Against 'Auschwitz' — and Other 'Lies,'" 85 *Michigan Law Review* 277 (1986).

208) . . . *a constant reminder of our collective guilt.* I admit that there may be less charitable interpretations of political correctness in language. For example, the point may be to demonstrate that we belong to the educated class that has learned the proper way of referring to various minorities. Steven Pinker, "The Game of the Name," *New York Times*, April 5, 1994, at page A21.

INDEX